Black American Money

Book 3

A collection of lectures by
The People's Scholar Dr. Boyce Watkins

Dr. Boyce Watkins

CONTENTS

ACKNOWLEDGMENTS

I would like to thank everyone who has supported the work that we do to improve the lives of others.

LECTURE 1

HOW TO QUIT YOUR JOB AND MAKE MONEY

When I was teaching at Syracuse University, I did not know that even as a PhD I was stuck with kind of a slave mentality. I was in a situation where my brain was not equipped for freedom. I was still a better fit for slavery, and I had to acknowledge that. I didn't know that, because I thought "edu-ma-cated" Negroes were doing well. I thought that I was one of those so-called successful black people, right? I did not know that I was such a fit for slavery until I had an honest conversation with myself. Let me tell you how I became a slave. I became a slave, because I was trained to be one from birth.

From the time I was little, I had a little bit of an inkling of what it means to grow your money. My grandmother use to buy me these savings bonds. I talk about my grandmother all the time. She died right here in Atlanta. She's buried just a few miles from here, actually. So, every time that I'm here, I always think about her. She was that first person to introduce me to compound interest which I didn't know, at the time, was going to be so significant. It became very significant in my life. But outside of that, the whole conversation around money was pretty basic. It was, "If you want to make money," you do what? "You get a job." That's how you make money. And when you get the job, you have to know how to behave. Don't upset Massa, because he will cut your food supply. He will cut off your money and then you'll be destitute. You'll realize that there are consequences for being black and outspoken or whatever it is. Right?

So, I also kind of remember watching people that went to work every day and how they hated their jobs. I kind of felt like, "Okay, so part of being an adult means that you have to go to this place that you don't enjoy, come home, and complain about it every day." Then also, I saw this weird cycle when it came to money where you go to work, make enough money to pay your bills, run out of money, and go back to work to get more money to pay the bills again. Then you run out of money, and you just rinse and repeat. Just repeat that cycle over and over again until you're too old to work and eventually just die. Then your children start over exactly where you started, right?

There was rarely any conversation I heard anywhere about the pillars of wealth — about an equation to kind of emancipate yourself from all of this. I didn't know what that even looked like. I did not even know that even existed. I did not hear any conversations at all about stock market investing. Not at all. When I started learning about stock market investing as a college student, it was all theory. It was all something white people did. Even then, even when the knowledge was presented to me, and I was a very good finance student. I had very good grades and all that stuff. Even when it was presented to me, it just wasn't really real. I knew I could do it. I understood it, but it was all theory, and that really sort of speaks to the power of habits. It's almost like when I was ... I don't know if you guys know I've lost a lot of weight maybe in the last year or so. It's not like I just figured out that exercise would help me lose weight. I've always known that. I've always known that having Skittles and Twizzlers in your diet is probably not the best thing for a 40-year-old man. Right? I've always known these things. Right? This was not rocket science. This was not something like a revelation. It was something I always knew. What I learned is that habits actually override intellect, knowledge, and logic.

I mean, how many of us most of the time spend our lives...? Every day we know what we're supposed to do. Then we see what we actually do, what we want to do, or what feels good at the moment. Right? Probably about half the kids on this earth are born that way, right? You know that you weren't supposed to do it, but you did it anyway. Right? Now you got child support or whatever it is. Right? That's life. It's life. That's the power of habits. That's how it works.

By sort of following one path without giving critical thought to what would give me economic strength and freedom, I falsely thought that extensive amounts of education, going to school, getting more school, more school, more school would give me that economic strength and freedom. I didn't realize that my habit formation was built around extensive training on how to be a slave. I thought I was heading toward freedom, but really, I was going down a path with more extensive forms of slavery. More deeply entrenched slavery. Right? I was becoming more and more committed to the very system that we complain about on a daily basis, and this was not something that just happened overnight. It was something that happened from when I was five. It was something that happened from kindergarten onward where they start teaching you that white people are the greatest thing in the world: that they've done everything significant. Where they teach you that the greatest sign of success for a person of color in America, or a black person, is to get close to white folks and get them to like you, so they'll give you money for being well behaved. Right? That's kind of what it is. I call it the "good Negro behavior protocol." If you follow that, there are rewards that come with that. Right?

This goes back to slavery. It is what Dr. Claud Anderson of *PowerNomics* refers to as meritorious manumission: where slaves were always rewarded for protecting their masters, entertaining their masters, et cetera. Oh and also, the biggest reward came for undermining any slave who was trying to defeat the system: any slave trying to escape or form a rebellion. If you went and snitched on that slave, then they would take good care of you. There was some Negro that was so appreciated by his town in Virginia that they put up a statue of him in the middle of town. When [the slaves planned] a revolt, he told the local law enforcement, and they went and shut down the revolt. They killed all the slaves who were about to do it. They loved that snitching Negro. His statue was up until, I think, the 1960s or 1970s. That's how real it was.

So, ultimately, if you are black and you want white people to build you a statue, you pretty much know what the formula is. It's very simple, very basic, right? The question is, which formula do you want. Do we want the formula that's been given to us and sort of establish over the last 400 years, or do we create a different formula? Do we want the old equation or a new equation? For me, as I sort of analyzed my own extensive slave training – everything that made me into what I was before I figured a few things out – I started saying, "Okay, I need a formula that's gonna get me away from all of this shit." I realized that I needed something that was gonna be different, break some rules, and probably upset a lot of my relatives. They were warning me against this. I mean, think about this. I mean, I was a black man with a good job. You don't mess up a good job going off trying to do this independent black stuff. I mean, my goodness, who wants to be black, right? So, it was really difficult. I had to kind of do a lot of soul searching, figure things out, gain some courage, and also confront and break some habits. Right? I had to confront some uncomfortable truths about who I was.

I break all this down for you, because I want you to understand that much of this process of going from what they call a "wantrepreneur" to an entrepreneur, is a scenario where it's gonna require you to do a lot of soul searching. It's an emotional process as much as it is an intellectual and logical process. I mean, let's just be real. Let's keep it real. Look, everything you need to know to go start, build, and grow a great company is out there. You know where the knowledge and the information is. You know who the gurus are. You know which classes to go take. You know you can turn on the internet. You know that if you spend 10 hours a day doing nothing but studying business and reading about investing, you could be really good at all of that, very, very quickly. Right? Just the same way I always knew that if I got off my fat ass and went running every day, I was gonna lose weight. If I had put down the Skittles and picked up some vegetables, it would have made a difference in my body. But remember, there's a reason why I did not do that even though I knew what I was supposed to do, needed to do, and wanted to do. I wanted this for myself, but at the same time, I wanted something else that was related to habit formation and instant gratification. It's always comfortable to stick with what you know. That's why many of us stay in bad relationships. If you haven't done it before, then you aren't human. I bet all of us have done that: been in a bad relationship and stayed in it because it was comfortable and familiar. Some of y'all are in relationships like that right now. I apologize to the person who will be your ex within the next few weeks after this conversation.

So, how do you do it? How do you break away from this abusive marriage with white supremacy? You love this system. You love all of it. This is who you were born and trained to be – some of us. Some of us. Many of us. Right? How do you deal with this abusive marriage, and how do you form a process that will allow you to take those steps necessary to put yourself where you want to be? Where you become an asset to your people and a greater asset to your family? Where you've got a legacy? My God, a legacy. And, it's gonna be huge. It's gonna be huge. Whatever legacy you leave, it's gonna be huger than you can imagine. Let me tell you why.

My grandmother, rest her soul, who's buried five miles away from here...I mean, she's in heaven. I hope that she can watch. I hope she's got Wi-Fi in heaven or something. Big screen TVs. They tell us all these great things that happen when you die, right? So, I hope she can see how significant her legacy is when I'm speaking to all of you, and I'm speaking with her voice. The voice she gave me in the 1970s and 80s when she was buying me those financial toys and educational gifts for Christmas instead of just buying me the same old okie doke stuff. Right? And, this is the beginning. This is the beginning. I mean, think about what you're teaching your children because of things that you might have heard from me or from other people you see at this conference? Every day when I'm online, every week, I'm talking to about a million people a week, and it's shaping their thinking. All this came from my grandmother's tiny little legacy. Her tiny little thing that she did years ago. This is not the only example. There are tons of examples out there where somebody did something in 1945 that they thought wasn't gonna be a big deal, but it ended up being a huge deal.

So, I need you to do something. I need you to make sure that you're doing something that, even if it's not a big deal to you, it's gonna be a huge deal to somebody else. Most of y'all have something that exists in your life that is huge to you, that was small to the person who gave that to you. Good or bad. Good or bad, right? You've got families where they have generations of abuse. Maybe to the abuser it wasn't a big deal when that man touched his niece, or whatever it was, but it became huge later on. The same applies in a positive direction. Little things you do. Little things you put in position. That little life insurance policy that you get. Whatever it is. That little business that you start. Those little concepts and ideas that you teach in your household. That decision to take your child out of public school and homeschool your child or send them to an African-centered school. Those little decisions you make are going to have a huge impact, so never underestimate the power of you, what you are, and what you're doing right now.

The best way to control the future is to prepare when you're still in the past. Or, the best way to control the present, is when you have prepared for the present back when the present used to be the future. The people that controlled 2018, are the people who were planning for it in 1988. Just go look at gentrification. Look at gentrification. I mean, do you think that they just started preparing gentrification plans last Tuesday? No, they were talking about this in the 70s and in the 80s. They said, "By 2018, we're gonna have billions of dollars in extra wealth." Right? Planning ahead is the key to everything.

Let me give you some specific information that's gonna help you in that transformation — some things that I learned and figured out along the way. I'm going to start with mainly the three pillars of wealth. The three pillars of wealth that you want to understand are stock and bond investing, real estate, and entrepreneurship. Each of these is very basic but goes extremely deep. When we teach our children in the Black Millionaires of Tomorrow program in The Black Business School, what we tell our kids is the same thing we would tell any adult, because these kids are gonna be adults one day. We tell them to keep your poise. Poise is P-O-I-S-E: producer, owner, investor, saver, and entrepreneur. What does that mean? Why do we tell them that? Why do we remind them of that? Well, because you see, capitalism in America is what you would call a horse and jockey type of race. Everybody's in the race, but some people are horses, and some of us are jockeys. Think about the way the horse race works. The jockey gets on the horse's back, and the jockey don't really do much work. He just smacks the horse and tells the horse what to do. The horse runs fast, and the horse wins the race, but when the race is over, they don't give the money to the horse. All the rewards go to the jockey. The horse gets sent back to the stable to get his hay or whatever it is. The jockey is the one who gets the glory. The jockey is the one who gets the wreath around the neck. The jockey is the one who gets the big payday, right?

Capitalism is a horse and jockey system in the same way. There's a massive amount of wealth being created in America. There is a wealth divide in America unlike anything we've seen in the last 100 years. That wealth divide, the divide between the haves and the have nots, is not going to shrink. It is not going to go backwards. They are not going to be able to undo this. They have opened up that rabbit hole, that Pandora's box, and eventually America will have the same wealth disparities that they have in many Third World countries where you've got the one percent then everybody else. That divide is not going to go anywhere. I don't care what the politicians tell you. I don't care what dreams they feed, the Democratic party...all of that...that's not gonna work. None of it's gonna work, because when these wealth gaps in pretty much every country occur, they don't usually go backward. The only way they might go backward is if there's complete revolution, and the whole society just descends into chaos. At which point, you need to go buy a bunch of guns, learn to grow your own food, and build a bomb shelter or something. It would be a whole different game at that point.

Truth be told, these gaps do not shrink. The way these gaps work is that in the horse and jockey context, you've got the people that accumulate wealth and then those who build wealth for the accumulators. For example, if you grow up like I did, and you're thinking, "Okay, I need a place to live. How do I get a place to live?" Well, you can go rent an apartment. Okay. Who do you rent an apartment from? You rent an apartment from a landlord. Okay. All right. So, you're paying rent to the landlord every month, and y'all know how that game works. The rent money, you don't get it back. We know that, right? The landlord takes that money, because the landlord is the jockey. You're the horse. You're feeding the landlord's wealth. You're giving him $1,000 to $2,000 a month or whatever you pay in rent. They're taking that money, and they're putting it into the value of their property. They're taking the seed you've given them and positioning it to grow. That seed is gonna grow through what they call capital gains which are taxed at a much lower rate than regular income. They opened the Pandora's box during Reaganomics. They didn't go back, but they didn't shut it again, right? So, the landlord is accumulating this wealth through capital gains. In addition to the fact that now he owns the building and gets whatever price appreciation comes from the growth in value in the building, he's making income from the building the entire time. So, his tenants are all paying his mortgage which is allowing him to build wealth for his family. Basically, if you're paying say $1,500 a month in rent, and you do that for a 20-year period, you have made your landlord a millionaire. If your landlord takes that $1,500 and invests that money in either real estate, stocks, or bonds, they can easily take that $1,500 a month and turn that into a one million dollar asset.

Now, contrast this. Pay attention. There are a lot of people out here who pay up to $1,500 a month in rent or more, and they swear up and down that they don't have any wealth. They swear up and down that they can never become a millionaire. Like, it's not possible. I don't know how to do it. I was born poor, so I'm supposed to die poor. Well, if you can't make yourself a millionaire, how is it that you can make somebody else a millionaire. That doesn't make any sense. Right? It's almost like when the film *Black Panther* came out. There are people who say that black people can't afford to build our own school system, because it would cost hundreds of millions of dollars to build our own schools. I said, "But we raised half a billion dollars for Disney in about three weeks." They gave us entertainment, and we gave them half a billion dollars. They're not giving that money back. It's like we took a bunch of money, flushed it down the toilet, then said, "Damn, I ain't got no money. It's hard being black out here." Think about this. You give your money away then complain about having no money. So, who should you be mad at? Are you mad at the person who took your money? No, you give me money, I'm gonna take it. Right? Or, should we be mad at ourselves, and kind of say, "Well, maybe we need to rethink this thing," right?

So, let me talk about the second pillar of wealth. When it comes to stocks and bonds and studies examining the gap, everybody's obsessed with this growing wealth gap in America. Everybody's like, "How is this happening? How is the one percent getting all the darn resources? By golly, how is this occurring? This is outrageous." Right? They're confused, they don't get it. They're like, "What the hell is going on?" When the scientists – financial scientists, people who do what I do – look at the data, what they find is that the number one driving factor is the fact that people that have more money, or an investor's mindset, are putting their money in the stock market. Not only are they putting their money in the stock market, they're doing it on a regular basis. In the last 30 or 40 years the stock market has shot up like a rocket, and that is not a recent trend. The stock market has been doing that for about 100 years. Even the Great Depression was an excellent time to invest and buy everything as cheap as possible, because all those assets went up in value.

John Rogers in Chicago wrote a great article about this. He's a billionaire – a black billionaire out of Chicago. He said that when the 2007 stock market crash hit and many black folks got scared and took their money out, we probably gave away two or three trillion dollars in wealth that would've been accumulated if we'd been taught to wait out the storm – if we had just held steady and remained consistent. This guy, Warren Buffet, is a really good investor. One of the things Warren Buffet did to show the power of compound interest was show how the $113 he invested in 1942 became about $450,000. He's a big believer in stock market investing, but he does all different kinds of investing. By the time he hits the 100 year mark, that money...it'll be, I think...six million dollars. Six million dollars. Just wealth out of nowhere. So, think about this again. Remember how I told you little things turn into big things? Imagine if you lived in

1942, and you didn't have much to leave your children or grandchildren. You're thinking, "I ain't got much money. I ain't got much education. I ain't got much of nothing." But let's say somebody convinces you to gather, as a family, $113 to invest in the stock market. Back then, that amount of money wouldn't buy you a car or anything. It might buy you a raggedy used car but not a good car, right? So, it's not as if in 1942 you couldn't do that, right? You gathered the $113 and put it in the stock market. A hundred years later, that's six million dollars for your great grandchildren. That's huge. That's a game changer for them. I mean, how many of you have a life that would change tomorrow if somebody left you six million dollars? Even if you had to split it with your cousins. That would still be a lot of money, right? Again, the little things turn into the big things. I want you to always ask yourself, "What are the little things I can do even if I can't do the big things?"

There was a brother in my class the other day. We were talking. We meet a couple times a week, and he was talking about this beautiful plan he has to transform the entire black community. Building a school system, making it extremely profitable, reinvesting the funds, and doing all these amazing things. Just flipping the whole black community on its head. I said, "That's amazing man. I hope you do it. I'm so excited for this plan. This is awesome, but I need you to just do the little stuff first. Show me the little stuff." The thing is, we can talk all day about the big stuff. I hear big talk all the time, so I'm not impressed with the big talk. I'm impressed with the little actions, because the little actions give you the confidence to eventually pursue bigger actions. Then next thing you know, you're doing the big stuff. Right? Before you can hit the half court shots, you've gotta just practice and hit the little layups. If you're LeBron and you're missing all your shots...Well, Lebron might get back in his rhythm by just hitting some layups and free throws. Then he might start scooting back away from the basket. So, that's what I want you to focus on – the little stuff. The little stuff is what gets you there. If you were to walk out this door right now and somebody gave you marching orders to walk to California, you could get to California, but you're not gonna get there in one big step. You're going to take a million, or whatever, tiny steps. Then one day, you'll be looking in front of you and the Pacific Ocean will be right there. It's the little stuff that makes the difference.

The real leaders in the black community, in my opinion, from what I have observed, are the people doing the little things every day. Why are the little things important? The little things matter, because the little things also keep you from being overwhelmed. You don't want to carry the weight of the world on your shoulders every day and just be stressed out over all the things that you feel like you can't do, because you don't have enough capital. "I don't have enough money to do this and do that." To hell with all of that. Start with the little stuff. The little stuff will open the door to the bigger stuff. At least, that was my journey. I had to start with the little stuff. Now I can do bigger stuff, but there's bigger stuff I want to do that I can't do yet. So, every day I still gotta do the little stuff relative to where I want to be one day in the future.

The third pillar of wealth is entrepreneurship. Real estate. Stock and bond investing. Entrepreneurship. Every person in the black community who cares about the future of black America, must be committed to the idea of understanding at least the fundamentals of entrepreneurship. Everybody doesn't have to go run a business, but everybody should know all the different ways you can be an investor in a business. Also, entrepreneurship is critically important for the community, because we have been controlled by others. We are overly committed to a system that does not work to our benefit.

This thing that we call racism – which is very, very real – is actually more specifically the idea of walking in somebody else's house and wondering why they're not treating us like a relative. Now, again, we built America. We know this. We know that we own a percentage of this country. We should fight for reparations. I believe in all of that. I support all of that. But again, I also believe white people ain't ever gonna stop being white. I don't believe that they're ever going to willingly give up the 13 or 14 trillion dollars that they really owe us. I don't believe that. I just don't. So, when I first started thinking about racism, I would get tempted to get in these depressing internal dialogues about how hard it is to be a black man. How everything's stacked against you. How white folks will only let you go so far. But then, I started really thinking about it. I said, "I'm trying to solve this problem within the box of white supremacy. If I try to solve white supremacy within the box of white supremacy, then I'll never come up with an adequate solution. The only solution I can come up with is lay down, be still, and quiet, and make sure I'm well behaved, so I can survive this system." Upon reexamination, I realized, "Wait a minute. I can actually walk out the door."

Systems are designed and built. This system that you're in was built by somebody. Why don't we, the black community, commit to training millions of our children on how to develop and build systems. In this room, if we were all adequately trained on developing systems, organizations, and corporations, we could develop a system that sustains, employs, feeds, and takes care of every single person in here. We would not have to walk outside this room to get what we need if we understood the basics of how to develop a system. How do you develop an organizational structure? How do you fill out the paperwork necessary to file to become an LLC? How do you hold meetings, and how do you structure your employee handbooks, and all of that stuff? Why are our children not learning this at an early age? I mean, think about this. What is it? I don't understand this. There's, I think about, 18,000 hours of life that a child lives between the age of six and 18. They spend that 18,000 hours...I think...or, actually...they spend about 18,000 hours in school or something ridiculous like that. Why is it not that in those 18,000 hours at least 200 - 300 of those hours are spent training our children on how to prepare for the future – how to develop systems so they can escape white supremacy? You see?

Ultimately, when you look at an obstacle like racism, you could fight through it. You could overcome it. Or, you could get the fuck away from it. Excuse my French. Just leave. Just leave. I mean, look throughout history. Look at people in the past who have been oppressed. There are people who have had to just get up and fight, die, bleed, and everything else. That's powerful. That's extraordinary. That's incredibly brave — the fact that there were some people who just said, "Let's just pack up our stuff and go." I'll give you an example: the Mormons. These were some oppressed white people. They were out east, and they were being mistreated. They were being oppressed, because they were Mormons. And so, there was this guy, the leader, Brigham Young, who gathered about 250 families, and said, "Let's just go west. Let's just pack our covered wagons and go west to the great Salt Lake. There's nothing out there but freedom. There's nothing out there but opportunity to build our own. It's gonna be hard. We won't have much. There are no jobs. There's no McDonald's along the way. There's nothing out there, but if we can make this work, it'll be ours." So, he got these families together, 250 of them, and they all started going out west looking for this great Salt Lake. At that time, going west was a really scary thing.

About a third, literally a third, of the families died just from illness, getting killed by animals, or getting killed by some of the Native Americans out there. The Native Americans didn't want them out there, right? So, they were really dealing with it, but a few of them got out there. The last third got out there. When they got there, again, there were no jobs to go apply for, no schools to enroll their kids in, none of that. There was no government, no nothing. So, they just planted some potatoes, so they could eat. Then, they said, "Well, we need a bank," so they set up a bank. It'll be like a little...in their cardboard box or whatever, but they set up a little bank and put up a sign with the word "Bank" on it. That's the bank, right? Then somebody became the dentist, and the guy that's the dentist is maybe a guy who knows how to put on horseshoes. He knows how to hammer a horse's foot, so he's like, "I can do teeth, too, right?" It was real sloppy. It was really ghetto in terms of how they set it up, but there was just sort of this idea that, "This is ours. It's gonna be what we make it into, and we're going to make it into something great. It's gonna take time, so let's start with the little things, and the little things can become the big things." So, they start with the little things, and they create. They need a university, so they open up Brigham Young University and some other schools, eventually. Now, if you go out there to Salt Lake City, you see one of the wealthiest cities on earth. One of the wealthiest cities on the entire planet started off with a group of people who just said, "We don't want to be persecuted anymore. Let's pack up our stuff and go." Right?

For us as black people, I think our best option in this white supremacy thing is to pack up our stuff and go. If you're complaining about the public schools and how the public schools are doing your kids dirty and all of that stuff, just pack up your stuff and go. They don't know how to train a black boy on how to be a black man. They have no incentive to do that. Just pack up your stuff and go. You don't like your job? They're mistreating you on the job, or whatever? Well, you find a way to pack your stuff and go. You don't like the media? Pack your stuff and go. You say, "I'm going to support black media. I'm just going to get my media from black people." Right? For every single system that bothers you, oppresses you, or makes you uncomfortable you always have the option of packing your stuff and leaving.

Why do most people not do this? For the same reason that not every Mormon was ready to get in that covered wagon and go to the great Salt Lake. The journey ain't for everybody. Some people are scared, and it's okay for them to be scared. Maybe they'll come in a generation. Once other people found out how well they were doing out west, guess what? Other people started to follow. I know this feeling. I remember this feeling when I was first kind of doing this thing. I wasn't the first one to do what I did, but I kind of felt by myself. I didn't have much support. My own family didn't get it. My colleagues. I hung with these hoity-toity Negroes with doctorates and stuff, and they thought I was crazy. They were like, "Oh, you're gonna get black balled. If you keep talking this black stuff, they're not gonna hire you anywhere." I was listening to this thinking, "Man, yeah, they're right. I won't have a job anywhere, so I better do this right." So, I said, "You know what? One thing that I know is that I can't live like this anymore. I can't live like this. This is going to kill me."

You think there's no connection between racism, white supremacy on the job, and the fact that black men die earlier than anybody else? That's all that stress. That's that hypertension. I met a black man who was a successful Negro. He had an MBA, he worked at a bank or whatever, and he said the stress on his job was tearing his body up so badly, that he went to the doctor and the doctor said, "I don't know how to explain this, but all the testosterone in your body has disappeared." I'd never heard of that before. Like, he had...he literally...I mean, talk about emasculation by taking away his manhood. He said he had NO testosterone. So, he was having hot flashes and sleeping all day. He couldn't perform for his wife, because...you know. You need the testosterone to get at attention. You know what I'm talking about, right? He couldn't do that. He couldn't do any of that. He said the best day of his life was actually when he got fired from his job. He said that's when he started regaining his sanity.

Now, the interesting thing is that he didn't even know he was giving me this lesson at the time. He thought we were just talking, but I was sitting there kind of like, "Damn. I don't want to end up like that." He came downstairs and showed me this big basket of pills that he had to take just to keep his chemicals balanced and his mind right after going through the stress of racism on the job.

So, yes. Racism will drive you crazy. Racism will kill you. If you want to be safe, if even just for your own health, you've gotta pack up your stuff and go. What you'll find when you leave is that the amount of money you need to feel comfortable being free is not the same amount you needed to feel comfortable being a slave. Let's say you leave your job, and you were making $70,000 a year or something like that. Now, you're doing your own thing, and you're pulling $30,000 a year, or whatever. Yeah, it's a little tight, but it's not so tight that you're like, "Okay, I gotta go back to that job now. I gotta go back." Once you know freedom, you can't go backwards. Anybody know what I'm talking about? How many of you? Seriously? Once you know freedom, you can't go back. I remember thinking, "Man. Okay. So, this is how the other half lives. This is all the great stuff that happens in your life when you're not spending all of your time – literally, about 40.2% of your waking hours – working a nine to five job." If you add it up, what is it? Let's say you do 40 hours a week. Well, if you do that for 50 weeks a year, that's about 2,000 hours a year. Do that over a decade, that's 20,000 hours. Over a 40-year career that's 80,000 hours. So, most of us spend between 80,000 and 100,000 hours at our job. When you're free from that, you literally have another 80,000 - 100,000 hours which is almost like living to 150 years old. You have an extra 80,000 - 100,000 hours that you get to spend with your kids. An extra 80,000 - 100,000 hours to have conversations with your parents before they get old and die. Right? Another 80,000 - 100,000 hours you get to spend traveling, living life, and doing things you always wanted to do. That's the real reward. The money is not bad. Once you figure out how to make the money, that'll be nice icing on the cake. Once I started making more money I was like, "Yeah, this is what's up. This is cool," but money is not what you'll enjoy the most about the freedom. The freedom itself is the reward. I'm not kidding. That was my journey. That was my experience.

I had a special lesson this week. Yesterday morning I woke up and looked at my phone. I had a text message from my father, and he said, "Your uncle, Charles, was killed last night in a car crash." I was looking at the text, and you know. You get a message, and you just...it just doesn't seem real. I was like, "Am I really reading this?" This doesn't even seem real. My Uncle Charles and I were very much alike. He was my one relative. There were two men I knew when I was a baby – not including my father. He wasn't around. But my two uncles. He was the last uncle left. The other one died in 2012 from typical black male problems. He had a typical struggling black male life, if you can imagine what that looks like. He died young. This was my last one, and he was the most like me, so watching him die was like watching myself die. I don't know if anybody's had that experience: when somebody just like you dies in a car crash, so you can imagine how it feels. Imagine how they would feel if they knew that was gonna happen to them.

I started really thinking about it, and it bothered me. Death is such a horrible inconvenient thing in the sense that it doesn't really care what you got planned for next week. It doesn't care how many more years you thought you was gonna have. It doesn't care, like, what you're gonna do that day. Like, that day was his 41st wedding anniversary. He had just talked to his wife, my Aunt Janice, about what they were going to do that night. Three hours go by. He isn't home. It takes him 20 minutes to get home from work, so of course she's worried about the worst and finds out the worst. Then on top of that, it was the same day as my grandmother's birthday — my grandmother I told you was buried here in Atlanta. So, he was already...We were already feeling some kind of way, because it was Grandma's birthday. Then on top of that, it's his anniversary. Then his wife's birthday is one week after that, and his sister's birthday is on the same day. So, it was this crazy tornado of thoughts that came through when I was thinking, "This is unbelievable."

It's so unfair. It's so sad, sick, and ridiculous. Life plays these cruel jokes on you when you really think you're in control of things, and you find out that you're not. I thought about conversations I had with him through the years. I remember us having a conversation one day at Applebee's, and we were just sitting there talking. We were talking about financial stuff, and he was talking about his credit — how his credit score hadn't been what he wanted it to be. How he'd had some financial setbacks. He was talking about how he was gonna try to fix those things. He said, "Yeah, but it's hard to start all over when you're almost 50 years old." I said, "Yeah, but you don't know how much time you have, and whatever time you have, that's all you got. It would be nice if you were 20, but you're not. You can't let things go just because you're 50 and not 25. Like what does that mean? You do the best you can with what you got and where you're at. That's what you do. You just start where you're at, and you do the best you can with what you got, right now." He was on board with that. It wasn't like we were having an argument about it. It was just...I remember having that opinion like, "It's okay. It's gonna be fine. Just move forward. Take good steps. Do the little things. Do the right things."

Here it is 12 - 13 years later. I doubt if my uncle knew he was going to die like this. So inconveniently. That same week he had achieved his goal of improving his credit score. He and his wife had just...and again, this is tragic. It's tragic yet inspirational. It depends on how you look at it. Which side of the glass are you gonna look at? The tragedy is that he and his wife had just bought a brand new house. It was so new that they hadn't even moved in completely. They were sleeping on the floor. That's how new the house was. That's the sad part. But to me, the triumph is the product of the conversation my uncle and I had at Applebee's all those years ago. He made that comeback. He got that credit together. He got that money together, and he is able to leave this beautiful legacy for his family. Again, you don't know when you're going to get taken to the next level, but he prepared for it. He went out like a man. He did it right. So, ultimately, what I will say to you is that you don't know how much time you have on this earth.

I'm going to tell you this. I really believe that in this generation, we have an opportunity as a community. All of us in this space and all of us who are a part of these movements – the We Buy Black Movement and the Black Economic Empowerment Movement – have our shot at greatness. Yet, if we spend most of our time thinking about the despair and the challenges that come with being black, we're gonna miss all of that. What you do is realize that, yes, it sucks to be 25 points behind in the game, but that gives you a chance to have one of the greatest comebacks in history.

You got to go out there, line up, run the offense with complete precision, and show these people why we are the original man. Why we are the survivors of the middle passage. White folks couldn't have survived all of that. It's 250 years of slavery. We came out smiling and shining after 250 years of the worst slavery known to man. We went through 100 years of Jim Crow. We went through 40 years of mass incarceration, and we are still extraordinary people. Right? So, I say we tap into that, and build something that's amazing. I say we truly do what you would say is a corny phrase; make black people great again. That's what we are, right? It sounds like it's a Donald Trump thing, but I hope you understand what I'm saying.

To summarize, let me give you something that you can write down. I didn't know if this was supposed to be instructional or just me talking to you. Either way, I hope you benefit from this conversation.

With the students in our Black Millionaires of Tomorrow program, we tell them to keep their poise, P-O-I-S-E. That stands for producer, owner, investor, saver, and entrepreneur. That's what you teach your kids early. That's what you talk to your family about, because horses are on the other side of POISE. Right? If you keep your POISE, you get to be the jockey. If you lose your POISE, you become the horse. Right? On the other side of the producer is the consumer. On the other side of the owner is the renter, right? The investors and savers are contradicted by the spenders and borrowers. The entrepreneurs are riding the employees, unfortunately. Right? So, it doesn't mean that you can't be these things. All of us are consumers sometimes, but we shouldn't be consumers all the time. Many of us are employees at some point in our lives, but you can't let that be all of what you are economically, right? At the end of the day, you have to be in those three pillars of wealth. Stock and bond investing. So, as Christmas comes, promise yourself right now, if you're not invested in the stock market, you're going to start now. Start today. You can download Acorns, Stash, or Robin Hood — one of those three apps – and start investing tomorrow. You can start with just five dollars. Just have some amount. I don't care if it's two dollars a week. Have some amount that's automatically deposited into your stock portfolio, so you can begin that process. Same thing when it comes to real estate. If you can't afford to buy property, at least learn how. Doesn't cost you anything to learn how to buy property, right? Entrepreneurship, same thing. If you ever want to check out the Black Business School, we have everything you need. We have black professors who got tired of their jobs at white universities and decided to come and work with us. They're teaching every single week on every single thing that you'd ever want to know along with companies like Black Upstart and Jay Morrison Academy. All of us are basically building new systems and building a new nation that will allow us to educate our own at the highest levels. That's what we need as a community. That's what's gonna make us great. We gotta get away from the nonsense and start building up our dollars and sense. Alright, thank you guys very much for the conversation. I appreciate it.

Dr. Boyce Watkins

LECTURE 2

7 GOLDEN RULES OF LOVE AND MONEY

While my team and I were in the midst of planning our latest film, *The Black Love Blueprint*, one of the things that came up was how love and money intersect with each other. One person expressed that she does not believe love and money should have anything to do with each other. She went on to share her belief that if you love somebody, it does not matter how much money they make. The person saying this was about 22 years old, so I had to school her a little bit and let her know that money does matter. Money matters in every aspect of life. Money is one of the most crucial things that people talk about and deal with on a daily basis. It is one of the most important factors that will shape your life.

Anybody who feels money does not matter is probably someone who has the luxury of never worrying about money. This may be due to the fact that they have plenty of money themselves or a provider making them feel financially secure, but consider this example. Imagine you are the president. You have all of these Secret Service agents all around you. You may say, "Oh, security doesn't matter. I'm safe. I'm doing good." The only reason you have the luxury of thinking security is not that important is because you have the Secret Service agents always watching every little thing. If you are attacked, however, that thought process changes. The moment security has to jump in and save you is the moment you become more aware of the threats you did not initially believe existed. Money is the same way.

With all of this in mind, I decided to put together what I consider to be the seven golden rules of love and money. These are seven things I believe every couple should think about, talk about, and analyze before tying the knot. There are so many different ways that love and money link. There are so many different ways a marriage can parallel the merger of a business that it is not even funny, and I want to talk to you about some of those parallels.

First of all, love and money do mix. I need you to believe and understand when I tell you this. According to *Marriage.com* money, right behind infidelity, is the number two cause of divorce. Infidelity is number one. Money is number two. The general mentality seems to be that if someone gets cheated on they get mad and get a divorce. I think this is a really interesting thing when you think about, say, your grandparents who stayed married for 80 years. I bet if you were to ask

Grandma or Grandpa if there was ever any cheating they would probably say, "Yeah, but we just chose to stay together," but that is not my business though it is a fact. Number three is a lack of communication. Number four is constant arguing. I bet you that the lack of communication has to do with money, and the constant arguing has to do with money. Number five is weight gain. Number six is unrealistic expectations. Number seven is a lack of intimacy which can be linked to money. There are studies that show a woman is less attracted to her man if she feels he cannot provide and make her financially secure. Again, I am not saying that this is always the case, but I am saying it does happen. I have seen it. I have researched this. Number eight on the list is a lack of equity. A lack of equity, in many cases, links to money. Maybe the husband makes the wife feel like she is less worthy in the household, because he makes all the bread, or maybe the husband feels inadequate, because his wife makes more money than him. Either way, there are lots of dynamics to think about when it comes to love and money.

Based on my latest research on this topic and my doctoral studies in financial psychology, I believe one of our problems is that love is not rational. Love is not a rational process. Love does not follow the same mental process as mathematics does. Love also does not follow the same mental process as philosophy does. For example: thinking strategically, thinking about the long-term, or employing dynamic optimization. Love is one of those things where you say, "Oh, I really like her, and I don't exactly know why. She looked at me, and she was so beautiful," or, "Girl he has so much swag. He just stole my heart in that moment." Love is irrational in a way that is similar to making purchases. There are studies that show buying is also an irrational process. This is how companies sneak in and get money out of your pocket. They get you high. They get you in a little bit of a trance then they sneak in and grab your money. This is what they call unconscious buying. Love is often the same way. A guy may get a woman to sleep with him by playing a little music, getting her to drink a little wine, looking her in her eyes, and whispering sweet nothings in her ear. The next day, the woman may wake up saying, "Oh my God. Why did I sleep with this man?" Well, it is because love is an irrational process.

The irrational process of love is very interesting when merged with the highly logical, mathematical, scientifically driven concept of money. Money requires you to make a plan, set a budget, or even invest and understand a portfolio among other things. So, my theory is that mixing love and money is like mixing oil and water. It is like mixing two ingredients that really do not belong together. I believe that is why you see so much financial devastation in so many relationships when they fall apart. People often end up broke as a result, but my goal with the seven golden rules of love and money is to help prevent that from being you.

~

First Things First

The first thing you really want to understand is that family planning is critical to wealth building. I have a friend who lives in Botswana. She told me that her father has a lot of money, and the reason her father has a lot of money is because he has a lot of cows. I said, "Cows? Really? Where does he get the cows?" She said, "Well, he got them from his father, and his father got them from his father. Each generation, they have more cows." I visited the house, and they have a gigantic house with a Mercedes and a Hummer and servants and maids and a gardener. I mean, you must have some serious money to have a gardener: paying a person a full-time salary just to garden around your house. That is how well they are doing, and a lot of it comes from the money her father makes from cows. My friend expressed how she does not understand how African Americans survive. I said, "What do you mean?" She said, "Well, in our community, we do not disconnect family and money. Who you marry and form family bonds with is not just about who you think is the cutest, which girl has the nicest booty, or which guy has the most swag. When we form family bonds, we are thinking about the economic dimension of all of that. We are thinking about forming family empires and protecting that family unit, because that is critical to our survival." When I heard that, it made me really think about how African Americans view love and wonder if that view is healthy in the long-term. I mean, if you look at who has the worst net worth or the lowest net worth in America, that includes single black moms and single black fathers. It is probable that single black fathers are financially devastated, because they are dealing with child support courts. Meanwhile, many single moms experience financial devastation from caring for kids by themselves. Sloppy family choices cause financial ruin, and members of our community would benefit on multiple levels from breaking this cycle.

Divorce is one of the great economic death traps of America. Studies show that the average divorcee's wealth level drops by 70%. That is both the man and the woman. It ain't just the man. It ain't just the woman. It is both. The reason both of their wealth levels drop is because their attorneys are getting all their money. And child support? I am an 18-year veteran of the child support system. I have paid enough money in child support to fund NASA's mission to Mars. I tell you what, after I had that first baby and was writing those big ole $1,100 a month checks, I said, "Woo, I am not doing this again, because I do not want to write two checks like this every month."

On a brighter note, a strong family business can get you ahead. That is one of the bright sides to merging family and money in a good way. If you bring together your family and see it for what it can be – a tremendous economic asset – you can create a great family business. You have all these people who bring with them free labor, intelligence, love, trust, support, great ideas, networks that can be shared, and resources that can be pooled together. My belief is that every black family in America should have a family business. I do not care what anybody says. EVERY black family in America should have a family business. I do not care if your business makes $2 a year. Have a business, be proud of it, and work on making it a good business later on. It is the most fun you will ever have in your life. It is the easiest way to bond with the people you love. That said, family problems can make it tough to accomplish professional objectives. Have you ever seen somebody going through a messy relationship while they are trying to accomplish significant goals? Have you ever seen somebody who is dealing with fights with their significant other every day and still trying to finish school or raise a baby at the same time? Tell me those situations don't look like complete messes. Keeping that in mind, who you marry is probably one of the most important decisions you will ever make in your life. It has to be a lot deeper than a big butt, a smile, or flowers. Do you know how many women have been killed by men who bought them flowers? I am not saying your significant other is going to kill you, but I am saying you need to do a little more investigation before you make that big move and join your life with someone without really knowing who they are as a person or what they bring to the table. Marriage and dating are the most critical, risky, and sloppy investments people make. Remember that. Marriage and dating are investments.

When I was working on my doctorate, we did extensive studies, work, and research on corporate mergers and acquisitions. You would be amazed at how many theories for mergers and acquisitions can be instantly applied to marriage. Marriage ain't nothing but a corporate merger, and when two corporations decide to come together there is a lot of due diligence that must be done. You do not merge two big corporations together without first making sure the merger makes sense. You make sure each company is fully aware of what they are getting into. Every company also understands synergy: that two plus two does not equal when we come together. Two plus two must equal seven, because the whole must be greater than the sum of its parts. You bring the peanut butter. I bring the jelly. You bring the hot dogs. I bring the buns. If I have buns and you have buns, then we are going to have a big bun fest, and ain't nobody gonna eat good, because we did not analyze whether or not we were actually complementing one another or competing with one another. Buns and buns equals bumping heads. Buns and buns does not equal synergy. In many cases, you see people engage in sloppy mergers that knock them out of the game really fast. To keep that from being you, let us take a deeper look.

Rule #1

The first golden rule of love and money is making sure you are equally yoked. I am thinking about a story involving a professor I knew. She was one of those highflying black women. She was on top of the world doing great things, but she married a loser. I mean, this guy could not achieve his goals. He started law school then dropped out. He was not making much money. She made more money than him. He could not keep a job, but she always had job offers. Hence, she got all these awards and ended up achieving all these great things.

Meanwhile, he was not doing anything. One day he could not take it anymore, so he decided he was going to kill her. He killed his wife then killed himself. Their bodies were laying on the bed, and their two-year old and five-year old children walked into the room and found their dead parents lying on the bed.

I hate to share this horrible story, but these things happen all the time. I am not saying this woman is to blame for what occurred neither am I saying she should have known. However, I will say that people warned her for years about the fact that she and this man were not balanced. They were not of the same cloth in terms of being equally driven, equally motivated, equally skilled, or equally capable people. You want to make sure that you have a consistent understanding when it comes to your value system. Apparently, she valued hard work. He did not. She valued high achievement. He did not value it enough to pursue it. She came to the table equipped with all kinds of ability to be a highflyer in life. He was not a highflyer. He was a loser. Maybe she just wanted a husband. I do not know. At the end of the day, I think it is important to make sure that when you seek a partner you think about compatibilities. People talk about all kinds of compatibilities. They talk about emotional compatibility and professional compatibility. They talk about spiritual compatibility. They also talk about sexual compatibility, but they never think to talk about financial compatibility.

I want you to think about anybody you know who has gotten married. Ask yourself if you think they spent enough time talking about financial compatibility. Did they just say, "Oh well, I love so and so, because they are so cute, and they are nice to me," and the next thing you know they planned to get married? If so, they did not really think about the severity of the decision of marriage. They did not think of matrimonial union as a major corporate merger.

Rule #2

Opening your mouth early and often is rule number two. Talk. Similar to corporations doing due diligence, there must be an extensive amount of communication in order for you to decide that a love merger is going to work for you. Talking allows each party to know what they are dealing with.

I counseled a married couple one time: a beautiful woman and a brother who was lucky to have her. He loved her to death, but here was the problem. One of the things he never communicated to her before they got married and had two beautiful children was his desire to pursue his dream of going into Hip-Hop. He did not want to be a rapper but a big party promoter who did things behind the scenes on the business side. She did not care about all of that. All she cared about was having a good family and keeping everything together. This couple stacked up some credit card debt over the years and the wife, with her regular job, saved up the money to pay off the credit debt little by little. I do not remember what her occupation was, but she did not make a lot of money. Even still, she managed to chop away $10,000 in credit card debt. Because this couple had poor communication, the wife did not know he grabbed the credit card and maxed it back up to $10,000 to start a business. I guess it would have worked out if the business had succeeded, but it failed miserably.

Here I am in the end sitting and talking to a wife who is thinking about leaving her husband of 30 years, because of what he has done with the money. So, I believe it is really, really important for you to communicate: where you stand; what you believe in; how you think; how you perceive money; what you believe makes good financial decisions; the financial choices you have made in the past; your debt levels and such. If you do not communicate all of these things, you are going to end up with train crashes like this one.

I counseled another couple where they were mad at each other, because the husband thought that they

46

were going to share bank accounts. The wife was like, "I don't know what planet you're from, but where I come from, we don't share nothing. That money's mine." He thought, "What's yours is mine, and what's mine is yours." She said, "No, no, no. What's yours is mine and what's mine is mine." That was her mindset. Next thing you know, the couple ended up in divorce court. You must ask the right questions. Make sure you have these conversations. Talk about money. Maybe allocate a couple of hours or an hour at a time. If a person is not communicating, well, that is communication in itself. That tells you something right there about the person you are trying to get with. That means they are trying to hide something, or you have to decide if you are okay with being in a relationship with somebody who will not talk to you about money. They are not going to change their behavior just because you marry them.

Never think somebody is going to change their behavior just because you walk down the aisle with them or have a baby with them. No, whoever they are before the baby is who they will be after. Whoever they are before walking down the aisle is who they will be after. Make sure you are okay with the person you are looking at today. Do not think they are going to change tomorrow. I had a relationship once with a woman who wanted to marry me pretty badly, and I remember that one of things that really bothered me was how secretive she was with her money. I was very open with how much money I made, how much money I had in my retirement, how much money I had saved, what I plan to do with my money, and my future economic plans. She was as quiet as a mouse. She saved half of her income. She never told me how much money she made. She never told me how much she had saved. When I talked to her about starting a business together, she did not want to invest. I remember thinking, "Okay, we're not equally yoked. We're not financially compatible. Sayonara!" I did not want to be married to somebody who was not going to talk to me about one of the most important aspects of our relationship. Talk about your views and expectations before you make major commitments. That is absolutely critical.

Rule #3

Golden rule number three is making sure you know what you are getting into. You would be amazed at how many people I see who get married not knowing anything about their partner financially. They do not know anything about where they stand in terms of credit score. They do not know how they make their money. None of this stuff. It makes you think about the movie *Goodfellas*. You have this guy killing people and throwing bodies in a trunk. His wife does not really ask too many questions. She just enjoys living the good life. She likes the fact that her husband is an important man, but she does not know why he is important. She just knows that when they go to restaurants they always get a nice table in the back. Every Christmas they have whatever they want, and she can buy whatever she wants. She does not start really paying attention until the Feds are knocking at her door. I can tell you, there are lots of people who go to prison for things other people do. There are women in prison today, because their husbands were hiding crack, unbeknownst to them, in the basements of the houses they lived in. You must know what you are getting into.

Make sure you know your partner's credit score. If they will not tell you their credit score, that tells you something about them. If they will not tell you, go ahead and assume it sucks. If they will not tell you, that means that they are hiding something, because I do not know anybody in the world who has an 850 credit score and is not proud enough to volunteer the information.

Next, do you know your partner's debt level? A lot of people sneak debts into a relationship, because they know their partner can help them pay off their student loans. Do you understand this? Do you understand? This is so important. Students loans are now a national crisis. They are at crisis proportions. You have a whole generation of young people who were unfortunately misled into believing they had to borrow $100,000 to get an education that, in many cases, will not even get them a decent job. I am not making fun of you if you are in that category. If you are, do not worry about it. Join the club. A lot of people are in that category. I still have students loans. They are not such a problem anymore, because I started my business, and that gave me plenty of money to deal with it. Back to my point, however, you need to know that debt level. In fact, if you really want to do a thorough analysis say, "Look, if you show me yours, I'll show you mine. Here's my credit report. Let me see yours." It is almost like looking at each other's HIV test. You need to make sure that you know what you are walking into. If you are not sure, just make sure you are okay with the consequences or what can occur when something surprises you.

Do you know how much money they make? I think that is really important. I think that if somebody will not tell you how much money they make that is a problem. I mean, you want to know what your income level is going to be like in the household.

What does your partner have in savings? How a person views saving tells you how things are going to go down in case the two of you run into financial crisis. That view also sheds very important light on your partner's monetary value system. A person who does not save is a person who is living on the edge. If you are a person who does not like living on the edge and you have a partner who is not saving, I have news for you. You are going to be living on the edge now that you have merged your life with theirs. This is why, ultimately, you want to know how much they have in savings.

Is your partner skilled at income generation? This is really something that I think is important. You have a lot of women who are raised to appreciate a man who can fix the sink and fix the roof and stuff like that. Those are good skills, too, but I tell you what. I told my girls, "Try to find a man who knows how to just go ahead and make things happen in a good, healthy, safe, and legal way. Find a man who just says, 'You know what? I lost my job, but I got with my friends, and we started a business. Now we're making twice as much as we were making before. We needed to hustle up $1,000 for the rent. We went out and made it happen.' That's the kind of person you want to be partners with." These tend to be people who were trained to be entrepreneurs. Maybe you can get together as a couple and take a class on entrepreneurship, so you can learn how to start a business. These skills are out there. They are in books. They are in classes. There are so many ways to learn. The question is why are you not doing it? You are going to need it if you lose that job.

Rule #4

Rule number four is to use your ears more than you use your mouth. Do not just do all the talking. Do most of the listening. If you listen long enough, people will tell you who they are. You just have to make sure you hear it. Like Maya Angelou said, people are always going to tell you who they are. Because love is an irrational and emotional process, however, we often do not listen.

I encourage you to do what I tell my daughters to do. This applies to the guys, too. Just let people talk. If you just let them talk, eventually they are going to tell you everything you need to know. I tell my girls, "Listen to the way that man talks about money. Listen to him talk about when he gets money. Does he talk about what he is going to buy? Does he talk about whether he is going to invest? Does he talk about his savings? Does he talk about his long-term goals?" If your partner is obsessed with setting goals, saving, investing, building, and acquiring then they are going to become more of what they are already aiming to be. If they are aiming to be an accumulator and acquirer, then over time they are going to acquire more things. If they are monetarily wasteful, boastful, and flashy that means they are basically a walking ATM machine for every business that they go into. They are giving money away — making it rain on everybody else. Then when drought season hits, they — and now you, too — are going to be in big trouble. So, use your ears. Listen to your partner when they talk about money. Find out as much as you can. You can find out if maybe there has been trauma. Maybe they grew up really, really poor. People who grew up really poor tend to see money in a certain way, because they are afraid of losing it. This might affect how much risk they are willing to take. It might affect how much they really feel the need to save. It might affect how frugal they become. People who were born during The Great Depression, for example, tend to be extremely frugal.

Does your partner view money as something to be spent or as a source of capital? A person who views money as capital is usually going to be wealthy, because when they get money, they are going to invest it. They are going to build capital which will allow them to become producers and owners: things where they are making money. A person who views money as purely something to spend is always talking about what they are going to buy. "I want to get this car. I'm going to get those shoes. I'm going to get that outfit. I'm going to go on this vacation." People who think like that tend to run out of money.

How does your partner behave when they do not have much money? That is important for you to know, too, because money changes one's psychology. Professor Andrew Lowe of MIT actually found that money affects the same region of your brain as cocaine. When people get money, they get high just as one would on cocaine. Likewise, when people lose money they get depressed in the same way cocaine users do when cocaine is taken away. Ultimately, you want to know how your partner's behavior is affected in the presence and absence of money. I can tell you this. Somebody actually informed me, "Boyce, when your money ain't right, you get cranky." I did not even know that. A woman I dated a long time ago shared this with me. I thought about that, and I realized that not having financial security bothers me. It made me mad. I start thinking about all the people I loan money to and then have to ask, "Where's my money at?" I did not realize that those types of situations had the power to turn me into a real jerk sometimes, so I had to become more in tune with that.

Conversely, when some people get a lot of money they become very confident. They get really cocky. They get really comfortable and then they start wasting money. Then when they hit a financial crisis, suddenly they want to get on high alert again. You probably know this. You have probably seen your relatives. You know who I am talking about: those relatives you cannot find when they are doing well because they just got their paycheck. They do not want to hear anything that you have to say, but when they cannot pay the rent they show up at your house hat in hand all humble and meek making every promise in the world, because they need your help. So, yes. Money has a way of affecting people's confidence. Even men perform better sexually when they feel more financially secure. Women are more attracted to men when they are financially secure, because women have a natural ability to smell confidence. I believe it is Darwinian survival of the fittest: that the fittest men doing the best are gifted by Mother Nature to mate, procreate, and reproduce. At the end of the day, know what you are getting into and who you are dealing with.

Rule #5

Rule number five: pay close attention to the family dynamic. Every family has an economic dynamic. I remember what it was in my own family. On my mother's side of the family there was my grandma: the one who taught me about investing money and financial literacy. My grandma was a single mom with five kids, but she never had a financial problem. She never had to borrow money. She owned her house. She owned her car. She had money. She kept money saved. She had some investments. She had a retirement set up nicely. She also owned assets and had perfect credit. My grandma was on her stuff. I mean, she was just on her stuff.

On my father's side of the family they had a two-parent household, so you would expect that they were doing better. They made more money than my maternal grandmother did, but it just was not the same. We saw a lot of chaos, financial emergencies, and people coming over to borrow money. I remember my father getting calls saying, "Oh we need money to pay the rent. If you don't pay the rent by so and so date, this is going to happen." I remember watching my parents negotiate that within their marriage. I think my father handled all of that very well. Had he not handled it well, I truly believe it would have caused problems in their relationship. You will probably have a similar experience especially – especially – if you happen to link up with somebody who is one of the primary breadwinners and main economic vehicles for other people. When you become economically successful, it is just going to happen. It is inevitable. Other people are going to look to you to help them out and carry them. You are going to be subject to every sob story known to man. I know I am. I get sob stories about once every day or two.

Somebody calls and me and says, "Hey, Boyce, I need you to do this for me. I need help with this." It just happens. It is life. It occurs. You have to know what you are dealing with and have a partner who can handle it in a way that makes sense and feels good to both of you. If your partner has a little sister or brother they always have to take care of, and they are constantly taking food out of your children's mouths in order to take care of some adult who cannot take care of themselves, it is only going to make you mad. When you pay attention to your partner's family dynamic, you want to ask yourself, "Do they have relatives they are caring for?" They may have cousins or parents that they are trying to take care of.

Find out what your partner's extraneous financial obligations are. If you date someone who has kids out of wedlock, there will be child support. How do you feel about that? How will you feel if you find out they have a small business? A small business is worse than child support, because it is a huge financial drain. What if you are dedicated to giving to the church, but your partner is not? This can sometimes be a hard one to negotiate if the two of you are not on the same page.

Are there any risks to the income stream? That is very important to consider, too. A lot of people who marry professional athletes fall for this. The non-athlete will marry the professional athlete while they are doing extremely well. This example can go both ways, but I will use what I perceive to be the most common scenario. A woman's husband has just signed a big contract in the NFL but, there is not much conversation about what is going to happen once his NFL career is over. The NFL is really the worst, because NFL careers are very short. They are only about two to three years, so NFL, in my opinion, does not stand for National Football League. It should actually stand for "Not For Long." NFL careers end in the blink of an eye. Many professional athletes and their spouses or significant others think they are going to be financially secure for the rest of their lives, but nine times out of 10 it does not happen that way. Most of these guys end up broke.

Many women married to or dating men in the NFL are excited about the life. They think it is a big deal to be married to a baller. Everybody loves it, but many NFL couples do not stop to think about what they are going to do in four years when the NFL contracts are gone. Think about what the outlook is if the NFL player does not prepare himself for this? If he did not get a good education because he dedicated all his time to playing football, he has no skill. He cannot go out and make any money. If he never took a single entrepreneurship class or never learned about entrepreneurship on his own, he will not have any income generation skills. On top of that, he will be carrying the burden of his lifestyle. I mean, the lifestyle of some of these guys is just...it makes your head spin. It is so sad. Some professional football players have multiple women, multiple babies by different women, debt up to their eyeballs, a bunch of material trinkets that they do not really need, and maybe even a drug addiction that comes from playing professional sports. A lot of externalities, as they call them in economics, can occur as a result of this lifestyle to the point where some players wish they never had a chance to be a professional athlete in the first place. I see it all the time. You have to look at every scenario. You have to ask yourself, "Okay, what happens if we lose this money? What happens if he loses this contract? What happens if she no longer has her job at the bank?" That helps you understand the financial dynamic between the two of you and what you are both walking into.

Also, find out if your partner's line of work will require your involvement. For example, if you are a man married to a woman who is the governor of Iowa, she is going to require you to be involved in her career. Make sure you understand what your partner's career entails.

When thinking about the financial situation between you and your significant other, perform a stress test in your head. A stress test is when you change certain variables and observe the results. Here is an example. "Okay, if one of us loses our job, will we still be able to afford our house, the car, provide for the kids, and pay for food? If our investments go bad, what will we do? Oh, we've got money in savings. We're diversified." You and your significant other must always ask yourselves what happens if things suddenly go bad. The two of you need to know what you will do if the real estate market plummets, and all the wealth you have in your house suddenly disappears. Are you going to be okay? If the answer is no, you must make adjustments to make sure that you will be okay. A lot of people in Prince George's County, the richest black county in America, went down big time, because they had a lot of their money tied up in their homes. When the housing market went south, a lot of these people ended up filing for bankruptcy. For some, their houses to this day have not recovered economically.

Rule #6

Rule number six is to take note of the highway ahead. I knew a couple that was on the brink of divorce, and one of the reasons they were going to divorce was because the husband felt like he had been bamboozled. I asked the man if his wife had cheated on him, and he said no. I then asked if his wife had a baby with another man. The answer to that was no, as well, so I asked, "What did she do?" He said, "Well, she came in. We got married. We were both making $70,000 a year. I thought we were going to save our money, buy a house, and do all these other things. As soon as we got married, she quit her job and went back to school. She didn't even tell me." When I asked him if they had talked about her returning to school, yet again, his reply was no. I said, "Well, if you didn't talk about it, how do you know she's going back to school? She didn't bring it up? Maybe you didn't ask. Did you ask her what her plans were?" His response was, "Well, I guess I didn't really talk to her about it enough." There you go. That is the problem. You have to know, to the best of your ability, what is going to happen. Do not assume that what you are looking at is always going to be there after you get married. People change when they get married. They change all the time.

Let me tell you about a theory in finance called moral hazard. There are thousands of research papers written on this topic. Moral hazard involves a person waiting for someone to make a decision that transfers power in their favor and then suddenly changing their behavior. A famous example is when men date women long enough to get sex and then quit the relationship. Have you ever heard a woman complain about this? A guy she dates begs her to have sex. She finally gives in.

Then, he does not call her anymore. He starts acting like a jerk, because he got what he wanted. That is a moral hazard problem. Getting the sex then feeling like, "Okay, I don't need you anymore." It is not right, but it happens all the time. Marriage is another situation that can turn into a moral hazard problem. A lot of people do not want to get married, because they are scared the other person is going to change their behavior: suddenly gain a whole bunch of weight or stop having sex with them. Sometimes that happens. I do not think you should distrust your partner, but at the very least, you should do your due diligence to communicate as effectively as possible to ensure that you are aware of as many potential changes as possible. Some of these things can actually be put into a contract.

People think prenuptial agreements are a bad thing. Somehow they think it is communicating a lack of faith in the endurance of a couple's love. No, a prenuptial agreement is what Chris Rock used to call "in case shit." He was talking about insurance. Remember that? He said insurance should be called "in case shit" in case shit happens. So, think of a prenuptial agreement as something you sign just in case shit happens. You are saying, "Look, I love you. I love you, and I always want to get along with you whether I am with you or not. So, in case shit happens – in case we do not stay together – let us sign a contract that will define the terms of how we conduct ourselves in the event we no longer love each other to death. We do not want that to happen. We do not plan for that to happen. At the same time, we want to make sure that if in the small probability that we may end up divorced like the other 50% of all marriages, let us make sure we are clear. We will set terms on how we are going to divide our assets and execute visitation – how are we going to do the divorce in general – so we do not give all of our wealth away to lawyers." That is a smart couple. That is a couple that has really noted the road ahead and taken necessary precautions to ensure they will not allow this merger, if it goes badly, to ruin everything else in their lives.

So again, when you think about the road ahead, figure out your partner's financial plans. They might have a whole bunch of money saved, but they might be planning to take that money and put it all into their record studio, so they can get that first rap album out, and get signed to a record deal. They may be planning to go back to law school, because now they have you to pay the bills, and they do not have to worry about paying bills anymore. Know what the plans are.

Does your partner have goals and dreams? I tell my girls not to ever date men who have no goals or dreams, because those are not going to be men who will be successful. Success does not happen by accident. Success happens with a plan. Success happens on purpose. I tend to personally believe that a partner with goals and dreams tends to be a partner who is most likely to be successful. If you are a person who has goals and dreams, you probably want a partner who has some dreams of their own. If not, then I do not know how that works out. With that, is your partner planning to go back to school? Are they planning to buy a home or rent for the rest of their lives? Some people are trained to be owners while others are trained to be renters. Some are raised to own businesses, stocks, bonds, and property while others were raised in families where they never talked about that. They do not own anything. They just want to give all their money to white people until they die. It is easier to deal somebody who already understands these values than somebody who does not. The latter will probably lead to constant fighting.

I have students in my Black Wealth Bootcamp who ask me, "What would you do if your wife did not agree with anything you're doing, because she thinks that it's a waste of money?" My response is, "I don't know. I can't tell you to get a new wife." That said, some people do get a new wife or husband. I am not saying you should do this. I am not telling anybody what to do. I would never tell anybody to get a divorce unless they already want to get one. At the end of the day, what I really want to do is build a time machine, so they can go back in time and find a spouse more equally yoked with them: a spouse they can communicate with so they can ensure the person fits within their pre-existing life portfolio.

You see, everything I can teach you about money, investing, and wealth actually relates to things you already know. Based on your own life, you understand portfolios. You understand diversification. You understand risk-return relationships. You understand what investment means. You understand all of that. Here is the thing. You already have a portfolio that God gave you when you were born. Your portfolio is nothing more than all the things in your life that matter to you and have value to you. That is your portfolio of life. Now, with this portfolio of life, there are some basic rules that apply. One of those rules that apply, just as in real investment theory, is that you do not pick an investment, because it is going to make the most money. No, you do not do that. You choose based on what they call correlation. Correlation is how investments relate, connect, and fit with all the other things you have that are of value. If it does not fit, then you must get rid of it. If it does not fit, you do not want that. When you talk about bringing something into your life, it must fit with everything else. If I am a person who wants to be a deacon or a bishop or a pastor, I cannot marry a woman who worships the devil. I mean, God bless her, but she cannot be the pastor's wife if she is talking about all hail Satan. That ain't goin' to work. She does not fit. Such an investment of marriage with this woman would not be consistent or correlated with my pre-existing portfolio. Therefore, I would need to pick a different wife. When you are picking your partner, you need to pick based on correlation. How do they fit? This means, again, you must do your due diligence in understanding what you are investing in.

Next, are your partner's parents married or single? One of them will be coming to live with you at some point. That is very, very important to understand. People do not factor that in. I had a friend who was dating this wonderful woman, and the woman had a mom who was single, in her 50s, and eating cheeseburgers all day. She never ate vegetables, and she worked herself into the ground. When she was not working, she did not save her money. She spent it all at the casino. I told my friend, "Before you marry this woman. I need you to think about this. Her mama ain't going to be young forever, and her mother is doing nothing to prepare herself for old age. She's not eating healthy which means she's going to have a plethora of health problems, and she has no money saved. She ain't going to have no good health insurance. Make sure you're ready for all of that." Love does not always conquer everything. You need to make sure you know what you are getting into. What is the situation of your partner's parents? If their parents are financially secure, that is one less pressure point on top of you.

Rule #7

Rule number seven is very important. Make sure you know your partner's status. What does that mean? I am going to tell you. There was a lady who reached out to me via email after I wrote my book *Financial Lovemaking*. She said, "Dr. Boyce, I just want to tell my story. My husband was doing really well, and we were making a lot of money. We lived next door to Bob Costas. What I did not know was that my husband had a crack addiction. I found out the hard way. One day, I woke up, and he was gone. Our bank accounts were emptied, and suddenly I had no money, no house, and no husband." All along she had no idea that the financial security she thought she had was a complete illusion, because it was being drained right from beneath her by the one she loved. It was too late for her to change any of that.

This lead me to develop a concept called FIV: financial irresponsibility virus. The financial irresponsibility virus is characterized by four things I have seen destroy people financially: sex, drugs, alcohol and gambling. If not handled in moderation, these things destroy. Look out, so you do not get infected with FIV. Look at poor Camille Cosby. I am not saying that Bill Cosby did or did not do what he was accused of, but I can definitely tell you Camille Cosby is probably disappointed that Bill's lack of sexual discipline caused them tremendous embarrassment and probably at least $100 million in legal fees. Whether Bill raped anybody or not, one thing that is well known is that Bill likes the ladies. He liked and slept with a whole lot of them. That became his vulnerability.

Drugs are also a major way to lose all of your money. If you ever want to go broke, just become a drug addict. Three celebrities we all love – Prince, Michael Jackson, and Whitney Houston – were all drug addicts. The money they were making enabled their addictions which made them even worse, and drugs ruin not only your finances but your health as well. There are studies that show American productivity as a whole is dropping, because corporations cannot find any young healthy people to hire due to disturbingly high numbers of people being high on pills or using all these medications pharmaceutical companies are putting out. These are things you have to look out for.

Alcohol was actually rated as the most dangerous drug in the world in a recent study: more dangerous than crack, heroine, and cocaine. So you ask, why is that? How can alcohol be ranked the most dangerous drug in the world? Well, alcohol is ranked the most dangerous drug in the world, because people think it is safe. They do not factor in all the economic loss that occurs from lack of productivity. People commit crimes while they are drunk. Drunk driving accidents kill people every single day. Health related issues go with alcohol, as well. I am not saying you are a bad person if you drink. I am saying that if you decide to form a relationship with someone who does not, know how to drink in extreme moderation. That sounds like a strange term, but you know what I am saying. You are risking quite a lot.

Drugs aside, gambling is one of the worst addictions a person can have. I remember one time I was buying a car from a guy in Syracuse, New York, and he was 76 years old. I asked, "Why don't you just retire?" He said, "Well, I had half a million dollars in my retirement account, but I spent all my money at the casino. Now I've got to work to pay my bills." At that moment, I decided I did not want to be in that situation ever, especially not as an old man. So, beware gambling.

Be leery of shopping addictions, as well. You have

things like retail therapy where people are addicted to shopping as a way to soothe themselves psychologically. Those who struggle with this should find a different coping mechanism that goes beyond spending money in order to feel better.

Lack of financial literacy is also a bad little virus to have. If a person is not financially literate, that means they do not know how to save. They do not know how to invest. They do not know how to make financial moves. They do not know how to start a business. I always argue that a person who is financially literate and financially capable is a better partner than one who is not. It is the same as playing basketball on a team with somebody who knows how to dribble and shoot. That is a whole lot better than playing on a team with somebody who has never seen a basketball before.

The last piece I am going to throw in is lack of discipline. If your partner is not disciplined, look out. There are a lot of people who know what they need to do, but they just do not do it. If you find somebody who is financially disciplined, that is a person worth looking at. Obviously there are more factors you should consider. You deserve to be loved. You should be respected. You should look for all the other things in relationships. If you want somebody that is cute then go for that, too, but be sure to think about financial compatibility, as well.

~

Those are my seven golden rules of love and money. If you make the right decisions, you can really find that happily ever after. Anybody who says money cannot buy love or that money cannot buy happiness is full of shit. Excuse my French. I will tell you what. I know a lot of people whose ability to be attracted to another person comes down to provision of financial security. People might call them gold diggers for thinking that way, but that is not true. Financial security is a very important part of wellbeing.

People who are not financially secure tend to be stressed out. They tend to be unhappy. They tend to be miserable. They tend to make really bad decisions in life, because they do not make enough money. Why would you not want to be financially secure? Why would you not want a partner who could provide that security? It is no different than providing physical security. Why would you choose a partner who cannot help you be safe? Why would you choose somebody who is going to make your life more insecure than it is supposed to be? That does not make any sense. Stop saying money has nothing to do with love. I am not saying you should go give somebody money and say, "Hey, here's a bunch of money. Will you marry me?" However, I think examining each other's ability to provide some sort of financial balance and wellbeing should be considered a part of the relationship process no different from wanting to have a spouse who is good with children. The same way you want your children to be safe physically from the actions of your partner, you also want your children to be safe financially from the actions of your partner. It all goes hand in hand. Also, not buying happiness? Please. Anybody who says money ain't related to happiness has never been broke. I have seen a lot of people become very unhappy, because they did not have enough money. Find your happiness. Find your happily ever after. Do you your way. Do not let me tell you everything to do. Just make sure you factor these things in, so you can make good decisions.

It is not enough for us to just want money or want to learn about money. We have to go out and learn how to make money in an ethical, healthy way. I guarantee you that once you learn how to do that, you are going to be much happier than when you felt somebody else controlled your life. Visit:

TheBlackWealthBootcamp.com

It is one of my programs where we break down things such as discussed here. So, if you are not in the Black

Wealth Bootcamp, yet you may want to go check it out. Our goal is to make sure that there are 40 million or at least 10 or 20 million financially literate black Americans. Now get together, have some sex, and have a good life. I want you to be happy.

LECTURE 3

7 GOLDEN RULES OF KIDS AND MONEY

I put together something for any family that is really looking for a way to get ahead. One thing we have going on in this country is a lot of struggling. There are a lot of people suffering economically and buried under debt. In addition, there are a lot of people who are unhappy with their jobs. Even more, there are a lot of people who are not prepared for retirement. Finally, there are a lot of people who do not have any savings and some people who do not have any assets. What is interesting to me as a person holding a PhD in Finance is that I also see a lot of people who are on the other side of the fence. I see a lot of people who have money to burn. Usually, these are the people who own plenty of assets, and often times they are people who possess a ton of wealth. They are people who are doing extremely well and, if they so choose, have the ability to go on $10,000 luxury vacations. These are people who can afford to rent or buy private jets. Some of them own companies and make money in their sleep while other people are actually doing the work. I always ask myself what the difference is. Why do some people live the easy life while other people seem to be in a perpetual struggle? After teaching college students for the last 25 years I have come to the conclusion that a lot of the difference has to do with know-how. In other words, it has to do with what you are taught, how you are taught to play the economic game, and the culture of your household among other things. So, I created these seven golden rules of kids and money in order to help those parents that really want a way out. The parents who really want to create a different legacy and a different life for their children. Also, I created this to make sure that parents do not feel that they have to spend $50,000 – $60,000 a year for their child to attend an expensive university to get access to the secrets that help rich people become rich people.

The seven golden rules of kids and money are very simple blueprints you can follow, and it is not hard to do. I get in a lot of trouble with a lot of people who are perhaps from the liberal establishment who believe it best to tell black people there is nothing they can do to earn wealth. They believe it is best to tell black people, "Unless the government or white people decide to become polite and help you out, you cannot possibly get ahead." I am going to tell you the truth. I am not trying to sit around and wait for anybody. That is not something I want to do. Therefore, with my PhD being the gift that I am offering to you, I want to lay out what I consider to be seven golden rules of kids and money. Thus, without further ado, let us get started.

Why I Created This

Here is why I created this list. First of all, black people are behind in the wealth race. We fell behind because of slavery, oppression, Jim Crow, and discrimination. There is no question about the fact that for hundreds of years black people have been unfairly treated. For example, black people have had our property stolen. Black people have been blocked out of economic opportunity, and black people have been put at the back of the economic bus. There is no question about it. It is well documented.

At the All Black National Convention every year we talk about reparations. My answer in response to whether or not we deserve reparations is absolutely yes. It is a complete no-brainer. There is no question about it but, the question for me is this. If you know that you were robbed and you know the thief is never going to give back the property they stole from you, do you sit on the side of the road in destitution complaining? Do you say, "The reason I don't have anything is because they robbed me and took my stuff"? There has to be a point where you accept the idea that the police are not coming. The racial police are not coming. They are not going to come and allow black people to suddenly get what we deserve. At least, they are not coming in my lifetime or yours. Even though it is not fair, there are points where you have to do something about it.

The problem is that while we fell behind due to racism, slavery, and Jim Crow, we remain behind. We are focused on what others have instead of what we can have on our own. We tend to not talk about financial literacy, and we do not have a culture of wealth building in our families. Instead, our culture tends to be one that is based on consumption. Even if you look at a lot of the studies that are out there which talk about black folks and money, most of them are focused primarily on spending power – not actual wealth, assets, or asset-building power. They have trained you to think of your money as a tool to support white supremacist corporations, and help them get rich.

The reason they do these studies on spending power is to get big corporations to market products to black people and engage in the doctrine of unequal exchange. The doctrine of unequal exchange, as explained by Dr. Claude Anderson, is one where black people are giving white people real value and real money while they give us something that is not worth much of anything. Effectively, conversations that are only about spending power are not healthy conversations. You should not be proud of how much money you are able to spend. Rather, you should be proud of how much money you are choosing to invest and choosing to save.

Here is what we have to understand. Number one, telling our children to get jobs only embeds them more deeply into the white supremacist system. Let me explain why. Let us say your child goes to a great university, and they make good grades. They may or may not get their dream job. There are millions of black kids – I meet them all the time – who do the right thing. They have master's degrees from top universities and work their butts off, but they are really disgruntled and unhappy. Mostly, they feel that they were lied to. They feel that they did what they were supposed to do to allegedly have access to the American dream, but for them the American dream turned into a big ole lie. They go to work every day. They feel surrounded. They feel like everyone they report to is not black, and no one understands them. They are dying to quit their jobs. They cannot wait, but the reason they cannot quit their jobs is because they do not have any savings. They do not have any investments. They do not have any alternative streams of income. They have no knowledge whatsoever on how to create a business. On top of that, jobs are scarce, and jobs are also volatile. So, telling your kids to get a job does not really liberate them. What it does is make them more committed to the system we know is oppressive.

A lot of the key to wealth has to do with psychology just as in fitness. You'll have people that say, "It is impossible for me to lose weight," but it is not really impossible. Most of the time losing weight is difficult, because you are addicted to eating the wrong food. You are not accustomed to looking at the nutrition labels of the food you are eating. You are not trained to know which foods are healthy and which foods are not. You are not able to understand any of that. What happens is that you end up wondering why so and so loses weight. You wonder why other people are in shape but you are not. "Why are they doing better than me?" you ask. A lot of it is because they know things you do not know. They do things that you do not do. They have habits that you do not have. It is not because it is impossible for you to lose weight. It is because you have not been trained to do it, and you have not developed the habits necessary.

If our kids spent as much time learning wealth as they spent learning how to dribble basketballs, throw footballs, and dance I personally believe that within one or two generations we would take the lead in the wealth race. Asians right now, for example in America, have higher incomes than whites. There is no reason black people cannot be in that same position. Black people simply have to do a few things in terms of understanding the importance of creating businesses and holding their wealth.

One thing about Asians is that they really love to save. Asians love to invest more than they love to spend. In America you have to work hard to get people to stop spending. In Asian countries you have to work hard to get people to stop saving so much. That is why their economy works differently than our economy. Ultimately, if we could shift the paradigm in terms of how black folks think, I believe that within one or two generations we could actually become among the world leaders in terms of assets and wealth building. We can make this happen especially if we connect with other black people around the world.

If you teach your kids properly, they can become assets not liabilities. You will run into problems in life if you do not train your children on money and how money works. Train them on how to be intelligent with money or your children will become a drain on you as they get older. They will come to you asking to borrow money when they are in their 30s. They are going to come and try to live with you when they are 38 years old. They are going to come to you every time they have a financial crisis, but when you have a financial problem, they will not be there to help you. A lot of this starts when children are young and go to college. You take on all that debt. You pay for every little expense. You give them money like it is not important, like it grows on trees. Well, they begin to see you as a bank. They start to see you almost like the federal government, as a place they can go to get whatever they need.

As you work to form strong economic habits in your kids, remember that you have obstacles. You are competing with media and music that pretty much teaches kids all the wrong things when it comes to money. It teaches them how to waste everything they have. It teaches them how to not put themselves in a good long-term economic position. It teaches them that going to the club and throwing money up in the air is the best way to use their money. Basically, you are dealing with a world where financial intelligence is not the norm. You are going to have to raise your kids in an abnormal fashion to make this work. Keep in mind that repetition is the key to habit formation. Whatever you decide to do with your kids, even if it is very basic, just be extremely repetitive, and that will go a long way. The things you teach your children will probably remain in your family for many generations. I have seen families where maybe a great grandparent taught something to their children when they were very little. Next thing you know, those children teach their children, and the children's children teach their children. I remember I met a guy from India. I asked him, "You own your own business? At what point did your father or your mother start talking to you about owning a business?" His response was, "Well they never talked to me about getting a job. It never came up. We did not even know if that was an option until we got older. We always knew that we were going to have a business."

Rule #1

Start teaching your children about money as soon as they are born. Starting a family business is a great way to bond with your children. It is also a great way to teach them on the job. Also, when kids become intelligent and capable they actually become a great source of low-cost labor for the company where they are learning. They are then apprentices. They are getting money from you, and you are getting the benefit of getting some help in terms of labor. Rather than them going out and giving 40 hours of labor to a stranger who does not care about them, they are giving 20 to 30 hours of labor to you.

A family business is a great tool for teaching when it comes to children. Make it part of your daily conversation. Talk about money. Just make casual statements like, "Make sure you own your own business when you grow up. Make sure you save your money. You should invest. Tell me how your stocks are doing. You own some stocks? Did you make any money this month?" Little things like that can go a long way in terms of getting the child geared to economic thinking at an early age. I think it should be a lot like church in the sense that most kids cannot even remember the first time they attended, because their parents took them as infants. They had a mother, grandmother, or father who took them to church so early that they did not even understand what the pastor was saying. They did not know what was said. They may not know much else, but they do know they are supposed to go to church, because grandma said so. Wealth building should be the same way. Start teaching the concepts – savings, budgeting, investing money, and ownership – to your children before they understand what you are talking about. Then when they finally become more aware, they are going to reflect on what you have said, and it is going to start making sense to them.

The concept of ownership is really important. Particularly emphasize that a job you acquire rather than build for yourself is not your job. You are borrowing someone else's economic power. Owning something is really what gives you power that is yours. Put your children in a consistent program on wealth building. Those who tend to think the most about wealth building tend to have the most money just like people who pay the most attention to the lyrics of their favorite rappers tend to be the best rappers. The same thing is true when it comes to money. People who talk about money and think about money tend to have the most money. You cannot tell me money does not matter, because everybody needs money. If money does not matter to you it is only because you have been afforded the luxury of having somebody who has thought about money enough for you to never need it. If you have ever known what it is like to starve to death, be evicted, or not have any food in the refrigerator to feed your kids, then you know the importance of money.

Rule #2

Rule number two is to start investing before your kids are born. Start teaching when they are born. Start investing before they are born. The most important variable in wealth building equations is actually time. I will give you an example. If a person started investing in *Amazon.com* say in 1997, today they would have about $500,000. The stock prices back in 1997 were almost at zero. Or better stated, the value of the investment is almost at zero. Today, however, our figurative person has made 500 times what they originally put into *Amazon*. This is not the only example. There are other ones out there. There are literally about a 1,000 different stocks I could show you with that same layout. You have Nike, Coca-Cola, Walmart, a lot of companies that if you had invested in them as maybe part of a broad investment strategy, you would have had a ton of money after just 20 or 30 years.

So, what I want you to do is imagine that it is 1917. Let me tell you this. If you had a relative in 1917 who just took whatever pennies they could afford and just put a little bit of money in the stock market every month, just a little tiny amount every month and did that consistently, your family would probably have millions and millions of dollars in wealth. The same way your grandparents could have done that for you in 1917, well somebody can do that for you in 2017. You can do that for someone else. Do whatever you can afford: just tiny amounts on a regular basis. If you are in my Black Stock Market program or The Black Wealth Bootcamp, you have heard me talk about the $5 a day investment plan. If you were to do $5 a day over a long period of time, then you would not be poor anymore. There is no way, historically, that a person investing $5 a day can be poor. If they did not spend that money and leave it in the market, they can have hundreds of thousands of dollars in wealth which technically makes them not poor.

I had a friend whose grandfather worked at University of Chicago in the 1940s. When he was there he had access to a small investment that he made in a company that he was part owner in. The grandfather got those shares of stock and held onto them. Years later around the year of 2010, his granddaughter was able to take that money and make a down payment on her house. Now her house is worth hundreds of thousands of dollars. The original investment was probably a few hundred bucks, maybe a few thousand dollars, but it was not much. Because her grandfather had the foresight in the 1940s to think about his grandchildren at that time, however, his grandchildren were able to have a better life. The little things you do right now will make a big difference in the lives of your children, grandchildren, and great grandchildren. Now, there are the exceptions. There are some huge investment opportunities. Bitcoin is a big one. I wish I had been smart enough to buy it back in the day. Bitcoin could have been bought for just a few dollars early on for even as low as 30 cents. Now Bitcoin is worth over $4,000 today. I do own Bitcoin, but I bought when it was at the $3,000 mark. I thought maybe $3,000 was too high, but now it has gone up to $4,000. A lot of black people missed out on this, because we were too busy working and not spending much time investing.

Rule #3

Rule number three is to teach your children to play the game from the top down. You have to play to win. In the wealth game if you do not play to win then you are playing to survive. That means you are probably playing to lose. One of the things I give students in The Black Millionaires of Tomorrow program is an acronym called POISE. I always tell them, keep your POISE. POISE stands for producer, owner, investor, saver, and entrepreneur. That means that when you are entering the economic system you want to be a producer more than you are a consumer. You want to be an owner not just a renter. You want to be an investor not just somebody who borrows money. You want to be a saver not just a spender. You want to be an entrepreneur not just an employee. The people that produce products for other people to buy tend to be wealthier. People that own assets tend to do better than people who do not own anything. Those who invest tend to do better than those who do not invest. Those who save tend to do better than those who spend, and those who run their own business instead of working for others do not have to deal with the stress of on-the-job racism.

Another model we use in The Black Wealth Bootcamp is COST. This is a model I created for black people, and COST stands for contribute, own, save, invest, and target. I feel that if you want to have freedom you must be willing to pay the cost for your freedom. In the words of James Brown, you have to pay the cost to be the boss. As a community, if we truly want freedom we have to establish economic freedom on our terms by using our mechanisms and our methods to get there.

The "C" for contribute means that every black person who cares about the community should contribute 2% to 7% of their income to some institution in the black community other than their church. That means out of every $100 just give $2 to $7 towards something you believe in. It could be the NAACP, your local T-ball league, or your local community center. Whatever it is, just give to something that is going to benefit black people.

The "O" stands for own. Everybody must train and plan to own something. Every black person in America must own assets. There is no excuse. Everyone must own something. You start with very basic things like owning shares of stock. You can buy a share of stock in five minutes for $5. The idea is that ownership is a mindset, and people that don't have an ownership mindset tend to be those who rent, and they do not think renting is a bad thing.

The "S" is for save. Investing means that you save your money, so your money can save you. You invest your money so your money can work for you.

The "T" is for target. When you spend your money, your money is your power. You do not give all your power away. When you spend your money, target black businesses, so you can build your community.

Then, I also have something called The Five - E Philosophy which I likewise put together for black folks: economics + education + expectations = empowerment. That is very basic. What it means is that, number one, every child in the black community should be economically trained. I do not care who you are. I do not care if you never plan to start a business. You need to know how to start one just in case you end up unemployed. Your kids do not want to hear that they cannot eat, because Mommy or Daddy cannot get a job. That is not going to fly. You cannot feed your children with excuses. You can only feed them with results.

Secondly, education must be the most important thing in your household. Educated people do not usually end up feeling that they are being kicked by white supremacy. Educated people who are economically intelligent do not usually feel that white folks control their destiny. So it is very, very important as a black person that education be the most important thing in your household. You do not have to go to school to get an education. You do not have to go to college to get an education. You can get an education on your cellphone. Everything you need to know is right there on your cellphone.

Set high expectations. Do not accept mediocrity. I taught on college campuses for 24 years, and all those years I have been on college campuses I have seen so many young people trained to accept mediocrity. They would be extraordinarily prepared for the step show. They would be extraordinarily well dressed. They would be incredibly good at doing the latest dances, and they would be really good at knowing the latest rap lyrics. However, when it came to the things that actually matter, the things that play the greatest role in survival, they were not ready for any of that. So, expectations are really important. Because we set low expectations, our results are typically low.

Tell your kids about the horse and jockey system of capitalism. Capitalism in America is a system where there are people who get all the benefits over people who do all the work. If you think about a horse and jockey scenario, the horse is doing all the running. The horse is running around the track. He's running hard. He's running fast. The jockey isn't doing much work. He's just telling the horse where to go. When the horse wins the race, the jockey gets all the money. The jockey gets all the praise.

Well, capitalism is kind of the same way. The jockeys are the people who own assets. They are the people who own stocks and bonds, the people who own real estate, the people who own businesses. The horses are the laborers. The people who are not thinking about an investment but about getting a job are the ones who support businesses. They, in turn, make the business owners wealthy.

Another type of horse might be the person who rents an apartment. They are just thinking about having a place to stay that month, so they pay rent, sometimes over several years, while the landlord is able to build wealth, because he owns the house. After 30 years of paying rent they have literally given their landlord enough money to afford down payments on maybe five houses. During that time and after it is all said and done, the tenant has nothing to show for it while the landlord has assets.

Another example would be the stock market. You have a lot of people who have made lots of money in the stock market. They cannot understand why the wealth gap between the rich and poor will not go away, but I am suspicious that it is because you basically have two different types of people racing down a freeway. One group of people is using a jet airplane, and the other group of people is walking. A person who is walking can never compete with someone who is on a jet airplane. The jet airplane is always going to go faster. The issue is when you talk about wealth, you must ask, what is your wealth building vehicle? Are you trying to even get a vehicle?

As much as we would like to say that ownership is impossible in America that simply is not true. I could show you how to buy shares of stock in five minutes with $5. You can buy shares of stock for the same price that it costs you to go to McDonald's or to buy a pair of shoes. The difference is that some people are trained to go buy the shoes before they will go buy the stock. They are trained to go buy some chicken before they will put money into a business. Ultimately at the end of the day it does not mean that you are a bad person for buying chicken. I mean I ate some chicken today. What it means is that you have to really pay attention to where your money is going. Just realize that when they do all these studies bragging about black spending power and how great it is, they are subtly saying black people are trained to only see their money as spending power. In some countries money is seen as something to be saved, preserved, and capitalized.

Do not tell your children that they should avoid the stock market. A lot of people are afraid of the stock market, and that is not wise. There have been trillions of dollars made in the stock market, and you want to participate in that. Also, do not train your children that money is something that should be spent. Money can be spent. We know that everybody spends money. However, spending money should not be the first thing that comes to mind.

Rule #4

Reinforce delayed gratification. Warren Buffet, one of the richest men on earth, says, "The stock market is a wealth transfer from the impatient to the patient." He is basically saying that impatient people show up and give their money away to people who are able to wait. If you cannot delay gratification then you are going to end up poor. If you look around our community, we do not have any mechanisms in place that really teach people to delay gratification. Everything is based on instant gratification. Everything in social media, entertainment, and all of that teaches instant gratification. You have to break your child away from some of that.

Thinking like an investor in every aspect of life is important. You want to tell stories and give examples to your children. Say, "Hey, you know so and so has that Lamborghini, because when he was young he studied the hardest and made the best grades. She owns that business and makes more money than everyone else, because she made the sacrifices and investments." Just tell stories. You don't even have to teach your kids per se. You can just tell the stories, and your kids will fill in the blanks. They're not dumb.

Another person I want you to meet is another Warren – Warren Cassell, Jr. He is a 15-year-old kid who is worth hundreds of thousands of dollars. He has made a lot of investments. He lives in the Caribbean, and I met Warren. I talked to him a couple of times. I really like the kid a lot. Warren actually runs an equity management company, and he pretty much already thinks like an investor. I can tell you that it is not hard. Warren is not going to be a guy who is running around saying, "Oh I cannot get ahead, because the white man will not let me." He is not going to be saying, "Oh, mama they locked me up again, because I was at the club, and this dude stepped on my shoes, so I had to shoot him." He is not going to end up like that. You can already tell that.

He is going to be a millionaire. He is going to be a multi-millionaire, because he was trained to think like an investor at an early age. You see how he carries himself. I have communicated with him. He communicates like a smart, mature, respectful young man. He values knowledge. He sees the world in the right way – in a way that breeds success. Somehow, we have been led to believe that our outcomes have nothing to do with our choices, but that is absolutely crazy. Let us keep going.

Rule #5

Rule number five is that you need to show your kids that money does not grow on trees. In some families I see dads take on this "daddy's little girl" approach to money. This is where you are just rolling out money left and right and letting kids think about money in an unrealistic way. Under such circumstances, they see money as something that is easy to get. All they have to do is ask for it. They don't have to actually work for it. That does not help you, and it does not help them. You want to make children earn their money to establish a psychological connection between work and reward. "The harder I work, the more money I get."

On top of that, maybe have your children read books and write reports for money. Make them do intelligent things for money. What that will do is establish a connection between intelligence and money. We do live in a world where those who are more financially intelligent tend to have the most money. That is just a fact of life.

For example, my friend made $10 million selling Bitcoin. He made $10 million selling Bitcoin, because he thinks like an investor. If he did not think like an investor and did not have that economic intelligence, he never would have known to invest in Bitcoin. He would probably be working at Subway or something unsuccessfully trying to get rich. Intelligence is definitely connected to wealth.

When I was 19-years-old in college I called my mother, and I told her, "Mom, I do not have any money for food." I thought she was just going to send me a check like all my friends' parents did. Instead, my mother said, "Well what are you going to do about that?" I replied, "What do you mean?" She said, "Well if you do not have any money, you know you can get a job. You are a grown man. You are able-bodied. Go get you a job." I did not like it. It made me mad, but in retrospect I think it was great for my mother to push me to get a job. It made me independent at an early age. I was not like my friends. I did not have to burden my parents by asking them for money all the time. I felt more confident in myself. I learned at an early age that my outcomes are controlled by my choices. I learned that I could not feel bad, because my mom stopped sending me checks. As a result, it made me an asset to her. Later in life as a grown man I could do things for my mother that a lot of people cannot do for their parents. If I saw that my mother was struggling, I offered to help, because I saw myself as an asset to her and not as somebody who should be dependent upon her.

Rule #6

Remind your children that their work is to benefit the community and not just themselves. We do not need more wealthy sellouts. We do not need any more offs. We do not need that black person who is on the cover of a magazine telling everybody to look at them and how rich they are. That does not really help anybody. We really need people that are connected to the community. We need people that are going to bring their expertise back to the black community.

We have a chronic unemployment problem in the black community. This is especially true among black men. Black men have the highest unemployment rate in the United States. The only solution is going to come from black people. It is not going to come from government programs. It is not going to come from the president, and it is not going to come from Congress. It is only going to come from black people. Black entrepreneurs are the ones who have the ability to solve the black unemployment problem. I am asking you right now to volunteer your child to be part of the economic army for the next generation. I am asking you to enlist your child in the battle to make sure that our community is strong, self-sustained, and a world leader when it comes to economic strength, development, and intelligence. I am asking you to do what you can to put your child in a position where they understand that their success is not just about them. It is about them elevating a community: a community that desperately needs people who can shine a positive light over those shining a negative light.

Black children have to be trained to institutionalize their talent. What does that mean? That means that being good at something is nice, but it is even better when you can develop a company around your skills and hire other people to work for you.

One reason that nobody tells me what to do is because I realized that America's racist system really is not for me. You guys have heard me talk, and you know that white supremacy does not allow black men like me to function for very long. I learned this, and I accepted it. I did not get mad about it. I just left the system and decided I was going to create my own situation. I did and made sure every step of the way strategically that I did not put myself in a position where I would be beholden to anybody who did not have my best interests at heart. Now as a result, I can say whatever I want, and there is nobody who is going to show up and say, "Boyce you cannot say that anymore." There is a strategy to all of this. It does not just happen by accident. It does not just happen overnight. People do not just give it to you. You have to find a way to create that for yourself.

Rule #7

Number seven is to make sure your children know how to build an institution. This is really important. Every black child, especially boys, should know how to start a business before the age of 12. Period. That should be a rite of passage. That is the most important thing that they will learn. I have seen a lot of my former students who have master's degrees, PhD's, law degrees, even MD's be unable to get jobs or get jobs then hate them. They are stuck. They cannot do anything else. When you feel trapped, when you feel like things are happening to you and there is nothing else you can do about it, studies show that can lead to depression.

Individual success is nice, but group success lives forever. If you take what you know, teach other people, and build an institution around the ideas you embody that institution will live long beyond the time you are on this earth.

Billionaires are created by economic machines. I heard a billionaire once say, "Being a billionaire isn't about what you do. It's about what you get other people to do." The ability to buy time from other people is extremely important. That way you go from working 80 hours a weeks to working 800 hours a week. Knowing how to scale up is really important. A lot of businesses, most black businesses, are mom and pop shops, because we have a community that is committed to a superhero complex. The superhero complex is where someone thinks they are supposed to do all the work by themselves, because they are the only black person in the world intelligent enough to get things done. That is just not true. You should be replicating yourself. That way, you have an entire group of people to carry the load – not just you. So, you want your children to know how to create jobs. You want them to know how to develop an economic legacy. Most of the American families that have billions of dollars in wealth are that way, because they have economic visionaries who put plans in place. Even when they had no money, they put a plan in place.

I was recently reading the story about Walmart and how Sam Walton started. He bought a little five-and-dime store in a small town in Arkansas with only 2,900 residents in the town. He had the very basic idea of selling his products for a lower price than the competition. That is all he did. The first store did very well, and then he opened a second one. Once that store did well, he opened a third, fourth, fifth and so on. Soon, his stores spread all throughout Arkansas. Then his stores started spreading all throughout the United States. Today Walmart is worth a quarter of a trillion dollars.

You do not have to have a gigantic idea in order to achieve an economic powerhouse. You just have to have something small that you just do repeatedly that works. These are things that you are not taught in school. One of the things about state universities and HBCUs that I have observed is that they just train you to work for other people. That is because they are training you to support the capitalist systems that are designed by other people. Elite universities like the Harvards and the Yales tend to teach you how to hire other people. They teach you to have other people work for you. You want to be on that end of the stick. You do not want to be on the employee end of the stick, because black people end up getting the short end.

One thing I want you to know is that most great businesses do not die. They are actually never born to begin with, because the would-be founders are afraid to even try it. They do not even make a move, so nothing is ever born. What is your child capable of achieving? I believe that your child is capable of anything you set them up to do. I believe that it is all controlled by you.

Do not wait until your child gets to be 18-years-old before you start giving them college-level training. Give them college-level training at the age of four. Four-year-olds, seven-year-olds, and 10-year-olds can understand the very same concepts I taught college freshmen at Syracuse. We just have systems that push people through at a specific pace. Those who tend to be the most extraordinary are people who break out of the system and move at the fastest pace they possibly can.

There is one kid I know named David whose mother and father just said, "We do not want our kids to go to college at 18. We want our kids to go to college at age 14." So, they had their kids learning at a higher pace. They spent as much time learning as people would spend working a nine to five job. Spending maybe 30 to 40 hours a week studying, by time the kids were about seven they were doing work at a high school level. When the local school said these students could not go to high school at the age of eight, their parents just said, "Okay, we will keep them at home and home school them." They kept their children at home until they were 11 – the age at which their kids were allowed to go to high school. By then they were doing college-level work. By the age of 14 and 15 David and his brother went to MIT. They did fine. They were well adjusted. They were very happy. They were glad that they were placed on an accelerated track. The point of the matter is that you cannot allow these systems to tell you what your child is capable of doing. You are the founder and the creator of the best system for your child. You know your child better than anybody else. You gave birth to your child. That is your baby. That white lady from the suburbs does not know your child better than you do. Why not put your child on a track that is going to allow them to be strong in this racist society and not fall behind? Point blank.

The solutions are out there. The reason you see so many people struggle is because they just do not pay attention. They do not want the solutions, or there was nobody to share the solutions with them, or somebody made them more complicated than they have to be. Somebody possibly distracted them with the wrong stuff. That is why you see so much death and chaos and ridiculousness around you. That said, children are able to escape a lot of that if someone teaches them the solutions needed to do so. If you want to learn more, we have a program for children. Feel free to check it out at *BlackMillionairesOfTomorrow.com*.

LECTURE 4

HOW TO BE A MILLIONAIRE BY RETIREMENT

Okay, so, I want to jump into this. I want to talk about becoming a millionaire by retirement. Lots of people talk about becoming a millionaire as if it is something that just happens, because you get lucky. They say you joined the right MLM company, or you did day trading, and you made the right trade.

Day trading stocks is not something I really teach. I do not teach day trading. This is not because people do not make money with it but because it is a rollercoaster. If I send 100 people to go day trade, half of you are going to make some kind of money. The other half of you are going to lose money. A couple of you are going to make a lot of money, and a few of you are going to lose a ton. I cannot ethically send you off to day trade. You can learn that from a different person. Day trading is a reflection of every nightmare your grandmother had about the stock market and how scary the stock market is. That is where you see the fluctuations, the ups, the downs and crazy stuff like that. Day trading is a lot like moving to a city. There are some parts of the city you can live in where you are nice and safe, and there are some places that are like the hood. Some places represent the dark alleys.

I am not going send you down the dark alleys of investing. I am more interested in leading everyone to the nice comfortable, safe suburbs. In this case the suburbs happen to be black. With that being said, what I want to talk about are systematic, structured ways to become millionaires by the age of 65.

If you are 35 – 45 years old that is still a really good age to be thinking about investing even though the younger the better. You are at that stage where you are reflecting on your life. You are realizing that maybe about 80% of what you have been taught all of your life is nonsense. However, you are still young enough to change a lot of things. Maybe you are reading this book because you are ready to consider possible transitions either in day-to-day choices or in career choices overall. I am seeing people in their 30s having wake up moments where they are climbing out of everything they might have been taught. They are not walking away completely from what they were before, but they are enhancing who they were to become a better fit for who they desire to be. They are really just circling back into their strength.

Not too long ago I had a meeting with a woman who was a business associate. She was about 32 or 33. She said, "You know, I used to just really think that a lot of the stuff you did was too much and too radical." She was very political. I think she was the Democratic representative for her section of the city. She was hobnobbing with a lot of elite people and trying to get in those circles. She went on to express her realization that racism is everywhere – that she hated it and decided to just be herself. I said, "Yeah, I know racism is everywhere. You know you were amazing before white people started to acknowledge you, right?" Her decision to just be herself is an example of circling back to one's strength. That is what I want to encourage you to keep doing.

Keep circling back to your strength. You are never going to be your best if you are imitating somebody else. The original is always going to be better than the substitute. Do not be the substitute. Be yourself, and you are allowed to have a wakeup call. That is why you are reading this book today.

If you are over 55, you are allowed to have a financial wakeup call, too. You, too, can still correct financial errors. It is just going to take a little more work and be a little more challenging. But, here is the thing. I do not care if you are 114 years old. There is a reason you are reading this book, and it really goes to the core of why you invest in the first place. You are not investing just so you can die with a whole bunch of money. You are investing, so your family can build a legacy of wealth, an endowment that is going to last long after you are gone.

If you want to be a thorough investor, you want to think of your family as an ongoing concern. You must get over yourself. You must stop thinking about me, mine, and what I am going to have. You have to stop thinking, "How fast can I get money, Dr. Boyce?" If you are just doing it for yourself, it is very difficult for you to really dig into this. A lot of people do not invest — not because they do not have the money or know how but because they have no incentive. They have not fully internalized the why. The why has to be greater than you for you to really be committed to it. When you learn about investing, start making moves, and positioning things. You are passing things down to your children that give them the chance to take it to the next level. So, even if you are 87 or even 97 years old, your job is to really start setting a trend and a pattern that will help your descendants escape the economic and psychological traps that hurt our community.

This is even important for children to understand. Not too long ago, a 12-year-old girl was asking me about investing, and I told her, "One day, you are going to have kids. You are 12 now but, you may have kids in the next 15 years, maybe 20. Who knows. Your kids are going to need resources. You should start investing today for your unborn children." The same thing applies to grandparents. You have unborn great grandchildren or great great grandchildren. Start investing for them now. That is what I am doing. I am thinking about kids that do not exist yet, so I can make sure that when they finally get here to this place called earth they are ready to live well in the afterlife – my afterlife. After my life is over, I want to make sure those people are living well.

~

The rules I am about to share with you on how to be a millionaire by retirement can be called Dr. Boyce Rules, because I do not take theories as they are. I enhance them based on what I have seen, what I know, what I know about being black, and the unique challenges that come with being black. There is uniqueness in terms of why we are doing this. We are trying to overcome oppression. This is similar, not entirely similar but somewhat similar, to what the Jews were dealing with when they left Russia to create Hollywood. Also, we are dealing with: limitations in terms of capital; challenges with family; 400 years of slavery and oppression; the trauma from slavery; and the list goes on and on and on.

The first thing I want you to keep in mind when figuring out how to become a millionaire by retirement is the finish line. Think about hitting the finish line as an accumulation of thousands and thousands of very tiny efforts. Thousands of efforts you repeatedly make over the course of time. That is how people become wealthy. That is how people die millionaires.

Rule #1

Here is the first rule, you want to invest early, and you want to invest often. Time is the most important parameter in any investment equation. Now, if you pretty much put up $5000 a year in your investment portfolio, that is a little bit more than $400 or maybe $500 a month. Maybe $400 to $425 a month. That is about the cost of a car note.

If a 25-year-old starts off investing early, he will be ahead in the race before his elders get started. They will not catch up with him, because by the time he hits the age of 45 and 50, he will be making money, on top of money, on top of money. By the time he hits 50, before a 55-year-old even gets started, he has already got a quarter of a million dollars in a capital base. You see, you ever hear people say, "It takes money to make money?"

Well, it does not take money to make money all the time, but having money, makes it much easier to make more money. The more money you have, the more money you can make.

There are different kinds of people in this country. There are people who cannot find two nickels to rub together. Then there are people whose number one problem is, "I have too much money, and I do not know where to put it." Think about this. Who buys Treasury bills from the Federal Government when the interest rate is like 0.1%, 0.2%, or almost 0%? Who would buy an investment where the investment rate is so low that it almost does not even exist? Well, the people who buy those assets are people who have so much wealth that they do not know what to do with their money. They are literally looking for places to put their money.

And so, by the time the 45-year-old gets started, the 25-year-old has accumulated a $200,000 head start. The 25-year-old is not only starting at a better place, but their rate of growth of their wealth is much higher than the 45-year-old, because the 45-year-old is starting with a tiny base of nothingness. My God, look at universities for example. Harvard University has an endowment of about $36 billion. If you look at their annual rate of return, I think they are able to generate over 10% a year by $3.6 billion dollars a year which would be about $300 million a month. Yeah, $300 million a month is about $10 million dollars a day. $10 million dollars a day! That is all, because they have a capital base. So, you need to go to your relatives and say, "People, what we need is a capital base."

A capital base is something that allows you to keep making money even when you are asleep. Now, capital base is not just financial assets. It is not just liquid money. It is not just a bunch of cash, a bunch of treasury bills, or a bunch of stocks and bonds. No, a capital base is anything in place that allows you to generate the resources that you need. So, a capital base could be a family business. A capital base, if you are a farmer, could be a cow. You can get milk off that cow every day, or an apple tree can be a capital base. We don't get any money off the apple tree, but it's our tree, and it keeps generating apples which allows us to eat. Anything you have in place that allows you to keep getting the resources you need – that you can live off of – is a capital base.

The reason black families struggle economically is because we have no capital base. What happens is we go to other communities to get capital that we need in order to survive. We are eating apples off somebody else's tree. Nobody is telling black folks to go and plant apple trees. Instead, everyone is thinking, "How am I

going to get an apple today, so I do not starve to death."
However, somebody has to say, "Let's plant some trees,
so our children's problem is not how to get apples to eat
but figuring out what to do with so many dang apple
trees." That is what you want.

So this 25-year-old, by starting his investing early,
has gotten so far ahead that those who invest after him
at the same rate are never going to catch up with him.
Not only is he far ahead, but his rate of growth is much,
much higher. I have a lecture titled Financial Fertility. In
that lecture I talk about rabbits and how the birth of
additional rabbits means having more rabbits in each
generation based on the number of rabbits you had in
the previous generation. Yes, that's a mouthful, but
really think about it. Likewise, the amount of money that
you have at a certain time dictates how much wealth
you generate in the next cycle or segment of time.

So, if a 35-year-old named Bob says, "That is all
right. I can wait 10 years before I start investing. It is no
big deal," that is misguided thinking. Bob will catch up to
the 25-year-old — we'll call her Sally — first and foremost.
The gap at retirement is massive: $787,000 versus
$364,000. Sally is $400,000 ahead of Bob. And if Bob
delays investing further and starts at 45, Sally will be
$600,000 ahead of him. If Bob starts at 55, Sally will be, I
don't know, $700,000 ahead of him. Over $700,000

ahead of Bob. So, you might think, "Oh, it is no big deal. I will be making more money then, so I can just put more money in." Do you not understand that the 35, 45, and 55-year-old investors could double their monthly contribution, and they still will not catch up to the 25-year-old Sally. Sally will win the race, because she has the asset of time.

You know what it reminds me of? It reminds me of when I used to run track. I do not know if any of you guys ran track, but I used to run this race. It was a horrible race called the 400 meter dash where you run one lap around the track. It was the hardest race for me, because the body gets so oxygen deprived. By the time you get to the finish line, your legs feel like they weigh a thousand pounds, and you feel like you are about to pass out. I used to run this horrible race. It was like torture. I mean, the race was so painful that we would literally throw up sometimes after we got done. That is how bad it was. So we thought that in order to avoid the pain of the race we would simply just chill out in the first half of the race. Just kind of jog the first half. Let everybody get a little bit of a lead and then sprint and try to catch up. Our coach would say, "Boys that is not going to work. By the time you get done jogging and start running, they're going to be so far ahead of you that it won't matter if they're tired. You still won't catch them." I did not listen to my coach. I jogged anyway. I just kind of pranced about for the first 200 – 300 meters and then I said, "Okay, now I am feeling good. Now I am going to kick it in." Surely enough, by the time I decided to pick it up, they were so far ahead of me that I could not catch them.

Investing is the same way. The person who gets out the gate and is consistent gets so far ahead of everybody else. The youngest person in my example is 25 years old. Well what if he was 15? What if he was five? He might need some help at the age of five, because five-year-olds do not make $400 a month, but their parents do. So, if I start my example at the age of five, that $780,000 for the 25-year-old grows into the millions. So it is very easy, and this is only an 11% return. That is about the average return of the stock market over the last hundred years. It's really easy to turn a child into a millionaire. Children are already millionaires, because they have the gift of time. What is really hard is to turn a 55-year-old into a millionaire by the time they are 65, because they have let so much time go to waste. It is very, very difficult.

Rule #2

The next step is rule number two. You have to be very, very consistent. The number one factor that kills all people's ability to accumulate assets is the inability to remain consistent. You want money to be automatically withdrawn from your account. You want to set it and forget it. You want to make it into a habit. You want your investment to be as consistent as eating. Imagine if I took all the money that you spent going to McDonald's or going to Burger King over the years. You have done that very consistently if you eat fast food. Maybe you do not like those places, but you have probably gone somewhere, right? If I were to take all that up and show you what you could have made in the stock market, it would probably make you cry.

The interesting thing about it is that consistency is replicated in many sectors of our own lives. There are many things you have done thousands of times that you have never thought about. I mean, imagine if I made you count the number of times you have had sex in your life. I do not know. If you are lucky, I assume you are at least in the hundreds. Some of you all are in the thousands. Whatever. I am not judging. Imagine if you added that up. You probably cannot even remember all the times you have had sex. You cannot remember all the times you sat down for a meal. You cannot remember all the times you got up, clocked in, and went to work every day. You have done it thousands of times, but you do not remember. So, investing must be part of your consistency that makes up this thing called life for you. Imagine if I asked the moms to count the number of hours they spent talking to her children and raising their kids. That is something they have done very consistently, because it is very natural. Investing must be the same way.

A person who is a consistent investor will never be broke. They just will not, because they are going to have a consistent accumulation of capital. If the money is put to work, the money is going to make more money even when they are doing something else. You give that person 20 or 30 years, and they are going to be absolutely fine financially. In many cases, they are going to be worth over a million dollars. The key is to be very consistent. Whatever you do, just set it as a pattern, and stay with it.

Rule #3

Rule number three is to increase your income base through entrepreneurship. Most people talk about their income as if it is static. They talk about what you can do with what you have and how you can cut costs. I broke that trend in my own life, because I did not want to cut my costs. I did not want to live on a frugal budget. I did not want to not enjoy my life as much as I did before. I figured there had to be another solution. The mathematics was very basic. Instead of cutting the amount of money I spend, I decided to try to increase the amount of money that I make. That is where entrepreneurship comes into play. There are very few communities where there are more entrepreneurial opportunities than in Black America. That is because the community is so undercapitalized. There are not that many businesses, and there are not that many businesses that actually get to grow. Also, the community culture is not one that is built on entrepreneurship. So when you make your children into entrepreneurs, they literally become instant power brokers in the black community, because they will never run out of black people looking for jobs.

I share this information far and wide, I go to all these cities and talk to a lot of people, but there are more people who do not listen to me than there are that do listen to me. Maybe there are a couple million people who listen to me. Well, there are about 38 million people who do not, and those people, unfortunately, are still looking for jobs. So when you make entrepreneurship part of your family culture, what you have done is directly increase your capital base in two ways. One, you have decided to work together. When you come together, that is an automatic increase in wealth. When you are working together, you are taking your energy and turning it inward instead of distributing your best energy and expertise outward. Instead of going out and working for white folks and doing things for them, you are doing things for your own family. You are putting that energy toward your investment projects that relate to people you love. You see, no matter what you are investing your time in it can always go bad. If you go work at Target or Walmart that company could fold. You could lose that job. A family business could fold as well, but at least if it succeeds the rewards are higher.

You see, investment is almost never a certain kind of thing. Investment is always a risk. I do not care how much of an expert you are at business, when you put your time, energy, and money into a business there is always a chance it is not going to work out. So, what you want to avoid is a mindset where you can only make an investment if you know for sure it is going to work out. I hate to tell you this, but there are no certainties in this world. Nothing is certain. You might marry the man or woman of your dreams, and it still might not work out. You just have to make sure you are always ready with a plan B in case it does not work out.

Getting back to my original point, I encourage you to increase your wealth by turning your best energy back into your family, and expanding your knowledge. Share this information as well as other information with your family. Read articles. Read books. Have conversations. When you have people that come together and then become smart people who come together, wealth will come out of that. You cannot put a bunch of really smart people – all motivated to do something special – in a room together and not have something amazing come out of that. So, create a brain trust within your family. What this brain trust will do is give you a chance to increase your income base. I tell you this as a man who knows what it is like to be a millionaire. I am not bragging, but I have been a millionaire for a little bit. I was a millionaire on paper a few years ago, and then the money eventually came with it. I am not bragging about that at all, but I have to tell you that, so you know I am not just talking from theory. I am talking from experience.

It is a lot easier to make financial moves when you can move thousands of dollars around whenever you want to. It is a lot easier to make financial moves, as well, when you have got some money, and you have a crew of people who trust and love each other and really want to do well. You also have to have some knowledge and creativity in there. When I get together with my brain trust people that I work with million dollar ideas fly off the table. Not only do we have the ideas and the trust necessary to execute those ideas in our own little economy, we also have the resources to make necessary moves. We have our own bank. We stacked up our capital base, so that we do not need to go and say, "Well I hope Bank of America will give us a loan." That is especially good because they may not do it. We do not need to go out and say "I hope white America will support this initiative." We can go back to our own capital base, and make things happen.

It is much easier to get to where you want to get to if you are thinking entrepreneurially, because you are also thinking in terms of multiple streams of income. Therefore, if there is someone in the family that loses a job, it is not a sad thing. If a skilled person loses their job, it should never be a sad thing. You should never be sad, because someone who has talent and education does not have a job. Entrepreneurship and multiple streams of income are resources that can be available for the family if properly applied. They can be utilized to develop the capital base for your family. When I hear of relatives that have lost their jobs, if I have space in my organization, I am like "Hey, let's get on the phone and figure out how I can justify what it is going to take for me to put some money in your pocket, and for you to help us build up this family business." That is the kind of thinking you want to have. You do not want to have thinking that says, "I am going to push this fish back into the water and just hope that somebody picks them up. If no one does, they must be worthless." That is not true. You are worth something whether or not someone pays you for your time.

Rule #4

Okay, moving on to rule number four. If you have a job and a 401k plan, max it out. Max it out especially if your company is putting in matching funds. I got so angry last week. I was watching *Saturday Night Live*, and they had this segment called Black Jeopardy. It made me so mad that I get to say it twice. They were basing it all on stereotypes. The host said, "The next answer is, your boss says they want to take $40 out of your paycheck for your 401k." A black contestant answered, "Alex, what is you better give me my $40, so I can buy me some scratch-offs?" I couldn't believe it. It made me so mad. I am sure there are lots of black people that think it is the funniest thing in the world, because they are like "Yeah, you know how black people are. We do not invest. We want the scratch-offs."

Guess what? Scratch-offs can knock you off economically and leave you destitute when you do not have somebody else paying your bills. The scratch-offs are what will lead you into poverty, because a lottery ticket is literally one of the worst investments you could ever make in life. The lottery is designed for educated wealthy people to take advantage of false fantasies being fed to the poor. It is a really huge mind trick. They literally play with your head by asking you, "If you win the lottery, do you want your money in a lump sum, or do you want it over a 20-year period?" They could ask you that question after you win the lottery when it is more relevant. But, no. They ask you beforehand. Deliberately. They know that the more you make it real in your mind, the more fantasizing you will do, and the easier it will be to get you to buy that ticket. That really just comes from consumerism.

Consumerism is built on the idea that most purchases are made from an emotional standpoint. They are made for emotional reasons. They are also compulsive purchases. People do not really sit and contemplate what they want to buy most of the time. They buy it on the spur of the moment. So ultimately, that little stupid *Saturday Night Live* segment really made me angry, but that is neither here nor there. I had to bring that up. These stereotypes are killing us, leaving us broke, and leaving us hopeless. It also causes us to believe that investing must be for white people.

If you have a 401k on your job, especially if your company is matching any of that, max it out. Even before stashing acorns and everything else I have taught you, go to your 401k. Now 401ks are not necessarily always better than, let's say, IRAs. IRAs are Individual Retirement Accounts: another tax deferred investment vehicle. Tax deferred, not tax exempt. Tax deferred, means that you are still going to pay taxes, you just pay later. The 401k is a great tool, because companies provide that as an incentive, and that is where you want to start building your wealth. When you max out your 401k, you are using your money, Uncle Sam's money, and your boss's money. What a great way to invest. Plus, you get far more bang for your buck going that route economically than you get by investing on your own.

Rule #5

Rule number five is to make somebody else a millionaire, too. Just remember, you know, kids have all the time in the world, and investing is a legacy kind of scenario. You want to think of your family like a corporation. Your family is a business. Really you want to think to yourself, "Maybe I can or cannot make myself a millionaire, but I can certainly make my kids a millionaire." Take a little two-year-old boy or a 10-year-old girl. They have so much time. They are going to need money one day, as well. The fact of the matter is that basic investing programs for them at an early age can make a huge world of difference.

When you talk about long-term investing, one thing you may want to do is allow yourself to invest by taking your pay raises and automatically putting them in your 401k plan, or investing them. Just commit yourself to whatever standard of living you are currently at. When your income increases on your job or you make more money from a side hustle, decide for that money to go towards investing. That way, your life can remain the same, and this natural growth in your income over time will allow you to build assets and build wealth. That is one of the things that I did.

I will tell you guys the truth. I like to enjoy money. I like to enjoy life. I never believed in torturing myself in order to get ahead and build wealth. I have always been an investor, but I have always been an investor who feels it is important to enjoy life. Nonetheless, my biggest investment was actually time. I invested my time into positioning myself by making sacrifices when I was young. That way when I got a little bit older, I could live a better life. Even when I was 23, and I was studying seven to eight hours a day I would put in my hours of studying and then spend a few hours relaxing and doing whatever the heck I wanted. When I first started making a little bit of money I said, "I want my wealth to grow, but I do not want to cut my costs." To accomplish that, I decided to create extra income, so I made my first investment of time. Even if you do not have a nickel in your pocket, you can invest time. If you have a cell phone, you have access to the internet. Invest time, and realize that when you are investing that time, you are investing in a financial asset. Your time is worth money. That is why your boss pays you by the hour or by the week or whatever.

So, I invested time in entrepreneur-ship and then I created another stream of income. Now, here is what happened. When I became more of an entrepreneur, I was not making a whole lot of money. I was actually losing money. Then when I started making money, I was not making a ton. I was making $300 this month. Maybe $500 the next month. Maybe a thousand the next month. But here is the thing. When I was making that extra money two things happened. Number one, the financial physics of my income changed dramatically. Instead of being in my old life where I was waiting a whole year to get a 3% to 4% raise, I suddenly had a situation where I could increase my income by 20-30% in a month or two just by making the right business moves. It is almost like the difference between plowing your field with human labor versus someone buying you an industrial size machine that has the power of 5,000 human beings. It presented a whole different level of possibilities that came from thinking from an entrepreneurial stand point. Then I was able to take the money I earned from my job and enjoy that. I could take that and buy whatever I wanted and live however I wanted. When it came to building my nest egg, I had this extra stream of income that became my investment capital. That became my investment base. I was taking that money and investing it to build my long-term nest egg.

I am not certain when I became a millionaire on paper, but I am going to say it was around 2010 or something like that. When I hit that point, I still had to be an investor, because when you first become a millionaire, if your journey is anything like mine, you will feel illiquid. Your business will finally be worth a million dollars, but it will still be a small business. Small businesses require lots and lots of cash flow, lots and lots of economic food. We were making money, and I had to put that money right back into the business. There was still a sacrifice there, but, the dynamics changed over time. That is what I would tell you guys to do. See income and wealth as something where there are a million different ways to skin the cat. You do not have to think of it as, "Okay, I am going to live like a regular person, and just take my little regular person paycheck, and do what I can with that." When you get together with family, anything becomes possible. If you have a family where five of you all are trained at a high level and you want your family to be really wealthy, here is what I would do. I would challenge the family to do the Black Entrepreneurship Challenge. I would challenge the family for a year, to go through entrepreneurship training and the boot camp style training where we are talking and learning about entrepreneurship on a regular basis. For an entire year. If you do that, when you get to the end of that year and you have five people in your family all thinking entrepreneurially, suddenly the whole world will open up to you. You realize just how much opportunity there is out there.

Now, let us jump back to the specifics one more time. Here is approximately how much you would have to invest to become a millionaire by 65 assuming a 7% return on investment. It is a lot more conservative than the assumption we discussed earlier. The formula is an example of how much a person would have to invest in a diversified portfolio earning an average of 7% in order to be a millionaire by the time they hit the age of 65. First is your age, second is the amount of savings that will be needed for each month, and third is the average monthly income of the average American at your age level, and that is an important assumption to keep in mind. If you know how to hustle, you know how to position yourself, right? If you're a 20-year-old and you're making the average monthly income of a 20-year-old, you only have to save about 13% of your income if you want to be a millionaire by the age of 65. So the 20 to 25-year-olds, pat yourselves on the back, because you just won the lotto. You can be a millionaire by the age of 65 if you take these very basic steps.

Now you get to the age of 40 where you're not young anymore, but you're not old. You gotta move, because, you know, time is running out. Well, 40-year-olds would have to save approximately 35% of their income. The pressure kind of grows, but again. I would say if you have a double-earning household or a family that says, "I'm only making $4000. I want to get that up to $6,000," guess what? You can hit that $1,465 number, and not change your lifestyle one bit. You don't have to change anything about how you live, but you do have to change how you make your money – just not how you spend your money.

When you get up to the 50's it starts to get a little tough. You have to save 94% of income. If you're 50 and you waited this long, it's not over for you. You can always change the parameters. You can always retire a little bit later. You can always increase your income, but a 50-year-old or a 55-year-old would have to break out of the box in order to make this work. The only option a 55-year-old might have if they're trying to become a millionaire by 65 is increasing their income. Again, that's where entrepreneurship might come into play or whatever the case may be. I have an entrepreneurship program. If you guys are interested in it, you can go to BlackMoney103.com. Anyhow, a 55-year-old will have to be kind of creative. Maybe retire a little bit later. Maybe set their standard a little lower and say, "Ah, you know, I don't need a million. Maybe three quarters of a million might work." Those are the three ways a 55-year-old who hasn't saved for retirement can potentially get caught up. You'd either have to increase your income, retire a little bit later, or set your standards a little bit lower. One of those three things would have to apply, or a combination of all three.

Those of you who are under the age of 50, don't wait. Do not copy the investing behavior of the average American in this country, because, the average American in this country is going to financial hell in a hand basket. The average American has ruined themselves economically, and what they are doing is just hoping for the best. They're just assuming that everything is just gonna find a way to work out. I'm not making fun of these people at all. I'm just saying if you don't have to be in that category, why do it?

The other thing as retirement goes is to make sure you're taking care of retirement. It is kind of an interesting space. It's 20 or 25 years of life where you have to figure out how to get by with no income or very little income. Now you have social security which gives you a little bit. Maybe some retirees work part-time. Some people have their 401ks, IRAs, and other investment vehicles that kind of help supplement their income. Some people are able to go live with their children and things like that. We tend to take care of our seniors in our community. White folks are a little bit interesting with their senior citizens. I've seen them throw them all out and put them in a home. I think that's crazy. Black people don't typically do that as much, but some of y'all might have some trifling kids. If that's who you are, I give you my condolences. At the end of the day, when you're thinking about this retirement thing just know that it's real. I've heard a lot of people say that it's silly for black people to save for retirement or put money on social security, because we don't live long enough and all that. Yeah, you might die before 70, 75, or even 65, but you know what else? You might live. So if you do live, you wanna be prepared. You wanna be protected. You don't wanna just sort of be out here.

~

So that is pretty much a straightforward blue print. I see becoming a millionaire by a certain time as very straight forward in the sense that it's not hard for me to explain to you how to become a millionaire. I just have to get over the myths. The myths are, "I'm gonna get a record deal, or I'm gonna get into the NBA, or I'm gonna join this multi-level marketing thing." No disrespect to multi-level marketing, but I don't know a lot of multi-level marketing millionaires to be honest with you. The hardest part is dispelling the myths, and helping people find intelligent and responsible ways to build wealth and understand the accumulation process. So, it's not straightforward in terms of the instructions being very very clear.

The hard part is that while it's straightforward, it is a long road. It's just like me trying to explain to you how to walk from New York to California. It's easy to explain it. "I say, "Here's the GPS. Here's the map. California is west. Just keep going west, and you're gonna get there." The question is, "Are you willing to start walking?" If you don't start walking now, what are you doing with that time? Meaning, if you're not invested in preparing for the future, what are you doing with that money? What other things are you doing with that money that could be used for something that's more meaningful for your family. I'm not saying that you can't still enjoy your money. I'm saying that you have to make sure that your investing is equal on the priority list to all the other things that you're doing. I've told parents, "Look, just keep doing what you're doing with your kids. Just put entrepreneurship coaching on the same par as going to football camp or sending them to cheerleading camp every year." These are fundamentals that they need to know in order to be successful.

Same as you as an adult. When it comes to investing your money, putting your money aside for you, and protecting your future, put them on the same par as going to Popeye's Chicken every couple of days or whatever it is you do with your money. Put that on the same par as going to the Beyoncé concert, getting your hair done, going to buy the new Jordans, spending money with your boys to go out and get drinks, or whatever it is you might want to do as leisure. If you take that money and match it...I'm just thinking about hair 'cause my daughter is in the hair industry. If a woman took the money spent on beauty and makeup and just said, "I'm gonna make sure I invest the same amount in my future as I invest in my head. I'm gonna spend as much money making sure I am good as I put into looking good." If black women did that, you would have a whole lot of black female millionaires in this country. Point. Blank. Period.

Guys, we're not off the hook either. We waste our money on all kinds of ridiculous stuff. When I wrote my book *Financial Love Making* and was analyzing and interviewing couples, I discovered that most of the time the financial tragedies actually came from men's irresponsible behaviors. The four vices I warn black men of getting caught up in because they can ruin financially are sex, drugs, alcohol and gambling. I have noticed that those four things are common. At the end of the day, everybody has their demons. Everyone has their weaknesses, myself included. What you do with money, is a very emotional process. It's a very irrational, illogical process sometimes.

Andrew Lowe, Professor at MIT actually said that spending money and receiving money affects the brain in the same way as cocaine. So literally, sometimes you make bad financial decisions, because you're economically high. You're financially high. You're just in the mall, and the outfit looks good. The music is playing, and you're caught up in some sort of emotional trans that leads you to part with your money. That's why, a lot of times, one way to keep from spending is to keep your money where it's tough to get to. If your money is in your stock portfolio, and it's gonna take three days for it to be released, then you're less likely to let that money go in an impulsive decision, because you have to wait three days in order to make the purchase. I would compare it to sex. Imagine if people had to wait three days to decide if they wanted to have sex with someone. The world's population would drop by about 40%.

LECTURE 5

HOW TO START AN INVESTMENT CLUB

What is an investment club? In the simplest terms, a group of people that wants to build wealth. How do you start such a club? By finding and gathering other people who want to build wealth, too. Remember, a lot of wealth building and cooperative economics, meaning black people working together to help each other succeed, is hinged on teamwork. It's about finding other people who think the same way you do and believe in the same things, so you can work together to build the kind of nation you want to see built.

A more specific definition of an investment club is a group of people that puts money together to make investments as a group. Everybody puts together a certain amount of money, and the money is managed as a group. If you are buying stocks with your own money, you get to decide what you are going to buy. You get to decide what you are going to sell. If you're in an investment club, however, everybody gets to decide. Everybody gets a chance to make the decision. It's not just one person, so the group votes when it comes to decision-making.

How Investment Clubs are Different from Mutual Funds

Investment clubs are almost like mutual funds except different. The government looks at a mutual fund differently, because there are thousands of people involved, and these individuals do not know the other people who are investing. With an investment club, you know every person in the group. It could be your family members. It could be some of your friends. It could be both. Usually groups are very, very small. Also, they are usually organized as partnerships between people. A partnership is a type of structure in business. For example, a business can be created as a partnership or as a corporation.

Investing Consistently is Key

The key thing with investment clubs is investing consistently, so you might want to have a rule that says everybody in the club has to put $20 a month into the pot, or $100 a month into the pot, or whatever they can afford to put into the pot. That said, if you have different amounts being put in, it is a little harder to keep up with the numbers. You will want to make sure somebody keeps up with the math, so there is no confusion about how much each person has in the pot.

Reinvest Your Dividends & Diversify

Some companies pay dividends. This is when the company makes money but does not keep it. Instead, the company gives it away to people who own shares in the company. If you are in an investment club, I suggest the group reinvest dividends earned. You want them to go right back into the stock. You can set that up on platforms like Ameritrade. You can tell it to reinvest your dividends, or you can just tell everybody in the group that all the dividends that get paid are going to go back into the portfolio. Meaning we're going to leave that money in our group of stocks, so it can keep growing. We're not going to take the money out until the point of selling.

Also, don't forget diversification. You always want to diversify, diversify, diversify. You want your money to be spread out. You never want your money to be in one place. Having your money in one place is a very good way to lose all your money. Never let that happen to you.

Elect Investment Club Officers

The next thing you want to do with your club is elect a leader, vice president, and treasurer. The treasurer is very important, because the treasurer keeps up with the money. If your club has a bank account, the treasurer can get money out of the account and put money in. With that in mind, you want to pick somebody you trust. The president and vice president are very important, too. The vice president should back up the president, and the president should be a person who believes in the investment club, because your leadership determines the strength of your organization. If you have bad leadership, then you are not going to have a good organization.

Invite Guest Speakers

You may want to reach out and have financial experts in the local community come in and speak to your group. An investment club can consist of a group of kids. It can be a group of senior citizens. It can be a group of women. It can be a group of men. It can be your family. So, you can call people you know who are very knowledgeable in investing to speak with your club. Maybe select somebody who wrote a book on the subject or somebody who runs an investment company. Remember, one key to investing is lifelong knowledge. You always want to learn. You always want to be in school. You never want to stop learning.

If you ever start an investment club and you want to invite me to be a speaker, I may not be able travel to where you are, but I could potentially do something on Skype. I am pretty busy which makes booking me difficult, but hey. I do not mind you asking. We might be able to work something out.

Have Monthly Meetings

Make sure you have regular meetings. A good meeting frequency is about once a month. You can tell everybody, "Hey, if you want to be in this investment club, you have got to show up once a month." That is really important.

Each Club Member Must Participate

When you invest, everybody must participate in choosing the investments. There are no, as they call them, passive investors. What is a passive investor? Somebody who says, "I do not care what you buy. Just take my money, and invest it in whatever you want." That is not acceptable. You cannot have a group where two or three people are making all the decisions while everybody else just sits there watching. That is not legal, because your investment club then becomes classified by the government as a mutual fund. In addition to having thousands of members, a mutual fund involves some members giving their money while other members classified as the experts make all the decisions. To be a mutual fund, however, you have to pass a lot of regulations. There are a lot of laws in place, and it costs a lot of money to set up. It is not something that is very easy to do, so you do not want your investment club to be seen as a mutual fund. That would be bad for you.

Investment Clubs Cannot Exceed 100 Members

Investment clubs cannot have more than 100 members. The best number of members to have is six to 20. So when you start your investment club, start small. Start with six to 10. Do not make it huge. If it gets too big, it becomes very difficult to manage. Everyone having different personalities is hard enough to deal with, so make sure that you at least know the people you are inviting into the club. Like I said, you may want to start with family members or your best friends – people who really believe in what you are doing and think in a similar manner as you. Over time you can build wealth together, and you can also get the most important kind of wealth which is knowledge.

~

So, that is an investment club, and how it works. I want you to buy your first share of stock soon and figure out how you can start an investment club. Remember, keep the size of your club small. Everybody can invest

$10 a month or $50 a month or something like that. Just get started. That is the key. The key to investing in wealth building is consistency and getting started. Never ever sit still.

Dr. Boyce Watkins

LECTURE 6

THE SECRET TO FINANCIAL SECURITY

We are going to talk about wealth, what it means to build wealth, how to build wealth, and how to attain financial security. Financial security is very important. Let me tell you why it matters and why most Americans do not have it. The big problem we have in America is that there is this really interesting intrigue with luxury items. There are a lot of people that want to live like the Kardashians. I really think reality TV plays a part in this. Reality TV creates this false reality. It is funny that they call it reality TV, because it is not reality. It is actually a false reality that leads people to want to live in luxury. Everybody sees what is happening on these shows and the way so-called wealthy people live, and everybody wants to get that stuff.

According to a study reported by CNBC, one in eight Americans is willing to take on $1,000 or more in debt to depict an extravagant lifestyle. Now, one in eight is not a huge number, but there are a lot of people going deep in debt for things that do not always make a lot of economic sense. Even college education has fallen into the luxury category, because they started charging too much for it. Everything should have a price, and there should be a point where you say, "You know, I think I want that, but I don't want to pay that price for it." It really should not cost you $40,000 - $50,000 a year to go to school. Because we feel that it is mandatory, however, we feel like we have to do it. You have heard people say, "If you don't get a degree your hair's gonna catch on fire. You're gonna die on the spot."

People do not realize that you have to be creative about how you move forward in the wealth game. It is just like companies. Some of the biggest companies in the world that make the most money are bad investments, because they are borrowing too much to get what they need. It is almost like, if you say to me, "Hey I'm hungry, Boyce." I say, "Okay. You should eat some food." You say, "Absolutely, I agree." And I, knowing that you're hungry, want to eat, and like my food, say, "Okay, well to get a meal, it's gonna cost you $1,000 a plate." You would probably be within your rights to give me the finger and cuss me out. You would probably say, "I love Dr. Boyce's fried chicken, but it's not worth $1,000 a plate."

One of the fundamental rules of finance is that you have to know what the price is. What is your price? How far are you willing to go to obtain that bank? A lot of times when it comes to luxury items, education, or things we feel like we need we get to the point where there is no such thing as a price that is too high. I think it is important to avoid that mindset.

Another thing you want to know is that Americans are not saving. Twenty-eight percent of Americans have nothing in their savings account. Nothing. That is the epitome of economic vulnerability. If you are in that category, do not be ashamed, but you have to fix it. You have to fix it, because being black is very risky in America. There is a day you are going to get in a fight with your boss. Your boss is going to disrespect you, and you are going to want to...You might want to bless him out and walk out the door, but you are going to be stuck. You are not going to have options. Things break down. Things go wrong. Crises emerge all the time, so you want to be proactive as opposed to reactive.

People who tend to get ahead financially are proactive people. Proactive means that you do not just react to the crisis that happened yesterday. You are prepared for the crisis that might happen tomorrow. Proactive thinking is not popular in the black community. There, I said it. I said it. Get mad at me, but proactive thinking and planning are simply not popular in the black community. You know what is popular in the black community? Let me tell you what is popular in the black community. What is popular in our community is to live life on the edge – on the brink of economic destruction – and then cry, scream, holler, go crazy, and pray to Jesus when the economic calamity you could have prepared for occurs.

Think about funerals, for example. How many times have you seen a funeral where the family is devastated financially and cannot afford to bury the person who just died? So the family goes to the church and begs them to take up a collection plate to help bury Uncle Willy. Well, the whole family is in complete chaos, because Uncle Willy did not spend $30 a month on some life insurance. Some might say Uncle Willy could not afford life insurance, but I saw Uncle Willy go to McDonald's every other day. I saw Uncle Willy spend money on liquor, weed, and sneakers. I saw Uncle Willy spending money to go to the movies. So, why is it that Uncle Willy had an easier time spending money on things that added no economic value to his family, legacy, and position in the world? He had a serious problem.

People do not seem to want to do the dirty work. They do not really want to handle necessities. Necessities are boring. People tend to aim for the extravagant. They enjoy saying, "Look at the new car I bought. I got the Chrysler. It looks just like a Bentley," or, "Look at the outfit I got. I look so fly tonight." There is that instant gratification. There is that desire to look good as opposed to actually being good and in a good position. That is very prevalent and very, very popular. It is marketed consistently to the community.

I'll give you a good example. This is going to make you all laugh. A lot of people – and not just black people – go in debt, because they really are trying to keep up with the Kardashians. They watch Kim Kardashian and her family make $100 million a year with this lifestyle empire they have built, and they want to be like them. Right? So, they go in debt trying to be like the Kardashians. Well, here is the interesting thing about that Kardashian lifestyle. Some of you may laugh at this. You know Kim Kardashian is famous for that fake butt where she is trying to be like a black woman. Well, her butt, from what people have said has now deflated and deformed because of the injections wearing off. At about 40 years old all of those butt injections she got so she could look good in the short term may cause her to look crazy in the long-term.

So, a lot of us, in a way, can be compared to Kim Kardashian. A lot of us can be compared to that mentality, that instant gratification mentality. That mentality that says, "Now. The future will never arrive. Therefore, I'm just gonna do what's best for me now and not really think about the consequences." That's kind of everywhere. I encourage you to find a way to understand, that if your desire is truly to look good, if you really want to look good, there's nothing wrong with that, but I really encourage you to also find a way to be in a good financial position while you do it. To not ruin yourself and ruin your future and sacrifice your future in order to have what basically amounts to instant gratification. That's all it is. It's just the desire to have everything now, now, now.

Twenty percent of Americans don't even have a savings account, and 70% of Americans are in debt. Thirty percent have no plans to pay off the debt. So, a large number of Americans are not only going to die without any wealth, they are gonna die in the hole. They're gonna die leaving a legacy of debt. That's a very scary thing, because when you talk about death, death is scary. Death is already traumatizing to the people you love. The debt compounds the emotional damage that comes from losing someone that you didn't expect to lose.

Here a couple of rules of thumb. First of all, when it comes to financial security, just know this. Let's get this out of our heads about this whole thing about how much money somebody makes. Who cares how much money somebody makes? Earning money is not the key to financial security. It is having more money that can make a difference. It is keeping the money that you get that matters. It is what you hold onto that makes all the difference.

They make fun of black people on this issue. They make fun of us! All of us. That's why the Jews have a nickname for black people. They call us liquid money. This old Jewish man said, "Yeah, you know, we call the African-American community liquid money." You know how liquid flows through your hands? If I take this water and pour it in my hands it's gonna flow through and land all over my pants. That's why I didn't pour it out, but that illustrates liquid money. The fact that we're seen that way should be an absolute insult to all of us.

Now, everybody's not gonna change. Here's what I predict. The black community at large is gonna maintain some of its very bad habits. One of the bad habits of our community is not picking up books as much as we should. We also watch more TV than other groups of people. That's why they build entire TV networks off of our sluggishness. We use social media more than other people do. With that, a lot of people build their economic success off the backs of black people. That's not gonna change.

What can change is you. What can change is you saying, "That ain't gonna happen in my house." In my own house, we don't think this way. In my house, we embrace the idea of economic intelligence. In my house, we preserve wealth, and we build wealth, because the wealth that you build becomes your protection. It protects your dignity. It protects your family. It protects your sanity. There are a lot of black people who are really going crazy. They're out here begging. There are a lot of people who are stressed out to the point that it's effecting their physical and mental health, because they're worried about money.

When your children grow up, the world isn't gonna change. America's still gonna be a capitalist society, and they're gonna be stressed out about money. The question that we must ask ourselves as parents is if we really want our kids to be stressed. Or, do we want our kids to be strong? Do I want my kids to be stressed, or do I want them to be blessed? You can bless your kids by planning and making very basic steps to create financial security that lasts a long time.

I'll give you a little secret. My daughter and I – she is big on hair, fashion, beauty, and makeup – hold daddy-daughter business strategy meetings. We talk about her business, product lines, marketing, and distribution. We talk about monetization. We talk about inventory. We talk about processes. We talk about everything that is going to make sure she knows how to keep her house in order economically.

Also, remember this. Money isn't the only solution to the financial security question. What you're actually trying to do is not just get money. You're trying to build wealth. Wealth can be money, but wealth is not always money. That's very important to understand. So, if you obtain some wealth – a business, assets, or a brand name that you want to protect, etc. – all these things can be put into your trust when you die. I know that the name Dr. Boyce Watkins is a multi-million dollar asset that I can leave my children, and I will put in my will and in my trust with my estate planning lawyer. This is how I want it to be preserved, and this is how I want the revenue to be doled out. You can do all of that.

I'm really encouraging black people to build empires. You came from kings and queens, and you will, at some point, become kings and queens again. It's up to us to decide how quickly we want to accelerate the process. The ability to be a king or queen really comes down to thinking like a king or a queen. A king or queen is not into foolishness. A king or queen is not easily swayed by the nonsense going on in the world. A king or a queen is a leader and not a follower. A king or a queen is able to build their house and defend it.

So, what I would encourage you to do is think like a king or a queen even if you don't have much. Pride is really important. Being proud of what you have is more important than the amount of what you have. You may not have a whole lot, but being proud of that and preserving that will make all the difference. It gives you the opportunity to go in for the kill and to accumulate that. You must protect what you have to begin that process of building more, and then you'll have more to protect.

I'm gonna give you a few things, a few symptoms, that will help you identify whether or not you might be a candidate for financial insecurity-itus. Number one, getting all your income from one job. A lot of people think they're secure, but they're not. They lose that job? They're done. If you wake up every day stressed out, because you might lose that job then understand that you're stressed out for a reason.

Next, being deep in debt. Too much debt is the devil. Debt and the overaccumulation of debt has become a huge problem for Americans. You want to be cautious about debt. I'm gonna give you some rules on when you should and should not consider debt.

Living paycheck to paycheck. That's a big problem, a lot of people live that way, because they don't think they can get out of that. I'm gonna give you some tips that can help you deal with that.

No savings. You save your money, so your money can save you. A lot of people don't save at all. They think saving is just...I don't know what they think about it, but they just don't do it. If you're in that category, don't be embarrassed.

No investments. Your investments are something where you're preserving capital to give yourself financial security and also give your money an opportunity to work for you. I was reading *The Wall Street Journal* today, and I was looking at different articles where they were talking about how the big players were working with their investment capital. I was reading about big companies like Amazon, and how the founder of Amazon, Jeff Bezos, made 3.3 billion dollars yesterday. He literally made 3.3 billion dollars in a day because of this company Amazon that he's been building for many, many years. Amazon is a company you could have invested in, back in the year 2000. Back then, I think the stock was selling for as little as $5, $6, $7, $8 a share. Now, it's up to almost $1,000 a share. There are other "Amazons" out there. There are other companies out there that can allow your wealth to grow, but if you don't invest, your money never gets a chance to grow.

Also, no alternative streams of income. If you've only got one source of income, and you don't have any alternatives out there then you're gonna put yourself in a bad financial situation. You're in a risky scenario. You don't have financial security, in my opinion.

No assets. What are your assets? In what places or in what things have you put your money, so you could sell if times get tough? Do you have any things that can generate additional revenue?

Insurance. Insurance is huge. A lot of people are in financial turmoil. They create a scenario of economic turmoil for those they love by not taking the time to get adequate insurance. Life insurance is a big one. I'm pretty mean about life insurance. If you've got kids and you don't have life insurance, you don't love your kids unless you are just absolutely so destitute that you can't afford a $10 a month policy or a $40 a month policy. Maybe that's possible. I mean, $30 a month is a dollar a day. Maybe that's possible, but if you are buying anything other than life insurance – Burger King once a month, a new pair of shoes once every month or two, going to the movies – you can have adequate life insurance.

Your goal is simple. If you want financial security, you have to close all the loopholes. That's it. Just look at that list, of Dr. Boyce's symptoms of financial insecurity and make sure to address the issues. You're not gonna address them overnight, though. Gotta allow time.

Step 1

So, here's step one. Create multiple streams of income. Now, that's easier said than done. That's why I'm your teacher. I can talk to you about ways of thinking that allow you to create multiple streams of income. Until you figure out a way to make multiple streams of income, treat it as if it is a family concern. This is a family emergency, if you will. You know you're vulnerable. You have to fix it.

I'll give you a personal example. In my own company, somebody might come up to me and say, "Hey, Dr. Boyce. This was a great month. Look at how much money we made over here." The first thing I think about is what will happen if that faucet turns off. I'm not thinking about how much money we have now. I'm thinking about what's gonna happen if that source gets shut down. So, first thing I think about when I accumulate anything is how to defend it. Well, one way you defend it is through diversification.

When you're celebrating because cousin Pookie got that good job with the law firm, he should be thinking about that next step: how to put himself in a position to have income from multiple sources. He will want preserve the lifestyle to which he hopes to become accustomed. Have family conversations about how you can get some other little streams of income. Streams of income have to be grown. They're not easily acquired overnight. It takes time. New streams of income start off small and very sloppy. Most entrepreneurial families get it wrong the first time or two. That's why consistent education is really important.

In fact, right now my team and I are in the process of seeking to acquire property all across the country to set up economic empowerment centers. Our goal is to, have places where people can gather, talk about what they are trying to do, and share their economic journeys, so we can support each other. I've gone to almost 50 cities in the last year and a half on the Economic Empowerment Tour to educate about economic power, financial literacy, and the like. I figured out that what we need as a community are gathering spots. That will allow us to have conversations with other like-minded people, so we can build our family empires.

I encourage you, until that time, to start with your own family. Have regular conversations about developing multiple streams of income. Not having that is a financial risk that you cannot bear if you are black in this country. A lot of black people are enslaved because of the fact that they are dependent on that other person to pay their bills. That's a vulnerability that you don't want to live with your whole life. It'll stress you out.

Step 2

Step two, start thinking carefully about debt. Debt has gotten many Americans into trouble. Millions of Americans are drowning in debt. Most of the debt is stupid debt or bad debt. Bad debt is debt that you take on for just any reason: to go out to eat, look like Kim Kardashian, go on vacation, buy the fancy new car instead of the good used car. Why is it that the brand new cars cost $20,000 more than cars that are two or three years old? In 2013, those were the coolest cars out. Now they're not cool anymore, because it's 2017? I'll drive the 2013 and keep my $20,000. Little decisions like that go a long way in terms of minimizing the debt that you have.

It's very, very important to avoid the mistake of not taking care of the fundamentals before you spend heavily. If you're doing well and working hard then enjoy your money. No question about it. Just make sure that you have your savings and investments in line before you go enjoy your money. It's like food. There's nothing wrong with eating ice cream or chocolate cake, in my opinion. If eating chocolate cake is a crime then I deserve life in prison. I will eat some chocolate cake all day long, but here's what I won't do. I won't eat chocolate cake before I've eaten the main course, vegetables, and all the healthy food first. Another thing

159

I'm not gonna do is eat an entire chocolate cake, because it'd be too much. It would be gluttony. What you see in America when it comes to money and the way people manage their money are forms of economic gluttony. You see people just spending until they have nothing left, and all the money they spend is on stuff that doesn't matter. Then, they go deep in debt to buy more stuff that doesn't matter. The banks are building wealth, and you're just languishing away. Don't let that be you.

Step 3

Next, step three. Deal with the paycheck to paycheck situation, and get out. Find a way to get out of that. You can get away from the paycheck to paycheck situation in a few ways. First of all, long-term savings plans. If you can't save a lot of money now, save something, because here's the thing. You can actually save more than you think, and let me tell you why I know you can save. Most of y'all can save, because I bet you that if I were to take all the money that you spent at fast food restaurants over the last 20 years, I would probably have enough money to go buy me a house with that. If I invested that money in the stock market, instead, I bet you that I'd be very wealthy. In fact, a person who spends an average of $5 a day on fast food over a 30-year period would have $281,000 in wealth if they put that money in the stock market. A lot of people I know spend $10 a day, and that would be over half a million dollars if invested. What baffles me is how many people say they really cannot afford to save when they have actually been an ATM machine for somebody else. You have served as a savings vehicle for people who have taken the money that you gave them, and they've put it into financial assets. They've put it aside for their family. So, long-term savings can make a difference.

Other streams of income can help you stop living paycheck to paycheck. So, when you have free time always sort of be thinking about ways you can make extra money. Don't feel that getting a job is enough. A lot of people will say, "I need money. I'm gonna go find a job." Then they go find a job, and they feel like they've handled their financial problem. Well, you're doing good until you don't have a job anymore, right? That means you're not really doing that well, because you're very vulnerable to actions that are outside of your control. While you're in the security of having a job, you should say to yourself, "Okay, I'm gonna live below my means, and I'm gonna take that last little 10%, or whatever, and I'm gonna start putting it toward initiatives that will help me get real financial security. Help me get off the plantation. Help me stop living paycheck to paycheck." Be in a position where you are economically strong.

The problem a lot of times is that many people only respond to economic emergencies. We only respond when times get hard. That's when we get serious. That's when we want to learn. There are people who only listen to me when they're broke. They only listen to me when they're scared. When you're broke and scared, sometimes I don't know what I can do to help you, because you're in the middle of the fire. The whole time I kept telling you to put on your fire suit, you didn't want to listen. Your wellbeing, your good situation, clogged up your ears.

I can just think about a relative I had who was kind of like that. When he was doing well with money, you couldn't tell him anything. He was very confident, very bold, very brash. Very just, "Whatever. I don't want to hear that." When crisis hit, though, he would turn into a little boy. "I didn't expect this to happen, I'm so sorry, I wish, I just need some help!" Suddenly, he calls you right back 'cause he thinks you're the person that's gonna give him the money that he needs. That is a reflection of very reactive thinking that you see from a lot of people. I encourage you to get away from that. When you're doing well is the time to prepare for the time you might not be doing so well. When the sun is out, that's when you go buy an umbrella. Don't wait 'til it starts raining to buy an umbrella. You're gonna get wet. There may not be any umbrellas left to buy, because everybody will be buying an umbrella when it starts raining.

Ownership of property gives you an economic cushion. When you own property and assets that appreciate in value, that gives you something you can hold onto, borrow against, or maybe even sell in case you run into what is called a liquidity problem. A liquidity is when you just need cash, and you gotta get some cash in a hurry.

Typical conversations about money often sound like, "Oh my god! I don't have enough money. It's hard out here. I'm struggling again. Can I borrow some money?" I personally think that the conversations instead should be, how do we take the money that we have and create security as opposed to spending that money? How do we make sure that we are positioned economically with economic intelligence, so we know how to identify opportunities when they arise? A lot of people feel that there are no opportunities. This is not because there are none. They feel that there are no opportunities, because they have never been taught to identify them. For example, if you put an antique in front of me, it could be literally worth a million dollars, and I wouldn't even know. If I were educated on antiques, however, then I might jump and say, "Oh my God! Look at how much money I can make." The ability to see opportunities comes from education. That's why we must educate ourselves, and we must educate our own. That's why my team and I created a resource called *TheBlackBusinessSchool.com*. If you want, go take a look at some of the other stuff we have. We created *TheBlackHistorySchool.com*, because we believe that black people should be teaching black people black history. So, I think that if you do that – educate yourself – you're gonna know where the opportunities are.

Step 4

Anyway, on to the concept of financial fertility. Financial fertility is basically when your money is positioned to grow rather than die. A lot of people end up struggling, because they let their money die. They wonder why they keep running out of money or why they keep having to constantly re-up their stash, so to speak. A lot of people see money as something that you're supposed to earn. Then, you run out. Then, you go back, and you earn some more. Investors see money differently. They say, "I'm gonna spend a little bit, but if I plant it like a seed, it's gonna keep growing. Eventually it's gonna grow so well that I won't actually have to go earn any more money." It becomes a self-sustaining situation. So like investors, we must understand that financial fertility is basically the understanding that money is capital, and capital should be preserved and grown. Think of it like an apple tree. If I give you an apple tree, you're not supposed to chop down your apple tree to make firewood. If I give you an apple, you're not supposed to just eat the apple and throw the seeds away. You're supposed to take the seeds, if you're really trying to have apple trees, and plant them. Grow more trees, so you can have more apples. Right?

When you get a dollar, you want to ask yourself how you can get that dollar to work for you. Tax season is a great example of that. People get their tax refund and become an immediate stimulus package for the local mall downtown. The Arabs, Greeks, Chinese, and everybody else sitting in the black communities are waiting for you to get your tax refund, because you have partnered with them in your own economic exploitation. Your mind has already made extremely detailed plans of how you are going to allow them to economically rape you once you receive that money. It's not like they're fooling you into it. They're not tricking you into spending that money. They're not even asking you to do it. Because you don't see the fertility of your money you are willingly asking them to economically ruin you and take everything you've got. A person who understands financial fertility, would say, "I got this $3,000 tax refund, and I'm in a bad situation. This money is helping me get out of my bad situation. I could use this money to give me a temporary remedy or a permanent remedy for my bad situation."

It all comes down to whether or not you think like an investor. Investors understand financial fertility, and financial fertility is where automatic millionaires come from. Many millionaires in America are not people who were born rich. They are not people who won the lotto. They are not people who got rich quick. They were people who got rich slowly through automatic investments over a long period of time that allowed the wealth accumulation process to occur. The equations used to describe the way money grows are actually taken from biology. The very same equations that would describe how a tree, flower, or baby grows are the equations used to describe how money grows. That's what money is supposed to do.

Step 5

Ask yourself...This is step five. This is another way to think about financial security. What do you own? How many times do you really see our people sitting around and really talking about what we own instead of how much money we make or what kind of fancy thing we got? When I talk to my daughters about picking a man that's financially secure, I just tell them if the man ain't got a plan don't get with him. If he ain't working hard to build that plan, don't get with him. He ain't got to have assets today, but he's got to at least have an investor mentality where he's investing time to build something for the future. That's just old-school me. That's just basic fundamental stuff.

There is 94-year-old lawyer who just died. He practiced law 'til he was 90 and made millions of dollars in the process. He told this funny story about how he met his wife back in the 1940s. He told his wife, "Look, I just want you to know that I would like to date you. I would like to pursue you, but I have to confess. I don't have much money now. However, I am working hard. I am educating myself. One day I'm gonna have plenty of assets and a lot of wealth, and I am going to take very good care of you." She ended up marrying him, and he kept his promise. That's what happened. There's a part of me that just loves stories like that, because I think that's a meaningful way for people to interact. Also, if you think about it, that's an investment decision. She had to decide, do I want to invest my life in this man? Do I want to attach myself to this ship? Do I want to draft this player to be on my team, or do I want to go along with somebody else? A lot of times in relationships you're making an investment. You're taking a huge risk. If you invest in the wrong person, you can end up being devastated.

So, I tell my girls all the time to find out if guys they are talking to plan to own things or even think about that. In fact, I tell them to talk to their potential partners about money. Just bring it up. Maybe you can just say, "Yeah, you know, my dad runs his mouth a lot, and he talks about money and investing and stuff like that." Just see what he says. If he says, "Oh, that's cool," and just goes on and does something else, then you might want to wait and see what his perspective is. If he talks about money and he says, "Yeah, I got some money. As soon as I get some money I'm gonna go buy me the new J's or whatever," you gotta be very careful. That tells you how he thinks about money and what he thinks money is used for. To me, a winner would be a guy who says, "Yeah, I saw your dad's video, and it made me really think about wealth building and investing, and I do want to own my own business. I want to actually accumulate some assets. I'm working hard every day." People like that are gonna be successful.

I know that when I was 24, I was working 10 hours a day to build a future for myself. I was actually investing to prepare for children that were not yet born. In fact, I still have that mindset today. Today, when I'm thinking about what we're doing now, we're not doing this for ourselves really. We're doing this for children who are not yet born, so they can fight the battles and win before they actually begin.

So, ownership has to become part of our culture. It has to become part of our standard dialogue as a community. We must talk about owning things and not always talk about buying things. We have to talk about owning things and not just talk about how much money you make. We have to talk about ownership and not just complain about what other people own. At the end of the day, you can complain about the Arabs, Jews, and Asians in your community selling you crappy things at the corner store, but remember they achieved an economic position that you could have accomplished. You also could have owned those corner stores. You also could have come together as a family and put your money together and bought an asset that would make you money. You also have the right, as an American, to sell things. Now, you're not gonna sell in their neighborhoods. They're not gonna let you do that. Honestly, some would say that we as black people shouldn't let them sell in our neighborhoods, but I think complaining doesn't really get us what we want. It's actually doing something that's gonna make the difference.

So, ownership has to be premiere. If you want to start with ownership, start by owning a share of stock. You can go buy a share stock in five minutes. If you're in my stock market investing program, then you have already bought stock, most likely. So, you are an owner. Now that you're owning things, own more. Accumulate a little more. Get in that habit. When I got into the habit of owning things and accumulating assets, I got really addicted to that. I used to be a spend-aholic when I was younger before I really started thinking about my financial future. I used to spend money. That was my weakness. When I became an investor, I was still kind of a spend-aholic. I still push money around a lot to the point that my brother gets very nervous. The difference though, now, is that the money I spend is going into my business. The more I spend, the stronger my company gets. Also, the more I spend, the more I own. You understand? Ultimately, find some way to keep doing what you're doing. Just think a little deeper about how you're doing it.

If money burns a hole in your pocket and you like to spend it, get together with your family, take that money, and put it someplace where you can go and actually make money from that. What will happen is you'll get even more money, and you can make bigger investments. It's just really a fun process. So, think about ownership.

Another step toward ownership is real estate. A lot of people tell me they can't buy a house, and I think that's so funny. People don't understand that, mathematically, if you've rented property for 20 years you've actually probably technically bought your landlord a house. You've actually bought a house. You just gave it away to somebody else. If you rented for 30 years you probably bought them two houses. The economic system is very interesting in the sense that you have people that are able to build empires with other people doing all the work. It's very fascinating to see how that works. I don't agree with it. Maybe it's not ethical, but that's just kind of the way it is. So, real estate is huge. Then obviously, owning your own business.

I think a family that has those three things — owns stocks and bonds, some real estate, and your own business — is gonna have some financial security from assets and income from multiple sources. Your family should be a business. Your family is a business. That is your first business. If you mess that business up, then it kind of makes it harder to do anything else. But if you do it right, then you will experience a type of heaven that you didn't think was even possible. You will experience a pride that will make you feel like you are King Jaffe Joffer from *Coming to America*. I kid you not.

I will just do a confession. Y'all, I'm sorry. I have to do this. Don't tell my kids this, but I love being able to sit at the table as the patriarch of the Watkins family empire, and when my children get out of line I do my James Earl Jones, "No, you will NOT disobey me!" I'm kidding. I don't do that, but I do actually like the idea of feeling like a king. I like the idea that my mother is elevated in a certain way, and we can do things for her. I also confess that I chose not to get married. I know some of y'all think that means I'm a bad person or that I must be gay. No, I'm not gay. I just didn't get married, but that's a whole other conversation. But, I have a relationship with an awesome woman, and in my mind I get to say to myself, "Yes, she is a queen, and she gets the security of being next to a man who has his masculinity intact." I love that. I'm getting personal here, and I'm not trying to tell you all my business, but that's the honest truth. I love the fact that because we have our family endowment —a pile of capital, a pile of wealth, a pile of assets — we're able to create jobs for our children, their friends, relatives, and things like that.

Most of my daily business doesn't involve responding to a boss. It involves being a boss. It involves having interesting conversations about possibilities. For example, today I was sitting on the phone, and I was negotiating with someone about making a movie. I said, "No, the budget's not gonna be that much. It's gonna be this much. No, I need him to make sure he gets this done in this way." I'll just tell you the truth. It makes life a lot more fun. You are never really completely totally devoid of any economic risk. There's always something that can rattle the ship, but it's better to be on a bigger ship, and it's much more fun to own the ship.

I encourage you to figure out how to get you a ship, and own the ship. That's what I teach. That's what we do in The Black Business School. I'm not really big on teaching you how to go and cater to white supremacy, so you can get a better job. I'm just not good at that. If you come to me for advice, because you're having trouble with your boss, I'm the guy that will get you fired. I will get you fired, because I'm gonna tell you that I don't think you should tolerate that. So, I'm not the guy to talk to about how to keep a job. I'm the guy that will teach you where empires come from and why everybody can have one. Empires don't have to be big. It's all about mindset. Is my empire the biggest empire on the block? No, it's not. I mean, it is worth a few million dollars, but even if you rewind and go back to when it was worth a few thousand dollars, I still drew a tremendous amount of pride from knowing that my family had something that belonged to us. That we had and still have something that will be around for the great-grandkids to talk about.

As black people, we lack pride sometimes. We don't feel any shame in begging. We have a lot of black men who are broken who don't really understand that there are certain kinds of behavior you should be ashamed of as a man. It's hard to be proud as a man when you're out begging for money, but there are a lot of guys who can do it, and I don't understand that. Tap-dancing to get into professional sports leagues because you didn't learn how to create any other economic or educational opportunities for yourself, is something men should be ashamed of. You shouldn't be proud of that. You shouldn't be proud of catering to and begging of people who historically hated you. Who don't respect you to take care of you. There's no pride in that.

I didn't mean to go off on that tangent. However, I think that ownership is really important. There are psychological studies showing that people who own something feel proud of it. They take good care of it. So, find something that you own, and be proud that it's yours. I don't care if it's a $5 share stock.

Step 6

Check your dang insurance. Make sure your insurance is intact. So many of us are underinsured. When you actually get something worth losing and you don't insure it properly, you're asking for tragedy.

Anytime there's a tragedy or calamity in my life or that of anybody else, the first question I ask myself is, "Could this have been avoided?" When it comes to black people, I would argue that the vast majority of things that happen to us when it comes to wealth and health can be avoided.

If you look at why black people die, we don't die for the same reasons that white people die. White people die, honestly, from genetic hereditary stuff that they usually can't avoid so much. Honestly, I think that we have something genetically that makes us very, very strong. That's why people are afraid of us. Black people, unfortunately, die from things like gunshot wounds, heart disease, and diabetes, all of which is avoidable. A lot of that comes from maybe grandma's fried chicken, being extremely obese, and not even thinking about going to the gym. Again, there's a mindset that was built that led to those sorts of decisions. It's not always our fault. We've been brainwashed. We have been conquered and brainwashed. That's why the black man is on his knees right now in America. It is because he's been brainwashed to live on his knees.

And so, what I have to encourage you to do, is to question everything. You must question everything in terms of how you were taught to live, think about money, and respond to things. For example, proactive versus reactive thinking is huge. The reason we have reactive thinking where we respond to rather than prevent tragedies goes to the highest levels. Dr. Claud Anderson, in the book *Black Labor, White Wealth* speaks extensively about how black leadership is flawed, because many of our leaders only react to crises, because we think that being black means always being in a state of crises. It means you're always in a state of emergency. It means your world's always falling apart. It means you're always playing struggle-nomics, and you'll never get a chance to play power-nomics. The leadership thinking this way trickles down to the people. If you have children, you're a black leader. You're leading your children, and your children are gonna lead their children. So, you're leading a whole bunch of people. It's just that most of those people are not yet born. If you don't have kids, you're gonna one day be a leader when you do have kids or anybody you influence. If you choose to be a leader, you're a black leader. So, I would argue that the best black leaders are people that can be proactive and prepare.

That's where insurance comes into play, because insurance is a reflection of your desire to prepare for all the things that can go wrong. I spend the majority of my time talking to my team about insurance plans. Talking about estate planning. Talking about what's in my will.

Talking about trusts. Talking about stress tests or what-if scenarios. What if we lose this revenue stream over here? What's gonna happen to that? Are we prepared for that? Check your insurance. Make sure you have life insurance for yourself and for your children. I know two children who died this year. Their parents were not prepared for the funeral, and it only made things worse. I know you don't want to think about having your children die, but life insurance for children doesn't cost anything. It's a few pennies, a couple of dollars a month or whatever, and it gives you security in case something goes wrong. It doesn't mean your kid is gonna die. It just means you're prepared in case something goes wrong. You don't have the emotional turmoil compounded with financial problems, as well. Life insurance for yourself is necessary. If you care about your kids, you're gonna get life insurance for yourself.

Health insurance is important. A lot of black people, especially black men, don't have health insurance. That only leads to more economic calamity, because one of the greatest pathways to lifelong debt is to get sick. You get sick, you're done. You can't pay those bills. Costs too much. And then, if you don't address the illness, yes, if it's something that's killing you, then it will kill you, because you didn't go to the doctor.

Disability insurance is for just in case you get injured. Whether it's on the job or off the job, it makes sure that your income can maintain itself. Look into disability insurance. Property insurance. Protect your property.

Key person insurance. If you run a business, you're gonna be one of the key components to that business. So, as one of the key components to that business, you want to keep in mind what will happen if you are gone. What happens if you are unable to maintain the business or if somehow you die? Key person insurance allows you to protect against that. So, when my company got to a certain level, I had extensive conversations about making sure that there would be some money available to my partners in case I wasn't here.

Estate planning. Estate planning is critical. Let me tell you a secret about estate planning. Estate planning is what happens after you die. Let me tell you a big secret about estate planning that I heard from a lawyer. There's a lawyer who told me that the way her firm makes most of their money is from people who don't properly plan their estate. She said, "I hate it, but we make the bulk of our money, because people live life as if they are never going to die." What happens is everything they have goes into probate. When it goes into probate, your kids aren't getting the money. The lawyers are getting the money. It becomes a big mess. It may destroy your family. You have relatives fighting in court. It becomes a complete fiasco, and when it's all said and done your biggest beneficiary becomes Uncle Sam. The IRS becomes the biggest beneficiary that you have. So, proper estate planning is critical.

I want you to think about the afterlife. In church, you're always talking about the afterlife, but you're thinking about it in kind of a different way, right? You're thinking about the pearly gates. You're thinking about salvation and life after. Well, I encourage you to think about the afterlife in a different way. I want you to think about the afterlife in a way where you get over yourself. Stop thinking about what's gonna happen to you when you die, start thinking about the people that you're going to leave behind. I can't tell you what's going to happen when you go to heaven or when you die. I don't know what's gonna happen to you. I'm just gonna be honest with you. I'm not an un-religious person. I believe anything is possible. I just need a little proof. My father's a pastor, and I listen to him, and I listen to other people, too, but I don't really know what happens when you die, 'cause I've never died before. It's never happened. What I do know is that in the afterlife you're gonna be gone, and your loved ones will still be here on Earth. Their time on Earth is going to be either heaven or hell depending on how much time you spent planning for the possibility that you might not be here no more.

You must ask yourself if you are prepared for the afterlife. That is where making a will comes into play. That is where life insurance comes into play. That is where estate planning comes into play. That is where spending time learning about trusts comes into play. If you don't plan for your death, your family's gonna suffer, because they won't have the resources they need. Everything they need will be locked up in court. Secondly, if you have accumulated something, it's gonna disappear, because 70% of all families lose all their wealth within one generation. So the question is, how are you gonna end up in that last 30%? Also, 90% of all wealthy families lose all their wealth within two generations. So, when I think about my wealth, I think about how I can make sure I'm not in that 90%. I'm not thinking about how much we can accumulate in 2017. I'm thinking, "How do I make sure that we allow this wealth to grow, so it'll be around in the year 2117? How do I make sure that my great-great-great-great-great-great grandkids who are not yet born can benefit from all the hard work I put in to become Dr. Boyce Watkins?" That's what I encourage you to think about. That's what matters. That's how wealth works.

The last type of insurance is what they call umbrella insurance. Umbrella insurance is kind of what they call insurance for your insurance. A lot of people don't know that your health, life, and all these other forms of insurance have caps. Especially the health insurance. Health insurance has a cap where you will get covered up to a certain amount of money. So when you get your insurance plan, make sure you look to see what the max is that they'll pay. A lot of people don't think about it 'cause you don't think you're ever gonna hit that ceiling. When you hit the ceiling, there's usually a reason. You've got some really horrible thing going on physically, and it ends up causing you to die.

I knew a kid in Illinois. I was advocating for him, because he was, well, like a lot of our boys. He was big into sports in high school, and they love you when you're doing well, but they don't love you when you're not. This kid was playing wide receiver. Big strong kid. He took a hit that went bad, and he got paralyzed at the age of 18. I mean, peak of his life. Prime of his life. He got paralyzed from here, all the way down through his entire body. When that happened, everybody's feeling bad. The school goes to his mother and says, "Mrs. Wilson, we love your son, and we're gonna take care of him. We have an insurance policy in place. It'll take care of him for the rest of his life." What the mother did not know is that the school did not plan for him to live that long, because paraplegics don't typically live that long after their injuries. They tend to die within four or five years a lot of times, because the inability to even move your neck is huge. You can't even lift your head to eat. You can't do anything. So, anyway. I guess the school underestimated the strength of black people. We're just so amazing that it's hard to take us down. Instead of dying in three or four years like they planned, the kid lived another...I think he was 31 when I met him. So, he lives another 13 years, without being able to move his neck at all.

It was the saddest scene ever. His mother dedicated her whole life to sitting by his bedside taking care of every need that he had and all this other stuff. I went to see them, because I was advocating for them. What happened was, his 24-hour care ended up costing more than they thought. It cost $100,000 a year. Something crazy like that. His insurance policy had a cap on it, and he hit the ceiling. They sent his mother a little letter saying, "Mrs. Wilson, your insurance policy has reached its limit. We're gonna cut your policy at a certain date." Long story short, we advocated, screamed, and hollered. I tried to shame the school into making a move. They didn't do anything. They let this black man die. They let him die, and his mother was devastated. She dedicated her whole life to taking care of him. A lot of it was because they did not know the insurance policy had a cap on it.

So, what I would say to you is, be cautious when you buy insurance. Make sure you know what the cap is. Get umbrella insurance, especially if you have something to lose, 'cause umbrella insurance doesn't just cover your insurance if it hits the cap. It also protects you in the event of things like lawsuits. Once you start making money and getting financially secure, your life will change in a lot of ways that are good and bad. When you get financial security, it feels better. You're happier. You're able to help people, but you also become a target. You become a target for people who want to borrow and or beg for money. You become a target for people that want to steal it. You become a target for people who want to sue you. Lawsuits can devastate everything, so umbrella insurance is the way to protect against the lawsuits.

~

When you think about investing, the first thing you want to think about is not, how do I invest my money? The important stuff you're investing is not the money, it's your life! That's why the investment of marriage is huge. If you invest yourself and your life and your future in the wrong person, that's far more financially devastating than buying a bad share of stock. So, think about your investments in a broad context, not just money. Investing goes far deeper than money. You're investing right now by being in this room. You could be doing a lot of stuff other than sitting here listening to me. You're listening to me, because you're investing for your future, and you have some belief that this information I share with you is gonna help you build a better life for yourself. For that, I commend you.

Black wealth and wealth building doesn't usually look like an NBA player or a rapper. Building wealth is a lot like building a building. When you build a building, you gotta go brick by brick. You gotta lay out the diagram of the building you want to build, and you gotta go piece by piece, brick by brick by brick. It takes a long time. Wealth building is not get rich quick. It's something that happens slowly but surely. Financial security is something that will occur if you give yourself time to get there. You're not gonna get it overnight.

I can't sit around, waste time, and do dumb things, because I'm thinking about everything that's being lost by me wasting time doing what everybody else is doing. I'm always thinking about wealth building. I'm always thinking about investing. I'm always thinking about the community in terms of what we as a community can do. What if we took everything we had and applied it toward building as opposed to applying it toward destruction or giving it all away? The tiny steps are what matters.

Andre wanted to own a home, and Andre was making $15.15 an hour. He just sacrificed. He did something that is literally taboo, almost like a curse word in the black community. He made a sacrifice for his future, and he saved every penny. He kept track of his money for two or three years. He spent a couple years living like nobody else would, so he could spend the rest of his life living like nobody else could. That allowed him to buy his first home at the age of 22. He's been a homeowner ever since. Get off of this nonsense that it's just too hard to own a home, because you need a down payment. If you just take the time to educate yourself on how to buy real estate, you'll find that there are options out there that require very little money down. Some of y'all in this room might be homeowners. Being a homeowner does not require you to be rich. It just requires you to not have a poor person's mindset. It requires you to re-prioritize how you think about your money.

Next, start the process today. You can do little things today. Maybe start by making a budget. Look at how much money you make. Figure out what your expenses are. Then, figure out where you can find a little bit of extra money to start saving right now. A lot of you in the stock market program, already have apps like Acorns, Stash, and Robinhood to start investing. I love Acorns, because you can put a few pennies in every couple of days, or whatever, and it can grow. I know a kid who works with me who is 23, and he said, "I've been able to save up $400 in my Acorns app, because I'm adding the extra change from my credit card." So, I encourage you just to start small.

Then also, do the free stuff first. Learning doesn't cost you very much. I mean, maybe if you're in one of our programs, yeah, it might cost you about the cost of going to the movies a couple times in a month. But for the most part, learning information doesn't cost you anything. When you're not here with me and learning from me, get on the internet. Read articles. Just consume information.

I'm gonna leave you with this, and then I'll be done. Thank you guys for bearing with me, 'cause I'm very reflective today. That's why you've seen me kind of going in certain directions, because I'm really meditating on this issue, and I want to make sure you internalize this and understand what I'm saying. If you want to be a strong black person in America, you must be informed. If you want to be a strong black person in America, you must educate yourself. You must learn. I don't care if you're 12 or if you're 112. Being black in this country demands, requires, and dictates that we are on the absolute cutting edge when it comes to competitiveness, information, forward thinking, and planning. If we get to the cutting edge of those areas, then we have the chance to not just assume equity in our own future, but the ability to surge ahead. I'm not talking about equality or inclusion, I'm talking about dominance.

It starts with your own family. Don't worry about saving the whole black community. You can leave that to people like me. I'm a public figure, I guess, so I'll lay out the big master plans, and I'll ask you guys to help me if you trust me enough to help. But, start with your own family. That's your own black community, and you control that. Be a little bit audacious about it. Say, "In our family, we want to build wealth. We want to be like the Rockefellers." Keep your values and your ethics intact, but at the same time, really have fun with the process. I'll tell you. Being empowered and being educated is a whole lot more fun than being a victim. It really is. I don't think this whole victimhood thing works for us. I think it makes us look silly. I think it makes us less than what we're supposed to be. I think that it makes us a fraction of what we're supposed to be as a community. I don't think we're gonna get anywhere with that.

Thank you, guys, for hanging out today. I hope you can identify what financial security looks like. Tell people. Go talk to your relatives about it. This was a lot of fun. It's an honor to be your teacher, and I hope that what I've said today has been helpful to you.

LECTURE 7

DR. BOYCE SPEAKS:
THE BLACK WRITERS EVENT

What's happening, black people? How are you doing today? All right, now that was a hell of an introduction. I'll tell you I enjoyed watching the introduction more than I enjoyed my own speech.

When I think about what individuals like Dr. Collin Anderson and others like him have done for our people I feel gratitude for the sacrifices they have made. In my opinion their sacrifices are a lot like playing for a basketball team that is going through a rough spot. You know? Think about how they let black coaches take over college teams when they are losing the most. What about when Obama became president? The state of the economy was at the pits of hell. A lot of times our truest leaders, those who are really advocating for us, are the ones who are not only disrespected the most by America but by their own people. They are disrespected by their own community. We know the brainwashing is really deep. The brainwashing is persistent, and it has occurred over a very long period of time.

One of the things I have heard Mr. Brown mention is that there was a study that said it is going to take about nine generations for black people to catch up with other people, mainly white folks, when it comes to wealth. That would be about 228 years. I thought about that study. Right? The more I thought about that, the more I concluded that the study is laced with just a little bit of bullshit. Let me tell you why in my opinion that is bullshit, and I hope I do not offend you. Every now and then a cuss word comes out. Blame my dad.

That particular study bothered me, because it assumes that if enough time passes black people are going to catch up. Eventually, the gap will just narrow, and black people are going to catch up. That is a very, very, very bad assumption. That is assuming that we are running fast enough to catch up. The study assumes that our opponent is not out-running us. It also is assuming that we are moving forward and not standing still. We have a whole lot of Negros who are running backwards. They are running south when they are supposed to be running north. I believe the gap will not close. The gap will widen. If you look at the studies across America in terms of how wealth is split up, spread out, and controlled by certain people you are not seeing the wealth gap between rich folks and everybody else closing up. I am not just talking about black people. I am talking about everybody. The gap is widening.

Another reason the gap is widening is because, in the game of capitalism, there are those who understand it and those who do not. There is inheritance absolutely, but then information is the greatest inheritance and the most important inheritance there is: even more so than wealth. Why do we say that? Well, because there are also studies that have shown that most wealthy families lose all their wealth within one generation. Seventy percent of wealthy families lose all their wealth in a generation. Ninety percent lose all their wealth in two generations. The reason they lose their wealth is because we think an economic inheritance is the most important variable. If you do not inherit information, discipline, financial intelligence, and a culture that breeds economic growth as opposed to struggle-nomics, then you are going to find that even a rich person can go broke.

When we look at these studies, see where we are and where we have to go. Remember that where you are right now means almost nothing relative to where you are going. We are only here for a blip in time. I have thought about this a lot, because I want to see black people built into a great nation. If you look at the history of how great nations are built, one thing you will understand is that the building process does not happen quickly. It does not happen in two or three years. It does not happen, because you have one leader nor does it happen because you give a few good speeches. It happens sometimes over many, many generations and hundreds of years.

Although we are only here for a blip in time we are running a long race called wealth building. It is not a solo race. Rather, the wealth race is a relay race that you are not going to win right now or all by yourself. You must wait for your teammates, and they are not born yet. They are the ones you will hand the baton off to in a few years when all of us are old, gray, dead, and gone. When you run a relay race you must understand that this is a race where your best shot is not to feel you have to build every empire meant to be built. Planting seeds then letting our children and grandchildren finish the job is the most important thing we can do. It is like watching a tree grow. For example, a sycamore tree is one of the biggest trees. However, sycamore tree seeds are very, very, very small. As usual when one plants seeds you must make sure they have plenty of sunlight, water, and fertile soil. Then with the passing of time, you will begin to witness the growth of your tree. Keep in mind that sycamore trees are not built in a day. Likewise, wealth is not built in a day. Most wealthy families are built over many generations with everybody playing on the same team and running the same relay race.

Now out of all the ways money and investments grow for any financial asset in the universe there are pretty much two or three equations. In those equations the most important variable is time. Those equations are actually taken from biology, because the way money grows is similar to the way a plant grows or the way a flower grows. My biggest concern for black folks is not where we are. It is not that we do not have as much as we need to have or that we are going through a struggle right now. My biggest concern is that we are not planting enough seeds, and we are not creating fertile soil for those who want to plant those seeds.

Let me give an example. How many of you all have families where if you go home and tell them you have a new job they want to pop bottles and throw a party? But then, you tell them you are starting your own business, and they act like it's a funeral. They feel sorry for you. "Well, the white man must not have wanted you. Well, just hang in there baby. One day we are going to get you that job." Right? Then they begin to subtly disrespect you. Whereas, if you had a job they know exactly how to define what you do. Your grandma be like, "Yeah, my baby works over at Frito Lay. He puts the writing on the backs of the bags." The whole family is so proud. They brag about you, because you are the vice president at Frito Lay making $100,000 a year. They do not share the same level of excitement for you if you are building a business for yourself as they do when you are building an empire for somebody else. They are so proud, because they see Frito Lay as the real deal. It is almost as if they have been validated when you work for a large corporation. Somehow their self-esteem is elevated, because some of us as a culture need other people to validate us. They feel like our culture is worth nothing unless somebody else comes along and tells us that we have value.

So, I repeat. When you work for the white man, people understand exactly what you do. However, when you start a business and you see those same relatives they are like, "What do you do again?" They act like you do not really have a job. "Since you ain't working can you go pick up the laundry, get the mail, and go get the kids." That is the true sign that they do not respect what you are doing. It is the true sign that they do not understand the fundamental reality of every great empire that exists in America today started as a figment of somebody's imagination. In order for any building to be built somebody has to imagine it first. Someone draws up the diagrams for the building. Someone else does the brick and mortar. Everything that it takes to develop a structure has to be completed by someone. Such is also the case when it comes to building in the black community. In many ways those who are truly committed to building for the black community are seen as a little bit crazy, but if black visionaries did not have wild imaginations there would be no vision. Therefore, I am telling you that it is okay to be a little bit crazy. We need crazy people who think outside of the box to help build our nation.

I do not know the answers to every problem that we have as a community. I do not pretend to be that person nor will I ever be. One thing I imagine all of us can agree upon, however, is that what we have been doing as a people is not working. Many of us are trained from birth to be part of an economic, social, and political cage that is built for us before we are even born. A lot of us are like animals in captivity. We do not even know that we are born in the zoo. We really are the animals who live in the zoo and think they are free. Just like the animals, we have never known what it means to be free.

People I know who have gotten free – gotten off the corporate plantation and started doing things for black folks – cannot go backwards. Animals understand freedom. You do not have to explain to an animal why it is better to be free than be in a cage. Just let him out and try putting him back in the cage. He is not going to go back, but many of our people are born in a cage. Think about this. The first thing that we do is hand our children over to oppressors. We hand them over to people who have hated them for 400 years and say, "Here. Educate my baby." Then we wonder why so many of our kids grow up screwed up. Think about that.

It takes about 187,000 hours to raise a baby from zero to the age of 18. I do not understand how that child in 187,000 hours spends about 14,000 hours in school then reaches the age of 18 and cannot read, write, or do math. Somehow that same child can memorize the lyrics of every song that comes on the radio. They have mastered nothingness. They have mastered all the things that are irrelevant to their development as a strong black person in this society. The brainwashing runs deep. You are being exposed to propaganda every day. You are being educated in a specific way every day. Whether you turn on the radio, turn on the TV, go to school, or work for a corporation you are exposed to propaganda. Whatever you are thinking is being shaped.

The first thing that we have to do as a people if we are ever going to build anything is reclaim the education of our children in every single way. Let me tell you. When I am talking to people I am looking in their eyes. What I am really seeing are people that are kind of like, what they call, preaching to the choir. I do not think you would be here if you were lost. I do not think you would even be here if you were a person who needed to hear this information. Thus, I believe that you are here, because most of the black economic revolution is going to be led by people that I call the early adapters. The early adapters are the people who are like economic soldiers. Think about the military. You do not need everybody to be a soldier. You just need a few good men and women. So my argument is that we as the economic soldiers, we as the choir, we as the people that are taking the lead on this, have a mandate. That mandate is to make sure that as we raise our children we teach them to develop businesses, to develop structures, and really get the most out of their talents.

We have to kill the old paradigm of what is considered to be black success: going to school, working hard, getting a job, and giving 40 years to that job. When you die at your desk and disappear, they replace you within a week and act like you were never there. That is not success. Somebody just told you it is success. For many of you there was a point where you started thinking about it and said, "Wait a minute. I think I'm successful. I was told I'm successful, but I don't feel successful." That is because you are not. You were told you were free, but you really are not free. You had to kind of figure it all out as you went along.

I would argue that what we can do for our children is make sure they do not go through that process. They are hearing this from birth. Hearing this from the very beginning, but no black child in America should be raised under the assumption that you grow up and work for somebody else. From the minute your child learns how to say, "Mama, can I have some money?" You shouldn't say, "Well, boy, one day you got to grow up and get you a job." No, you say, "One day you are going to grow up and start a business." That is what you do. Now if they want to figure out how to go to work for other people as part of their plan that is fine. However, that should be plan B. It should never be plan A.

Additionally, I believe that we as black people can be successful when we are able to do whatever we want without changing a thing about who we are. We are already extraordinary people. Let's be real. We are descendants of the survivors of the Middle Passage. We are descendants of the survivors of the worst slavery and the worst atrocities in all of human history. Other cultures really cannot kill us. The only people who can kill black folks are other black people. That is why they train you to turn the gun on yourself. We saw Hip-Hop as a tool for empowerment, so they flipped it over and said, "Let's use it as a tool to kill black people." The fact is that they cannot kill us. They cannot take us down. Who we are is fine. We do not require an overhaul in terms of how we conduct ourselves. We simply require modest tweaking. For example, I do not believe that it makes any sense whatsoever for a black boy to spend more time on the football field than he spends in books. Nor should he spend more time in sports than he does in the classroom or on learning how to start a business. Black men are the most unemployed group of people in America. At the foundation, the core, the crux, of why our families are falling apart and why black women do not respect black men anymore is because our men are out here begging another man to feed their children. If a white man knows that he is the reason your children get to eat every day, you are not the man of your house. He is the man of your house.

Black men. Black boys. If you are raising black young men you have to understand that there is nothing out there for them. You must get this down, because it is your responsibility to help your sons understand there is nothing out there for black men. There are no opportunities waiting for them, especially if your sons have been to prison. There are no opportunities. It is a lie. It is a false dream. It is some hocus sprinkled in front of you to get you to behave just long enough to let your guard down, so they can slaughter you. If you do not believe me look around and see how many black men you see committing suicide on a daily basis. I am not talking about killing themselves literally. Though, some of them do. I know a lot of former athletes who gave everything trying to get to the NFL. Then, they found out at the last minute there are not that many jobs in the NFL. I know some guys like that who have actually killed themselves. I am talking about the guys who kill themselves slowly over time like the guy sitting at home every day smoking weed and getting drunk. I am talking about the black man sitting at home every day in his drawers playing Xbox. Finally, I am talking about the black men who still live in their mama's basement, because a white man will not give them a job.

Black people have somehow been led to believe that their 40 hours of labor a week has no value unless white people agree to pay for it. Think about that. Why would anyone pay you to work 40 hours a week if your labor did not have value? Therefore, if he is not paying you for your labor why are you not applying it to something of your own? You can extract that value for yourself. If corporate America is paying you $20 an hour, that probably means you are worth $70 an hour. Why are you not equipped to take your own labor and apply it to something that is going to benefit your family? Is it not better to work for yourself and directly apply your skills to something that you own as opposed to benefiting somebody else's business? A lot of this mentality comes from spending more time learning how to be a basketball player, football player, or rapper than learning how to be a man. This is warfare, people. This is warfare.

That which makes a man marriageable, in many cases, has to do with his ability to provide for himself and for other people. That which gives the man pride is connected to his ability to provide. I can tell you I became deeply offended as I grew up and moved into manhood. I started to realize, "Wait a minute. Hold on. Wait. In order for me to feel like a man, I have to go beg this other man to take care of me like I'm a baby. I don't feel like a man right now. I feel like a little boy. I'm feeling kind of like a bitch right now." What I am saying to you is the assumptions that we make about what it means to succeed in this society have to go out the window.

About 70% or 80% of the so-called successful black people we see every day really are not successful. They are individuals who have been given financial rewards for bowing down and supporting white supremacist institutions. If you know anything about white supremacy, if you know anything about capitalism, then you understand that systems reward you for supporting the system. If you reject, question, or challenge the system, the system is designed to spit you out. In many cases the successful black person is not the one who got to the top of the pile. A lot of times it is the person who got booted out. We are trained to think in a specific way about what black success really means. Therefore, we have been taught to mistake success for assimilation. We will often celebrate the least successful people in our community. One good example of this is the guy named Lee Daniels who makes that stupid show *Empire*. Lee Daniels humiliates our community by making all these movies that are incredibly disrespectful to black people. However, many black people consider Lee Daniels to be a role model. Others consider him to be a successful man, because some white guy wrote him a check. We need to get off that. We need to let that go right now. We need to challenge those people for that kind of behavior.

Let's get into some specifics on some strategies we can apply in order to do what we have to do. Now one of the people that I love the most and respect the most is Dr. Mulligan. He mentioned that Dr. Claude Anderson wrote a book. Although he has written lots of books, one of Dr. Anderson's books that I consider to be one of the greatest ever written in the history of this world. The title of the book is *Black Labor, White Wealth*. Another great book written by Dr. Anderson is *Powernomics*. One of the things that Dr. Anderson specifically talks about that I think we should meditate on is that we need leadership that has a plan. The problem is we have too many leaders who will hoot, holler, complain, and get everybody riled up. Then nothing happens afterward. There is no structured, systematic, step-by-step, day-to-day process that we can follow that will help us achieve the empowerment that we are looking for.

The other thing that we have to accept right now, at least in this generation, is that we are not the popular kids on the block. There will never be a day where we are speaking about the power of black economics, not in our lifetime, that it will draw a crowd as large as, say, a Beyoncé concert. My argument would be that as we move forward, rather than feeling like we have to carry on our backs the burden of saving an entire community, we can do what we need to do individually. Each of us within our sphere of influence can do what we can to develop economic strength and security in our own families. People often talk about building the next Black Wall Street. How do you build the new Black Wall Street? A lot of times what they visualize is something that is tough to accomplish. They are visualizing something that is worth hundreds of millions of dollars. Their vision includes something that consists of lots of buildings, shops, and everything else up and down the block. Looking to build the Black Wall Street over time. If you study how economies work, you realize that an economy can be giant, or it can be small. However, the dynamics can be very much the same. A Black Wall Street does not have to be brick and mortar buildings. A Black Wall Street can also be digital.

I look at technology, and I see what is happening on the internet. Black people are coming together to form digital villages where they talk to each other every day. It is really powerful and transformative. Most black people who know anything about me now would never have known about me were it not for technology. They are not going to let a Negro like me on TV. That is not going to happen. We know that. If I had a show I would lose it in about a week. Right? Technology is one of the avenues of possibility that exists for us. Also, technology is an avenue for wealth building in terms of the ability for us to do business with each other. Actually, you may not know this, but 80% of the wealth generated on this planet in the last two years has been generated in Silicon Valley. Our children are aiming for the wrong dreams. If we generate children who are masters of technology and entrepreneurship then those individuals will create the next *Snapchat*. They will create the next *Facebook*. They will create whatever.

What we have to do as a community is create fertile soil for black entrepreneurs, so their businesses can grow. Imagine you have a kid that is really good with computers. He is as smart as Mark Zuckerberg who created *Facebook* and he says, "You know, I'm really good at computers. I have this great idea. Here's what I'm going to do." Is he really going to get support from every black person he sees? Will he hear, "You know you can create a billion dollar company"? More than likely somebody is going to say, "You know, Pookie, you're good with computers. They will pay you $200,000 a year to go work at IBM." That is most likely what they will do. That is what I was told. That is what people like me are told. We have to have fertile soil. We also have to understand how economies work and what that really means.

Your child's understanding of financial literacy and wealth building should start at an early age. It should be as fundamental as our commitment to sports and entertainment. It should be as fundamental as going to church every Sunday. If you ask a kid who grew up in a church, "When's the first time your grandma took you to church?" they will not remember. I would argue that we should have children who cannot remember the first time their parents taught them about economic intelligence or how to start a business. It should be a part of the culture. They should also have some degree of financial literacy training at an early age. Every black child in America should know how to start their own business by the age of 12. Just as a rite of passage. As fundamental as their responsibility.

There was a mother who came to an event we had in Los Angeles about two months ago. The mother showed me a video of her four-year-old twin sons who had memorized one of our online curriculums. She said, "Sometimes it's hard, because the other parents think I'm too serious. I don't let my kids watch TV, and I don't let them eat garbage like McDonald's. I make sure they're learning financial literacy and not Nicki Minaj lyrics." I said, "You know what? You're the key to all of this." Mothers are the key to everything. Mothers are the first master teacher. Fathers, we come in second. We know we cannot do this without the mothers getting on board with these ideas. I said, "What you've done is basically guarantee that your sons will never be unemployed." A person who knows how to think entrepreneurially from a fundamental sub-conscious level is a person who is able to see opportunity everywhere. They can walk into a room where there is no money and see wealth everywhere. It is the difference between somebody who knows how to just hunt for a job versus somebody who knows how to start their own business. It is the difference between somebody who feels they can only eat when restaurants are open versus somebody who knows how to grow their own food, hunt, and cook their own food. Who is going to eat better? Who has more food security? The people who only know how to go to McDonald's and Burger King or the people who know how to grow and cook their own food?

Here's the thing, though. A lot of you all were raised in wonderful families where consciousness was taught to you at an early age. I was not raised in that family. I was raised in a very typical, stereotypical family, where I was taught a lot of wrong things. I picked up these ideas in my 30s. I do not have the advantages that our children can have, because it took a long time for me to un-program myself from all the other crap I had learned. I had to re-program myself into something that was actually going to help me succeed in this country. Did you know that if they took every supercomputer on the planet and put them all together they cannot simulate one human brain? You literally are walking around with a supercomputer in your hands. The most powerful part of that supercomputer is the part that you do not even see. It is the sub-conscious mind. The messages that you get at an early age shape you in ways that you cannot even imagine. My argument is that we need to hit the sub-conscious of our children early. We hit it hard. We hit it consistently with messages of empowerment, economic intelligence, and all the things that they are going to need in order to be successful.

The thing you have got to understand is that economics is not a nice game to play. It is warfare. Global economic warfare is what runs this country. Economic protectionism is what occurs in every single community. Many black people, unfortunately, did not get the memo. When you drop your child in the middle of an economic system and they've never been trained in economics, that's like dropping them in the middle of the Super Bowl and they've never seen a football. They've never had football practice. They don't know which end zone is theirs. They don't know how to score points. What's going to happen to that child when they're not prepared to play? Well, they're going to end up having to serve a master who will offer to protect them, or they're going to walk up to their opponent and say, "Can you explain the rules of this game to me?" They'll say, "Sure. The first thing you've got to do is give the ball to me every time you get it. Don't worry about scoring your own points. I'll score all the points, and I'll give you some points." Then they'll wonder why every game ends with them losing 187 to 2. That's what we do when we send our children out into the a competitive global economic system without economic training. We are putting them in the middle of a battlefield without a gun, without a shield, without a strategy, without training, without nothing. When you're in that situation all you can do is serve people who offer to protect you. You'll end up learning the rules of that battlefield from the people who are going to oppress you in exchange for that information or in exchange for that protection. The information that they give you is going to be false. That's what we're doing when we're learning how to play the game of economics from the people who hate us the most and live off of our exploitation.

Capitalism, is a lot like the Kentucky Derby. Capitalism is a horse and jockey race. Think about a horse race. The jockey is training the horse, whipping the horse, riding the horse, and he wins the race. When the race is over, they don't give the trophy and the money to the horse. They give the horse some hay and put him in the barn. When he gets too old they kill him. If he gets out of line, they shoot him. If he breaks his leg, they kill him. Whatever it is, right? They give all the rewards to the jockey.

The reason I compare capitalism to a horse and jockey situation is because you have people in the system who are trained to be jockeys while others are trained to be horses. For years we have been trained to be the horse, but it is time to flip the script, take charge of our own training, and become the jokey.

New Black Power Cinema Sneak Peek

Filmed Documentaries and Events Adapted for the Page

DOCUMENTARY

DEMOCRACY
FEATURING DR. BOYCE WATKINS & ZAZA ALI

What are the Consequences of Being Descendants of Slaves?

Zaza Ali:

Well, I think that is a multi-layered question. For me, I think the more important question is, "What are the benefits and the consequences of being a descendant of God?" I think, at times, we limit ourselves in the conversation and in our perspectives of ourselves by asking that question. What is the consequence of being a descendant of slaves? Of course, there are consequences. I also think that on a broader scale, we need to broaden the question, and stop limiting ourselves to the suffering that we've experienced as people. Our people, particularly in America, have been shaped and molded in the image of a foreign people who have been extremely savage and brutal in every different facet of civilization and of life. You have to understand that everything that we knew, all of our culture, all of our religion, all of our language, all of our spiritual concepts, our religious platforms were stripped away from us. There may have been one to two generations from that initial start of slavery that held on to some concepts of our African culture, but from then on – let's say 300 years – you have 300 years and multiple generations of people who had no concept of any form of civilization. So, being born into a life of slavery, literally from childbirth. Can you imagine a woman having a baby strapped to her back being out in the fields and picking cotton from sun up to sun down? I mean, that is a very brutal experience. And then, no hope of change. Not even the concept or the thought of, "Maybe this will end." Knowing that for your entire life you are going to be immersed in a life of suffering and brutality, that's a hell of a way to live.

Boyce Watkins:

Well, the problem with being a descendant of a slave in the United States is that you are often born in situations that are beyond your control. You're dealing with factors that were developed long before you arrived in this country and long before you were brought to this earth. You have not just racism to deal with, but you also have typically depredation of your community. You have a lot of dysfunction in families from the trauma lived through as black people. A lot of poverty. A lot of devastation. A lot of difficulties that are unique to black people and unique to descendants of slaves. Anybody who tries to compare immigrants to black people is way off base, because immigrants haven't gone through what we've gone through. You talk about 400 years. You're talking about almost half a millennium of some of the worst treatment known to man. You really can't understand blackness in America or being a black American without understanding the history of what we've gone through.

Zaza Ali:

A lot of that directly impacts our family structures today. There's been a lot of conversation about molestation in the black community. Most of it, if not all of it, stems directly from the history of slavery, and it wasn't just black women who were being molested and raped. White slave masters were molesting and raping our sons and our men, as well. So, now you fast forward to 2017...When we really go into it and look at it, we have a very large population of people in our communities who are being molested. Men and women alike. As a community, we haven't taken any real steps towards the problem. We don't even have a large broad conversation about molestation in our communities. It's not just the act and the savagery of the act. It's also the rest of us who are standing back kind of shaking our heads like, "Okay, we know what's going on, but we don't want to talk about it, because it's too painful." So, it's molestation. It's the economic deprivation. There are a lot of different facets that come from being born just past slavery that have festered. Some of them have gone away. Some of them have actually grown and are being exploited now by music, television, and internet. It's growing in certain elements to this dysfunction that we see in our community, and we can tie it right back to the system of slavery.

What is Black Capitalism?

Zaza Ali:

Well, I think in order to define that question we have to ask, "What is white capitalism?" The concept of capitalism is based around labor and capital. Of course, in a white capitalist world we know who has the land. We know who has the capital. We also know who does the labor. For us to try to flip the concept of capitalism and turn it into black capitalism, I think we have to remember that, around the world, the concept of capitalism relates to oppression. It relates to economic dissolution. It is directly tied back to slavery.

Boyce Watkins:

Black capitalism really doesn't exist in my opinion, because I don't think anybody has a universal definition of what black capitalism is. I like to talk about it in terms of black free enterprise or black business development which I do think is uniquely different from white business development. We're at a different stage in our economic evolutionary cycle. This implies that the way we build businesses, the things that matter to us, are a little bit different from what matters to white America.

The biggest mistake that I think a lot of black people can make when it comes to economics is to think that you can do what white people do. The fact of the matter is that you can't. You're not white. I hate breaking that down to you, but the truth is that you are not white. This means that these institutions that are out here – these corporations that are out here, these places that are giving out these jobs – are controlled. These institutions are controlled and were built by people who don't look like you. They're there to benefit people who don't look like you.

In fact, the way white Americans execute capitalism is very damaging. It's built on greed. It's built on an insatiable appetite to literally eat up all the resources that are all around you. It's built on a model that destroys the environment. Even out in Oklahoma now, they've got earthquakes everywhere, because the oil companies are fracking below the ground. Oklahoma used to have hardly any earthquakes. Now they have crazy earthquakes every other week.

Ultimately, you have all these devastating consequences of capitalism going wild. Capitalism is not regulated, and capitalism is a funny thing. It's a beast within itself. It has no conscious. It doesn't care about people. It doesn't have a point where it says, "Okay, I've got enough money. Enough is enough."

Zaza Ali:

For me, I don't know if adopting the term of black capitalism is necessarily a good thing. If we do adopt it or just use it as a teaching point, I believe that black capitalism is our people making strides, from an economic perspective, to own and operate all of the different institutions in our community. To be united as far as taking our funds and investing them back into the black community. I think that it is us taking the concept of capitalism and turning it into something that will be beneficial for our communities, opposed to us being used for the white system of racism, white supremacy, and their form of capitalism. Black capitalism is building up a world for ourselves rather than building a world for white people and for the West.

Can Black Capitalism Create Black Wealth?

Boyce Watkins:

Capitalism, in its purest form, is a lot like the little fat kid who won't stop eating. He will eat all of his food, your food, the neighbor's food, and he will go to the grocery store and eat all of the food in the grocery store. If you ask him if he's had enough, he says, "No, I never have enough. I want more, more, more." That's what's unfortunate about capitalism in America. Because it's not properly regulated, you see the destructive side effects. You see urban decay. You see the fact that we spend more money on healthcare than any country in the world, yet our healthcare absolutely sucks. We spend more money on education than almost any country in the world, yet our educational system absolutely sucks. You see corporations in America going around the world and convincing the US government to declare war on their behalf, so they can go get more resources. That's capitalist greed in action.

I don't think black people have to be that way. I don't advocate for that in The Black Business School. I tell black people that money is very, very important. You want to understand money, because money's what you need to survive, but money is not something to be worshiped. It's not something that should be valued over human life. I don't think many white Americans get that, and that is going to lead to the inevitable destruction of this country.

Unfortunately, with the way capitalism is taught in mainstream America, it is only there, presumably, for the people at the top. The first thing we used to teach students when I taught finance and capitalism is that the job of the corporate manager is to maximize shareholder wealth. That means that the only thing they're thinking about is how they can make the people at the top richer. So, I don't know if black capitalism can create black wealth. I think black free enterprise and black business development can build black wealth. That's where people at the top do very well but also people in the middle. People at the bottom also do better. Suppliers do better. Customers do better. Employees do better. The environment does better. The community does better. The family does better. When everybody's doing better, everybody wins. In economics, we used to call it maximizing utility.

Maximizing utility means you're maximizing the happiness of everybody who's in the system – not just a certain few people at the top. So, my argument is if we as a people come together and do a few basic things, we can actually build tremendous wealth in our community.

Number one, we can start by simply circulating our dollars, spending 20% of our money within our own community, and finding ways to produce enough products. Black business owners have to step in, but consumers have to help with this, as well. If we spend 20% of our money in our own community, our wealth levels will instantly quadruple. Why is that? Well, when you spend a dollar, the dollar doesn't just go away. The dollar gets handed to another person. That person uses the dollar. Then, the person after them uses the dollar. So, if I circulate my money and four black people get to use the same dollar, that one dollar becomes $4. If we all go run to the white man, however, and spend money at Walmart, K-Mart, Target, or wherever he's at then that dollar ain't coming back. So, $1 is only worth $1. Literally, you get almost financial magic that happens when you circulate your money. It's almost like circulating air with an air conditioner. When you have air coming in and you shut the window, then the same amount of air can keep the room cool for a very long time. Conversely, if you leave the window open and it's 100 degrees outside, then you're going to need a lot more energy to keep the room cool.

By simply circulating our money in our community we can, overnight, quadruple black wealth and black spending power. Also, by teaching our children the fundamentals of how economic systems work at a very early age. Teaching them entrepreneurship, black wealth, how to create cooperative economics. Things like that. Really making them into economic soldiers where they understand very basic things like the fact that you don't have to have a boss. You don't have to go work for a white man in order to make a living. You can build something of your own. You can go make your own money. If you raise say 100,000 African-American children with that mindset, the first 100,000 will employ the next 100 million, the next 50 million.

At the end of the day, there are ways that we can build wealth in our community. We don't have to wait for politicians to do the right thing. White politicians have had 400 years to do the right thing, and they ain't done it yet. Study after study shows that pretty much what they're doing in congress now isn't a whole lot different from what they were doing 50 – 60 years ago. The question we have to ask ourselves is, "In 50 – 60 years, do we want our grandchildren to be saying, 'Wow! The same problems they had in 2016, 2017, 2018 are the same problems we have in 2056, '57 and '58?'" You don't want that to happen to your kids, so you have to take this into your own hands.

What is Wrong with Our Government?

Boyce Watkins:

Our government is flawed primarily due to the fact that we have been raised to believe it's so perfect. We're raised to believe that those who wrote the constitution were geniuses, and they created the most perfect government in the world. What that does is create a false sense of superiority amongst the American people where we truly believe that America has always been this great country. You have politicians saying things like, "Let's make America great again," even though it was never really great – at least in terms of how the government was structured.

Our government, unfortunately, has been structured in such a way that gridlock becomes quite automatic. They can't negotiate with each other. They can't work together for the betterment of the country. It's almost like two people on a sinking ship, and both of them are arguing over who's going to take over the wheel. The ship is sinking, but neither one of them actually cares that the ship is sinking, because they care more about taking the wheel than they care about saving the ship. All they care about is that if the ship sinks, the other guy's going to get blamed for it. That's what the Democratic Party and Republican Party kind of look like right now when they fight each other like children.

Zaza Ali:

For one, I think that this is not our government, number one, and I think that it's important for us to look at it from that perspective. There are two sides to that coin. This is not our government as far as a government that is willing to protect, provide for, and look after black people in America. Now, the flip side of that is that we pay taxes. We contribute to the economy. We contribute to American society in every single way. It would behoove us to not take some sort of active role in United States politics.

Our government...I wouldn't say that. I would say the American government, and I would say what's wrong with it is that it was built on a foundation of exploiting the indigenous people of America as well as Africans who were brought here and turned into slaves. This government has not made any strong move towards reparations or towards repairing the damage that they have done to us and the Native American people. Also, America has a strong hand all across the world, particularly in Africa, in raping the natural resources and not doing anything to add that back into those communities. The question is so large. We could talk about education. We could talk about economics. We could talk about a lot of different things, but I think the root of it is that the American government is not for the people and by the people. It is based on a specific agenda that is to protect the wealthy, predicated on black inferiority, and using their resources to continue oppressing people around the world.

Boyce Watkins:

So, here's what's going to happen. At some point, the United States government is going to default on the interest payments on the massive amount of debt that the country has. When that happens, the faith and confidence in the federal government is going to decline worldwide. When that occurs, your dollar bill which is not backed by gold anymore will steeply decline in value. It's already not real money and actually fiat currency. But anyways, that's when you're going to see the government fighting against hyperinflation which is where you might have a loaf of bread go up in price to $40 – $50. Something crazy like that.

Ultimately, there are lots of indicators that the best days of the United States are behind us. Our population is getting older which means our productivity is declining. Our children are not being properly educated. We're allowing entire sectors of our society to just go to waste – entire communities lie in ruins. What we're probably going to see is this falling apart of our country which could've been stopped by our government. Because they're so consistently committed to this gridlock and shortsighted thinking, however, none of them are thinking about what's going to happen 30 to 40 years down the road.

The biggest problem with our government is that they've been bought out. We don't have enough rules and regulations in place. We don't have the right value systems to protect our democracy from the capitalism. Capitalism and democracy in America are like brother and sister, and right now, the big brother capitalism is beating up the little sister and taking all her lunch money. Right now, the capitalism is eating and gobbling up the democracy in America to the point where your politicians are being sold, bought, and eaten up by the highest bidder. So, what happens then? Well, we naively think that because we're supposed to be a democracy that if enough American people are against something or want something that the government's going to stop or listen. Well, no, that's not true, because the government doesn't listen to votes or people. They listen to dollar bills. The dollar bills come from corporations. The corporations are driven by capitalism, which is a heartless beast that has really sick incentives.

You're not going to see things get better in this country. My guess is that you're only going to see things get worse. As we get more and more outraged, the wealthier are just going to have bigger militaries to shut us down, lock us up, and keep us silent. America is not a democracy as much as it's becoming an aristocracy, and it's only going to become more of that in the future.

Zaza Ali:

We can't just say what's wrong with our government. As a people, we have to start learning how to govern ourselves. When you govern yourself, you are not so dependent upon government. This goes back to what I said originally. Being disciplined, being focused, focusing on studying, focusing on your diet, [and] focusing on being physically strong. When you have a mindset of being self-governed and...if we go back to Africa, the concept is called ma'at: truth, balance, reciprocity, and harmony. If we use that in our communities to govern ourselves first as an individual, then as a family household, then on a local state level, then on a national level, I think that we will be a lot less dependent on what we call government.

Do African Americans Have a Choice in the Current Political System?

Boyce Watkins:

We have no choice whatsoever. We don't even have the illusion of choice. An illusion should at least convince you that it might be similar to reality. We know we're being screwed. We know that we're the victims of what I call voter jacking. Voter jacking is when somebody doesn't take any time trying to convince you that they're the best person to vote for. Instead, they spend their time convincing you that the other person is more horrible than they are. In a way, it's like giving somebody the choice between a rapist or a child molester. That's not a real choice. If you're given a choice between eating rotten dog food or a bowl of shit, that's not a real choice. That's what happened to the black community. At the end of the day, many of us have decided, "Okay, well, I've gotta vote. I don't have a choice to not vote, so that means I've got to choose democrat or republican. I'm not going to choose republicans, because they're going to make us slaves again, so I guess I have to vote democrat."

Zaza Ali:

I think that voting has had a minimal impact in the

black community. I think that there are certain instances that it can be beneficial. There was a law passed recently in New York. A brother put out a bill in order to have the local people there not have to check off that they are a convicted felon. This enables them to at least get into the interview process. It's a segue into allowing more convicted felons, or people who have records, to be able to have a chance at getting a job. So, that's one instance where voting can be beneficial.

A lot of times, we talk about electing black politicians – how once we get in the system, we can change it. Well, I think that's an oxymoron, and I think a lot of our energy unnecessarily goes towards politics when we could be putting that energy into our communities. Case and point when Donald Trump was recently elected, everybody was all up in arms saying, "We should've gone out and voted." You know what we should've done. First of all, clearly you don't have a clear understanding of Hillary Clinton and the background of her family and that political structure. But then also, how is it that our immediate response is to go back into the same agenda that just failed us? Wouldn't you say, okay, this is not working for us? First of all, we just had Barrack Obama in office, and there's an argument to be made about the gains versus what he didn't do for us as a people. But clearly, if we are still facing all of the problems that we've been facing for God only knows how many years now, why would we not immediately pivot and try something different?

Boyce Watkins:

This is really one of the biggest social-political hustles of all time. It works every single election. The politicians show up at your church, eat barbecue chicken with you, sway with the pastor, and tell you a bunch of lies. Then when they get into office and you come back and say, "We documented all the things you said you'd do for us. Which of these are we going to get working on first?" they delay, delay, delay. When election time comes around, they'll start paying attention to you again, and they'll say, "Oh, well, we were going to get that done, but we didn't have time, because the republicans stopped us from doing it. If you elect me again, then I'm going to do it this time around." The thing about it is, for most of these politicians their whole political career doesn't last that long. It's just a few years. So, they're only thinking four years at a time anyway. It's just sort of a rinse and repeat in terms of how black people get bamboozled. We really don't have any choice.

Zaza Ali:

You look at a city like Baltimore, the situation with Freddy Gray. You had a black mayor. You had a black district attorney. You had black police officers in the street policing the communities. You had a large number of black political representatives in a predominantly black city. When it was all said and done, there was no justice.

Kalief Browder up in the Bronx in New York. You had a black judge, black district attorney, a lot of different black brothers and sisters that were in the political arena. When it was all said and done and you look at the situation, this brother ended up killing himself. He was tortured and abused not only when he was in jail getting jumped and beat up by the guards, but from the beginning, the whole entire system failed him. This is an area where, locally, black people are in positions of clout. What's the real power in having black political instruments, if you will, in the community if they have no real say so as far as impacting the condition of our people?

We say we need to get our people into the political arena, but there's no guarantee that once they get there they're not going to turn into black men and women on the outside who have a European mind and represent the European agenda on the inside. So, voting has been a fix in certain aspects. One example I always give is the bill out in California about genetically modified food. Well, nobody, we weren't aware of that. We weren't in our communities talking about the importance of having genetically modified food labeled. You didn't hear the black political pundits on CNN and MSNBC talking about this, and it ended up failing. So, there are certain instances where politics can work for us, but I think that it should not be high on our priority list. We should support the brothers and sisters who have a political agenda, but as far as our communities, we need to spend our energy in ways that are better served.

Boyce Watkins:

The interesting thing is that we do have a choice if we're willing to make the choices. You don't have to vote. Now, I'm not telling people not to vote, but I will say that there are some very smart people all throughout history who have abstained as a political strategy. You go to congress. When congressional members feel that they're being given bad choices, they will abstain out of protest, because abstinence is a form of voting. It's a way of saying, "I would've voted, but y'all didn't give me a good choice." It's not as if we don't have a choice. We just allow people to manipulate us psychologically to the point where we feel locked in, and I would say that the essence of democracy is doing what you want to do. If black people want to have choices, maybe we could play chess instead of checkers.

I want you to think for yourself, and here's what you can consider. Let's say that black people said to the democrats, "Look, we're not doing what you want us to do. You ignored us last time. We're not going to vote for you at all." Then, the democrats lose to the republicans, and republicans take over the White House for four years. Don't you think that maybe next time the democrats are going to try a little harder to get your vote? Maybe the Republican Party will say, "Hey, black votes are up for grabs. Maybe we could do a little bit more for the black community." I think black people have to think about all the different strategies, and not just do whatever our favorite white democrat tells us to do.

How Did the Presidency of Bill Clinton Affect African Americans?

Zaza Ali:

Well you know, this is an interesting question, and it's always important for us to talk about this, because black people are so heavily invested in voting and the political spectrum. A lot of that comes from, you know.

234

We say black people died for the right to vote. I think we need to reframe that statement. No, we didn't die for the right to vote. We died, because we were living amongst savages. However, if we were living in a righteous environment, we never would have had to face that type of adversity in order to have the right to speak freely and to have our needs met as human beings.

Bill Clinton is interesting, because the three-strikes law was one law that was a turning point as far as the prison industrial complex. Here, you have brothers now who are being thrown in jail for 25 plus years for minimum type crimes that should be a slap on the wrist. Stealing a television. Getting caught with an ounce or a bag of weed. A domestic violence type situation. Because you have priors, now you are facing 25 years to life. We still have black men to this day in California who are serving long sentences for that particular bill. Now, of course, the law has been reformed. It is not still in effect. But, we talk about reparations. Who's going to provide reparations for those brothers who served those extensive prison terms now that the three-strikes law has been overturned and found unjust?

Bill Clinton was very instrumental in the Rwandan Genocide and what happened in Africa. We don't talk about it a lot, because he was blowing saxophones. We thought he was cool. But in Africa when there was a civil war going on, they played a very large part in the background as far as funding the opposing forces which brought on a large-scale massacre in Rwanda.

And of course, crack cocaine. Now, crack cocaine initially started under Ronald Reagan. Of course, we know about the war on drugs, and I talk about in my book, *The Scientific Intervention And Our Affairs*, the actual inception of crack. You have this drug now that's being dropped in black communities all across the country, and nobody really knows where it came from. Nobody really understands how a drug that decimates communities just dropped on the scene out of nowhere. Well, we can thank our United States government for that. Fast forward to Bill Clinton's era now. Ronald Reagan has already done his job. He's already used the media, the political spectrum, and the prison industrial complex to start the war, but Bill Clinton came in and really took it to another level. This is when the "three-strikes you're out" sentencing escalated. Of course, it was directly tied to the crack cocaine era and what happened with black men being incarcerated for being caught with and selling the drug as well as the mass epidemic of addiction.

Now you have brothers and sisters in the community who are addicted to this drug, and they are facing long-term sentencing for being an addict, basically. It's unfortunate for us as a people that we keep getting hoodwinked by beautiful characters, charisma, and people playing saxophones. We need to stop gearing towards the emotional mindset and really step back and look at people. Look at their agenda. Look at the laws and the bills they've passed, and be able to assess them based on that instead of just the feel good ties back to the preachers in the church. We want that feel-good sermon on Sunday, but we're living in hell from Monday up until the next Sunday. We have a tendency to get emotionally connected to personality opposed to using logic and reason to assess these people based on what they really stand for.

How Did the Presidency of Barack Obama Affect African Americans?

Boyce Watkins:

I think that Barack Obama was one of the best white presidents we've ever had. He was just as much white as he was black, and I think that what people did not understand is that he wasn't entirely rooted in the African-American experience. He wasn't entirely a part of what our community goes through. He wasn't able to entirely connect to that. But, what he did was brilliant in the sense that he allowed people to read into him what they wanted to see. They wanted to see their black messiah. He let them see the black messiah. He never said he was that black Messiah, though. He never really walked in and said, "I'm going to do this, this, and this for you." We just assumed that, because he communicated in certain nonverbal ways, his family looked a certain way, and we wanted to see that he was going to be a certain kind of president.

I think that Barack Obama executed the job, again, as well as any of the white guys before him. He was a darker version of a Bill Clinton. A little more progressive, a little more sensitive. I think that there's going to be a day where people are going to say, "Okay, wow. We finally have a black president." I think that will be similar to the day when Obama got elected, and we said, "Wait a minute. Bill Clinton wasn't the first black president." Remember, there was a time when everybody claimed Bill Clinton was the first black president. Then a darker guy comes along, a biracial guy, and they say, "Oh, well, wait. Now we have a black president." One day in the future, we're going to say, "Okay. Oh, now we have an African-American president." To this day, we still have not had an African-American president. We've had a biracial president who was part Caucasian, part Kenyan, who had very few roots on his Kenyan side. He was raised by a white woman and white grandparents, and he was very comfortable around white people. It allowed him to really navigate in spaces that a lot of black men may not feel comfortable. However, at the same time, to not take away from Obama, he was able to identify with some of the racism we experience, because he wasn't fully accepted in those spaces among white people, because he wasn't completely white.

But remember, he was just as white as he was black. In fact, some would say he is more white than he is black. I wouldn't even be surprised if having a black wife and beautiful black children was a strategic kind of thing for him to be able to endear himself to the black community. So, I wouldn't be one to disrespect Barack Obama, but I am a person that will say that he wasn't the messiah everyone may have thought he was or may still think he is.

How Did the Civil Rights Movement Help or Hurt African Americans?
Zaza Ali:

Integration was definitely a detriment to the black community. It kept us from moving forward on building our own institutions and basically made us more dependent on the system of racism and white supremacy. One example that I always give is the Negro Leagues and how you had the world's best baseball players in a contained black baseball league. They were traveling across the country, staying in black hotels, visiting black restaurants and different institutions in the community and basically creating an economic stronghold in the black community. Fast forward to Jackie Robinson integrating the leagues, and now you have one black man who is in the Major Leagues, and the rest of the teams were dismantled. All of those coaching jobs, players, businesses across the country that were depending on the Negro Leagues to sustain the community, basically, slowly but surely, dismantled.

Boyce Watkins:

Integration was really executed in the wrong way. Integration is a good idea in itself, but the problem is that it's almost like a marriage. If you marry somebody and you're not a whole person when you walk into the marriage, the other person may be determined to abuse you. You don't have proper leverage to negotiate the terms of that relationship. Then, you're going to end up in a marriage but abused and mistreated for a long time. So for black people, integration for the last 50 – 60 years has been like an abusive marriage. We've been included in America's society, but it's almost as if they live in the master bedroom while we live in the basement.

Zaza Ali:

Integration, in my opinion, was one of the worst things that could've happened to our people. You look at the Montgomery bus boycott. Because of the situation with Rosa Parks, we spent a year walking, carpooling, finding different ways to get around the community in order to stick it to the man, right. Well, what would've happened if we took that year and focused on building our own transportation systems? What if we had actually focused on having the mechanics and people who had inside information on how to start those types of businesses – actually started black transportation systems in that part of the country? We dropped the ball.

We tend to spend and exude a lot of our energy on being in a defensive position and doing what is needed in order to teach white people a lesson instead of putting that energy into building up communities and being sustained. If we had the know-how and the gusto for a year to walk and to do what needed to be done to teach a lesson so we could sit in the front of the bus, we could've taken that energy and applied it towards something that would have had a long-term impact on our communities.

The civil rights movement was a plus and a minus in several ways. For one, we can always look back at that time and see that our people stood up and fought for something. It pains me to see brothers and sisters sitting in diners and having milk and soda poured in their faces. You know, young sister Ruby Bridges went and integrated the school and had white people standing around and screaming at her and calling her all types of offensive remarks. I mean, you know. That is a very painful part of our history, but it also showed us what we can accomplish when we are focused on the end result.

Now, fast forward today. You ain't putting my son in a restaurant and expecting that he's going to get his face spit in, hit, poked, and prodded. No. But, I can only say that now because of what they went through then. I'm only able to stand on my square and speak as powerfully as I speak about it now, because we saw the end result of what happened to our people back then, so it was a win in that regard.

Boyce Watkins:

We've learned how to take a distant critical look at the civil rights movement. Not just appreciate what those individuals did because we know their sacrifice was absolutely paramount but also look at it with a critical eye. Say, "Okay, what are some ways that we can renegotiate this integration thing?" By coming back together and renegotiating the terms of that integration, we can go integrate ourselves into the global economy as equal partners. We're able to negotiate our own real estate, space, and sovereignty – if you will – without having to carry around the handicaps that come with growing up and knowing that our only hope to make money is to work for white people. Without bowing down to white people, believing the white man's ice is colder, following the white man's trends, and paying attention to his media.

When black people learn how to own things, they will have a better ability to integrate with white folks and everybody else in a way that is not devoid of dignity. That's the problem in the original civil rights movement. You're fighting and putting your life on the line to have the right to go sit in a white man's shop and buy something from him. That's just flawed logic to begin with. It only makes sense if you are a person whose self-esteem is so low that you really think that you can gain acceptance by giving somebody all your money. That just doesn't make any sense.

So, in this generation, this civil rights movement, we're upping the game a little bit. We will still sit next to the white man, but it might be in our shop, and he might be giving us his money. That's the type of integration I could live with.

Zaza Ali:

Once we got what we said we wanted as far as voting rights, being able to sit at the front of the bus, the different wins that we received in the political arena, we went to sleep. We dropped the ball on, "Okay, we made some wins in this area. Now let's come in our communities and huddle up. Turn the camera off. We don't need white people here. We don't need the media. Let's talk about coming into our communities and developing ways to be self-sufficient." We integrated the schools. Now we're satisfied with integration, but we didn't think about how they were going to start miseducating our children into the system of white supremacy. Instead of saying, "Okay, we have to send our children to these schools," let's start building small schools in the community, so we can still be teaching our children. After school programs so when they go into those schools and come out they can come to the local organizations and be trained with an African center perspective.

I can tell you in no uncertain terms that I feel like the generation that preceded us did a disservice to us in a lot of ways. They weren't prepared for crack cocaine.

They weren't prepared for sex trafficking. They weren't prepared for prostitution in our communities. They weren't prepared for a lot of the problems that we ended up facing in the 80s and 90s, because they breathed a collective sigh once we got what we needed from the civil rights movement. I think that there was no forward momentum. "Yes, we got what we needed. Now we're good." Just like Obama. "Yes, we got a black man in the White House, and we're good," instead of taking that momentum and building on it to actually build real tangible institutions in our communities.

What is the Black Woman's Role in American Feminism?
Zaza Ali:

Feminism is an oxymoron in a lot of ways, but I can never really fully discount it, because it was born out of women crying out for equal access to not just jobs, not just equal pay, but just to be seen, just to be heard. The European history goes back and tells a tale of white women experiencing extreme oppression and suffering back from Greece and Rome. Finally in America, they were able to express themselves and give a voice to their own suffering. Now, I say that tongue in cheek, because at the same time, they were very instrumental in the oppression of our own people.

Elizabeth Cady Stanton and Susan B. Anthony were the founders of what we know today as feminism, and their initial goal was to move the white woman's suffrage movement forward. They were not looking to cultivate a bond with black women or any women for that matter. They wanted to be recognized and respected by their own men. Black women got involved in the feminism movement, obviously, because they were suffering...but also because white woman pulled them into the spectrum in order to be able to have strength in their numbers.

Boyce Watkins:

I don't believe that the black women every really had a role in American feminism. I don't believe it was created for the black women to be other than a pawn to be used to bolster the numbers for white feminists. If you look at the origins of feminism in America, they're kind of murky. They're kind of, sort of espoused value systems that are not consistent with what we believe as black people.

Now, I'm a big believer in womanism and in the freedom of women to do whatever they want. I mean, you couldn't tell my mother, my grandmother, my daughter, my sister that they couldn't be self-determined in every single way. That they're not equal to men in every way. I've never believed that equal is the same, and neither do they. What's problematic is that feminism in many cases, sometimes labels the black man as this sort of barbaric Neanderthal that the black woman just needs to abandon for her own happiness and safety. As a black man who's never behaved that way who's always shown respect to black women, I resent that. I resent that entirely, and I think selfishness tends to be promoted in feminism. It's sort of like, "Well, I want you to treat me like a lady when I want to be a lady, but when I want to be a man, I want to do what men do." I think that doesn't work for family. I think family is not built on you always doing what you want to do all the time. Family is built on me believing that I'm a part of something that's more important than myself. So, as a man, I would never feel healthy or happy going into a situation where I always believe that I should just do what I want to do and to hell with everybody else.

Zaza Ali:

Now, the funny thing about it is that white women were simultaneously fighting against black men having the right to vote. They wanted white women to be able to vote but at the same time were very vocal about how they were against black men having the right to vote. I always say, "How did black women miss that? How did you sign on for an agenda and an ideology that was contrary to what was best for your man?" We as black women have to understand that our struggle is directly tied to the struggle of our men. If our men are not making progress financially, emotionally, and in this dichotomy, then we as women cannot win. Yes, we can have a nice house. Yes, we can have a nice car. Yes, we can be quote unquote "financially independent," but what are we leaving behind for the generations coming behind us? How are we lending our ear and our voice to be able to lift up our men? Feminism does not have a place and a conversation that talks about lifting up men, and that is why it is an incomplete ideology. That is why I can never support it.

Boyce Watkins:

There's no group of people in America that's more protected, more cherished, more put on a pedestal than the white woman. The world becomes sensitive to her feelings. When a white woman gets kidnapped, it's on national news. When a black man is charged with harming a white woman, it becomes the case of the century, and white people do whatever they can to get revenge whether you're talking about OJ Simpson, Nate Parker, or whatever the case may be. With that excess attention paid to the white woman, her feminist movement becomes one that's rooted in, and sort of saying, "Look at me. Look at me. It's all about me, me, me. My feelings. My, my, my." Right? I don't think that's healthy for anybody. I wouldn't agree with it if black men were doing this.

Also, what's so interesting is that when you talk about things like affirmative action, the people who've benefited from our affirmative action have been white women – mostly white feminists – and they don't care. They're not going to hire your black ass, but you'll make room for them, because you somehow think that what they want is more important than what your family and community needs.

Zaza Ali:

You have black women who only want to talk about the suffering of women instead of making the family, our people as a whole, and healing as a whole the agenda. Yes, we need to talk about the suffering of women. Yes, we need to have groups and organizations that only deal with what's happening to black women. At the same time, does feminism deal with the issues that black women have? Does feminism deal with the 370,000 abortions that black women are having every year? Does feminism talk about black women molesting black boys? Does feminism talk about mothers and how they abuse their sons and their daughters? Does feminism talk about the cattiness, the competitiveness, and the issues that women have with other women? Does black feminism talk about the color war that's happening between black women? Light skin versus black dark skin. Does feminism talk about the vanity and the materialism that is plaguing the minds of a lot of young people?

It's a victim type of mentality where we only want to talk about what's being done to us, and we're not talking about what we are actually doing to add to the problem. For me, I think that for black women to adopt the term feminism in itself, knowing the roots of it, is a mistake. If you want to create something that is specifically for black women, adopt your own terminology. Why do we always have to be followers? Why do we always have to latch ourselves onto what other people create? Create something new.

Boyce Watkins:

Black women certainly have a right and a reason to be upset with much of what happens around them. There are quite a few black men who traumatize black women. There's racism that's also traumatic for black women. Single black mothers have the highest poverty rate in America. I don't think feminism is the answer. I don't think feminism gets you there. I think that as a community, as families, we can overcome these things and deal with the trauma and self-hatred. We can deal with it in our way as a people as opposed to allowing our politics and our psychology to be imperialized by ongoing war between white men and white women. They want to recruit us into their battle as opposed to us simply having our own issues that we resolve in our own way in our own space. That's sovereignty. Black people rarely have sovereignty. Usually, whatever we have and whatever we do is given to us by white people. I just don't think that's healthy at all.

What Does Reparation Look Like for Black America?
Zaza Ali:

The root word of reparations is repair. Often times when we talk about reparations, we look at it from a perspective of having to cut a check. Of course we know the check is due and should be cut. However, there are a lot of things in our community that need repair. I personally believe that the crack epidemic in our communities warrants reparations. All of the families that were dismantled and torn apart, all of the years spent in prison, all of the murders, all of the convictions, all of the addictions. That needs to be repaired in our communities. The Jim Crow laws, slave codes, black codes, and all of the ripple effects that had in the community. Reparations are due. Slavery. The trillions, upon trillions, upon trillions of dollars that we pumped not only into the American economy but into the global economy. All of that untold wealth that has passed down through generations of white hands absolutely acknowledges that reparations are due.

Boyce Watkins:

To me, reparations look like, first and foremost, an apology. I think that the federal government needs to express a sincere apology for slavery. Tell us that they are sorry from the deepest part of their heart for what happened and that they want to make things right. Now, an apology is not anywhere close to reparations, but it's the beginning. I think a lot of people are very upset about the fact that America is a country that still thinks that we made racial progress, because they stopped beating, raping, lynching, and killing us. They think that when you stop committing a crime against humanity, that's the same as repairing the damage that has been done. It's not the same thing. If I spill some milk on the floor, the fact that I stopped spilling the milk doesn't clean up the milk that I've already spilt. I've got to go deal with what I've already done.

Zaza Ali:

It's a hell of a thing to look at. Literally hundreds

of millions of people who were put into a bondage type situation. It's like, when we left Africa, there was a pause. For hundreds of years there was no progress. There was no development. So now, we look at white people, and we credit them for technology. We credit them for the internet. We credit them for social media, but that's because you put us on pause. How do you know we wouldn't have had a *Facebook* that is 10 times what there is now if you would've just left us alone?

It's not just what we put into the economy as far as cotton and all of the different ways that we contributed with free labor. It's also, "You put us on pause." What did you take away from us? How many prophets did you kill? How many great leaders did you kill? How many scientists did you kill? How many mathematicians did you kill? How many great world leaders, thinkers, and spiritual gurus did you kill in 400 years? There's no amount of money that you can pay to replace that.

We talk about Trayvon Martin being murdered in cold blood and how justice was never served. What would his son have been? What would his daughter have been? What could his legacy have been if he had been given a chance to live out his life fully? Well, what happened to a slave, a young brother in 1800, who might've said something slick, gotten whipped, beaten, and killed? Sometimes when we talk about slavery and what we've been through, it's kind of like this tongue in cheek kind of thing. We didn't live through it. We don't have a human bond and connection to what our people experienced. The souls of black folk. What does that mean? What's in you right now in your DNA, spiritual disposition, and genetics that ties you back to those people? What do you owe them? What can we give the generations coming up in front of us that can supplement what we lost when they pushed pause on our people?

Boyce Watkins:

The next step, obviously, will be a conversation with relevant players in the black community. I'm talking about serious people, not these coons that they got up in DC sitting next to the president. I'm talking about black people who really care, are rooted in the black community, and have the trust of the community sitting down and really telling them exactly what reparations will look like. So, you bring in Dr. Claud Anderson. Maybe bring in Dr. Julianne Malveaux, and you bring in a couple other people, and you write out the plan.

It has to start with a Marshall Plan for urban America. You must spend as much money repairing urban America as you spent repairing Japan after

Hiroshima and Nagasaki. Germany after World War I and World War II and all these other European countries. As much money as you spent over there fixing those areas, Iran, Iraq, and all of that, you need to spend that same amount of money right here in your neighborhoods. You need to go to Detroit. You need to go to Milwaukee. Go to St. Louis. Go to Chicago. Go to Atlanta. Go to the most dilapidated communities and invest at least a couple hundred billion dollars repairing those communities – not just making them acceptable safe places to live with adequate schools but also providing capital for businesses to be developed in those communities.

Much of the black unemployment problem can be fixed by giving the small black businesses access to capital, so they can grow and hire other people. If they get capital and training...We can even give ourselves our own training. We have smart black people. We just need the money, too. Give them capital, and set them in scenarios where they get training. We can employ our own people. The answer to the black unemployment problem is not for us to get more jobs working for white people. That only puts you more indebted to white supremacy. It only opens the door to more lifelong frustration, because many of us hate our jobs. Many of us are being treated like niggers on the job. Why would you want more of that? We don't want more of that. We want true freedom and a commitment to that.

Zaza Ali:

I think that there should be guaranteed scholarships for descendants of slaves all around the world as far as college is concerned. I think that we should have guaranteed healthcare for our eternal lives as far as descendants of slaves are concerned. I think that there should be trust funds for our young people once they hit a certain age to make sure that for the prime years of their lives, from 18 up until about 25, they are financially secure.

Boyce Watkins:

All descendants of slaves should go to college for free. Why not? Let them go to college for free. In fact, fund us with enough money where we can build our own universities with our own founders, our own presidents, our own everything. True HBCUs, not these other things that we got. Not that they're bad. They're okay, but remember, many of them were not founded by black people. I'm talking about real schools that we build on our own to educate our own children. Now, that's what I would like to see with reparations. I don't know if they would actually do it, but I think that would be a good start. The beautiful thing about it is this. They could probably do a lot of this for half a trillion dollars. But really, if you want to be for real for real about what's really owed with reparations, you're talking about a debt that the federal government can never repay. I mean, the federal government debt is up to $19 trillion or something like that. Reparations would be about that much. They probably owe black people $15 trillion – $20 trillion, so we're just asking for half a trillion. We could do a lot with half a trillion. We don't even need the whole amount.

Zaza Ali:

Now, some people will scratch their head and say, "Well, America's never going to do that." Perhaps they won't, but even if they don't, the fact that we're having the conversation and talking about things that will help us sustain ourselves can perhaps move us in the direction of making it happen. What if we, collectively as a people, started thinking about creating a trust fund for our young people from 18 to 25 to make sure that they are financially secure, so they don't have to go work for the white man if they don't want to? Or, they can find their way without having to make bad decisions and choices in life. That is a starting point for us to start thinking like that.

Boyce Watkins:

Start with the educational system. Start really reviewing the prison system to the point where you're willing to break the system down and rebuild it in a fair and equitable way. I think that's huge for reparations. I think that if you out money into businesses so they can employ and hire black people that's important. Create scenarios where our streets are just safe and healthy, and we have access to the same things that white people have. Even basic things like grocery stores don't even exist in some black neighborhoods.

It doesn't make any sense that you can go to a lot of cities in America, and you'll go to the white parts of the city, and they look beautiful. Clean and pristine. Then you go to some of the black neighborhoods, and they look like fucking war zones. That's absolutely sick. It's absolutely horrible, and it's something that we should never accept. It's not because black people are lazy and they want this. We don't want this. It's because this is what you've done to us when you've given us taxation without representation. You're taking our money that we're putting into that government, and you're not putting that money back into our neighborhoods. You're taking that money, and you're giving it to yourselves, and that's simply not acceptable.

Zaza Ali:

So, reparations is economics. Of course, the check is due. Reparations is the mental abuse. Mental illness in the black community is flourishing right now into the hoods, the gutters, the cracks, and crevices of urban America where young black men are murdering themselves, killing one another, robbing our elders, and molesting our children. All of that dysfunction is happening in our communities. Who's going to cut that check?

The spiritual reparation. The emotional turmoil that comes with 400 years of suffering and abuse. We haven't even really gone into the deepness and the fullness of what has happened to us as a people. We have to keep the conversation going. We need all attorneys on deck that have that specific field interest at hand. We need the psychiatrists on deck. We need to hold the American government accountable...Even if they don't cut the check and they don't do what's right which leads to how they operate and who they are, [we're] having the conversation about what's wrong and what needs to be fixed. So, we have plan A: if they help us fix it. Plan B: if they don't. Here's what we're going to do. I think that is what reparations, which means to repair, means to me.

What are the Dangers of Black Role Models?

Boyce Watkins:

One of the problems with black role models is that black people don't usually get to pick the role models for our community. Media is controlled by white people. That's largely because for 400 years, they spent that time pretty much stealing everything that we had and locking us out of economic opportunities. For those reasons, black people are not able to really control the majority of the multi-billion dollar institutions that exist in America including the media, education systems, corporations, et cetera.

As a result, many of our so-called role models are tossed in front of us and tossed in front of our children without our permission. Our children embrace these role models. They look up to and admire these people, because they have a record deal, a book deal, a TV show, or a radio show, or something like that. Yet, nine times out of 10 those platforms were given to them by white people. That's a very dangerous place to be, because you don't want other people picking your leaders – especially people who are wired to hate you. Your oppressor will never pick a leader for you that is really going to empower you. So, many of the "chose" Negros or Negros on TV are not healthy for the community. There's a reason why a buffoon like a Charles Barkley gets a bigger platform every time he says something negative about the black community. There are white guys behind him cheering him on, and saying, "Thank God you're telling these Negros to shut up, calm down, and be quiet."

Also, what black people tend to do, unfortunately, is misidentify black culture as anything we see black that becomes popular. Anything in media. Certain TV shows, et cetera, whether it's *Love and Hip Hop*, or anything else. We will say, "Oh, well, that's black culture. That must be black culture, because there are black people doing it, and everyone's talking about it." That's not really black culture. That's really something that somebody gave to you, and when you start to worship these celebrities, it's unfortunate. In many cases, these are individuals who have very little incentive and very little cultural rooting in the idea that they are obligated to give you anything back.

The worst example, I would say, would be somebody like a Dr. Dre who goes and makes a $70 million donation to USC, the wealthy white school down the street. Now, what's ironic about that is that USC's endowment is bigger than the endowment of every HBCU in America combined times five. Basically what he did was say, "I'd rather take my money that I made by selling the hood all over the world, stand in front of millions of white people calling myself a nigger, act like a monkey, wear jewelry, act like I want to celebrate black genocide, and not even donate any of that money to the community. I'm going to donate it back to the same white folks who control me." USC spends about $70 million in a week. If you'd even given any HBCU even a 10th of that money, you could educated tens of thousands, if not hundreds of thousands of other black people. But because you think so little of yourself and you think so little of your people, you really thought that you were doing something special by giving that money right back to white people who don't even respect your ass or need the money. That kind of pathetic behavior is something that we as black people have to speak up against and let them know that we don't tolerate it. There's a precedent for that. Actually, other communities do that.

In the Jewish community, I'll be damned if you're going to go in there and milk the Jewish community for money and then not give something back. You won't be invited to synagogue. They will not consider you to be a part of the community. They respect themselves that much, but because black people have a self-esteem problem, we just take attention from anybody who gives it. We love people who refuse to love us back. That's something that has to change. If we're ever going to fight for true equality, we have to learn to love ourselves first.

What causes me the greatest concern is that not everybody is getting the memo. A lot of us, unfortunately, are falling for the okie doke. A lot of us have been just so traumatized by white supremacy, by the latest holocaust with mass incarceration, et cetera. Some families will take 100 to 200 years to recover. I think that this is only going to lead to a greater underclass, because capitalism is going in the direction where there aren't many protections for people who just, say, become workers. What I believe is going to ultimately occur at some point is that they're going to start sending people to prison for basic things like owing money.

What is Most Concerning About the Future of Black America?

Zaza Ali:

I think that the thing that concerns me most is the desolate condition a lot of our youth are in, and I don't think we really understand the massive scale of suffering that young black people, particularly young black brothers in America, are facing. Recently, I saw online Lil Wayne's daughter, Reginae Carter, got jumped at Park

Atlanta University. I mean, this is a group of college aged young black women with a beastly old savage mindset caught on film beating up another sister, and this is happening in our communities every single day.

Boyce Watkins:

What I really see is a lot of kids today who hit the age of 18, and they can't read, write, or do math. They don't know how to start a business, but they know every single song on the radio. They know every single dance that has come out. There's nothing wrong with singing, dancing, and rapping, but you've got to make sure you take care of the basics first. You live in a competitive society, a competitive world, a dog eat dog kind of situation, and you can't go into the middle of the battlefield when you don't have a weapon. You don't have a battle strategy. You don't have any armor. You don't have any protection.

Zaza Ali:

I think there's a lot of pain in our young people. I think that they are misunderstood. I don't think we are giving them enough of our time and attention [to]not only make sure they have jobs, safety, and comfort at home but their mindset. How insecure a lot of our daughters are. I mean, you have to think about a 10-

year-old putting up an *Instagram* video twerking. What's going on in her mind? What is she lacking? [There's] lack of male intervention in our communities letting our sons know that they are valued, that they are loved. Our sons and our daughters. And because the African proverb says that we're supposed to be operating in service of seven generations coming behind us, what is our future going to look like seven generations from now with the condition of our young people?

Boyce Watkins:

I see an underclass that's going to grow. I see a lot of black people that are going to rise and take advantage of the opportunities that exist, because our country is not without opportunity. I mean, anybody who says America has no opportunity is absolutely wrong, but there are obstacles. There are challenges. I think a lot of people are going to get caught in those bear traps, and they'll never escape.

Zaza Ali:

I say that we have a lot of star children: beautiful, young, intelligent, vibrant brothers and sisters who are going to make a lot of gains. I also know in working with young brothers and sisters in the inner city at the Boys and Girls Clubs, in the juvenile detention centers, that our young people are hurting. They are putting forward very destructive behavior. Whether it's suicide, whether it's alcohol and drugs, whether it's promiscuity and being oversexed and having children too young, whether it is looking for alternative methods of life in gangs, there is a very open wound within the community as far as black youth are concerned. I think that it is something that deserves our attention.

What is the Future of Black Wealth, and How did Black America's Condition Improve Over the Last 50 Years?

Boyce Watkins:

One of the biggest impediments to black wealth is a lack of access to capital, because whites spent 400 years stealing all of our stuff and blocking us from economic opportunity. Our predecessors were not able to leave us the capital that we need in order to do the things we want to do. When you talk about some of the challenges we have, the lack of access to a capital base is huge. Lack of financial literacy is huge. It's funny. A lot of schools will have sex education, but they don't have financial education, so a lot of parents have to give that to their own children. Some parents do it. Some parents don't. A lack of financial literacy is huge, because we don't understand how America is rigged.

For example, if you raise your kids just to believe that they're supposed to go work for other people, that they're not supposed to save any money, that they're supposed to go buy Gucci, and Louis, and Jordans, and everything else. Become 100% consumer. That they're not supposed to produce, invest, own, save, [or] any of that, then pretty much what you're doing is preparing your child for economic slavery. They're going to go deep in debt buying things that they do not need, things that have no value. Look at Beats By Dre headphones. They cost $14 to make, but they're selling them for $200. So, you go in debt $200 to buy some Beats By Dre headphones. What's happening in that transaction? You've given them $200 worth of real money. They've given you $14 worth of value and a $186 illusion. So, you're spending time paying back an illusion.

Also, student loan debt has become huge. Going to college is important. Getting an education is important, but an education ain't supposed to cost you $100,000. In this generation of millennials, this is the first generation in American history that is expected to literally die in debt. The average millennial will die in debt. They will never get out of debt. They will live with their momma until they're 40. They won't be able to do the normal things that people do as they get older like get married, have kids, own homes, things like that, or have a positive net worth. They're just going to be in debt. Why? Because you started off at the age of 22 with a mortgage, and you didn't even have a house yet.

Zaza Ali:

We don't live as a people. We survive. We exist in a mindset of today. I have to make sure that I have food on the table, feed my children, pay the bills, and everything outside of that is secondary. So, I think that our mindset as a people has to change. We have the poor man's mentality – just to get by. Surviving.

Well, for me, my mental well-being and spiritual growth comes first. I can only have that type of disposition, because I'm self-employed. I am doing what needs to be done to make sure that my household is intact. I don't have to answer to anybody else. Imagine working from 16 years old up until you're about 60 years old: 44 years of your life dedicated to building institutions for other people. Imagine if you took half of that and moved yourself towards building your own institution. Then, you are talking legacy. Whether you are a plumber, an electrician, a real estate agent, an author, whether you make dolls and clothes, whether you sew, whether you are in the health field, once you start to actually work for yourself you can start thinking about a legacy. [You can] think about what you're going to pass onto your children and to the generations coming behind you. It's a mindset that you have to adapt in order to really move towards freedom.

Boyce Watkins:

If you think that you're poor and you're supposed to always be poor then you probably will be poor. If you understand that wealth building is an intergenerational game, then you realize that it's not that difficult to build a capital base, but you have to give yourself 100 years to do it. You have to also accept the fact that you won't be the one balling at the top of the mountain of money. It'll be your grandkids and great-grandkids that'll be the ballers. You'll be the person that got the ball rolling, so to speak. So, one of the most important things we must do in this generation is begin the process of developing a capital base which can be done through consistent effort and activity.

Zaza Ali:

When you talk about being self-employed, you're talking about being self-sufficient. I remember Oprah Winfrey said, "Freedom is waking up and deciding what to do with your day." That is a very, very beautiful experience, and that is what I'm living right now. I wake up and decide what to do with my day. So, when you are living from a perspective of being self-sufficient, you don't only focus on money and paying the bills. I don't have to punch a time clock. I don't have to drive out in traffic for two hours in the morning and two hours in the afternoon and only have five hours left to myself at the end of the day. Now, I can focus on my spiritual growth. I can focus on sharpening my mind and studying things outside of things that have to do with my business. I can focus on establishing a proper and healthy connection with my son, making sure he gets to where he needs to go, and [ensuring] he has everything he needs outside of food, clothing, and shelter.

It's a very freeing way to live. I'm making my world. I'm building my world. I'm creating a legacy. You don't create a legacy when you work for someone else. I don't know any mogul, entrepreneur, or employee that has become wealthy from working for someone else. So, that's automatically a segue into being self-employed. You cannot become wealthy by working for someone else.

Boyce Watkins:

There are all these little economic traps. When we don't promote financial literacy or consider that to be important, we miss all these traps. For example, just recently, I went to a convention, and I spoke. There was a Mary Mary concert and another concert with some artist. I forget who it was. I was giving a financial seminar in the other room at the same time as the concert. The concert had 10,000 people. My room had maybe 50, and I talked to the 50 as if they were 50,000, but I remember thinking, "Wow, those people are distracted by the concert. [The convention attendees] are the people that are going to figure it out. The masses of us are not going to figure these things out." It's only going to be a small percentage of us that actually get it.

Zaza Ali:

That's why I appreciate Dr. Boyce Watkins so much in the platform that's he's built. The first thing he's doing is planting the seed. If you don't think about wealth, you're never going to be wealthy. Wealth is natural resources. Wealth is land. It's not just money, and we think about money as the end all be all when it comes to being economically secure, but the value of your money is going to be predicated on the value of the dollar. It's predicated on the stock market. It's predicated on what's happening in the political system. It's predicated on world issues. But when you have land and you have natural resources or access to natural resources like a lot of our brothers and sisters do around the world, now you can start talking about the concept of wealth.

The first step is to plant the seed. What does it mean to be wealthy? What does it mean to be rich? What does it mean to have your own business? Now that you've thought about these concepts, it becomes a matter of, "Okay, how do I do this? How do I get there?" Elevating your mindset into thinking about wealth, owning real estate, purchasing property, investing in stocks, making your money work for you, so that it works for you generations down the line. That's the difference between being rich and being wealthy: your money cycling down through generations coming behind you opposed to just having money right now like a lot of our athletes do. Understand those concepts and then be able to apply them to your own personal legacy. I'm not one of those people telling you, "You need to just focus on getting money." No. Figure out what your niche is, what your power position is. Master it. Whatever your field is that you love. Then from that perspective when you go into it seeking to get money and take care of yourself, you can go into those higher ideals of obtaining wealth.

What is Most Optimistic About the Future of Black People?

Boyce Watkins:

I think that the future of black wealth is quite

bright. I think that black people are gaining an increased understanding of economic systems. We're learning that, in America, it's very difficult to get rich by working for other people. You see a growth in entrepreneurship amongst African Americans. Each generation we're going to get better. We're also learning very basic things like having life insurance and how that's an important part of passing wealth on.

I really think that the future of black wealth is very, very bright. I think that you're going to start seeing our children really take things to a level that we can't even imagine, especially those kids who are raised with an understanding of wealth building, entrepreneurship, and cooperative economics at an early age. Those kids will grow up and not only build major corporations but also build things in a way that shows their love for black people.

You see, we have a lot of wealthy Negros in America right now. We don't need more wealthy black people. We need more wealthy black people who care about other black people. Historically, black people have been taught that if you reach a certain level or certain class in society that you have to leave blackness behind. You have to leave your community behind except in rudimentary simple ways. Like, you know. You can still do the line dances, rap the hip hop songs, and still say you're black, but what does that really mean? How much of your blackness is actually connected to the collective as opposed to you just sort of having these superficial expressions of blackness? At the end of the day, I think black wealth is going to grow, but it's not going to grow proportionally. There are going to be some people who get left behind, but there are a whole lot of black people who are waking up and who are going to keep it up.

Zaza Ali:

We've made a lot of strides. I can walk into any store I want to walk into and buy whatever I want to buy. I can start a business at any given moment without having to worry about someone standing in my way. The whole concept of walking down the street, and somebody [yelling], "What are you looking at, boy?" across the street, because a white woman's walking down the street, like, we don't deal with that. There have been lynchings in the past, what? There have been multiple lynchings, actually, in the past five years, but imagine living in a time where hundreds of bodies were being hung from trees. You [could be] walking and potentially run into a body hanging from a tree.

Boyce Watkins:

One way that conditions have improved is that it's a lot tougher for white people to just kill us, because we're doing something that they don't like. Now, there are still very subtle methods for killing off black people and committing genocide. It hasn't stopped. The holocaust continues through mass incarceration and things like that. The criminalization of black life. However, if you look back, say, in 1921 when we built Black Wall Street, what happened? White folks got jealous. They decided to run across town, burn everything down, shoot people in the street, and all this other stuff. I'd like to believe that in the new millennium, they can't do that as readily as they might've done back then.

Zaza Ali:

We've had a lot of gains as far as economics are concerned. They say now we spend anywhere from $1.3 trillion to $1.5 trillion. Now, of course, we can talk about what we do with that money, but we actually have $1.3 trillion to $1.5 trillion in America. Like, we have that money. I'm sitting talking to you, a brother who is established in his own right with his own profession. You being established in your own right with your own profession. Me being an author. Me being a public speaker. Me being able to teach my son about the power of being a melanated young man and having access to books about Imhotep, African kingdoms, warriors, scholars, and academics. Our people 50 years ago couldn't even fathom that.

Boyce Watkins:

Also, the internet has been an absolute game changer. The internet is the first time in human history that black people have been able to communicate with each other without getting a white man's permission. Before, we always had to go through a filter. That's why we couldn't communicate, and that's why we were so divided. Now with the internet, you're starting to see a lot more black unity. You're starting to see the mainstream middle class Negros connected with the conscious, and conscious black people who are connecting with brothers from the street. You're seeing connections formed that never existed before. You're seeing the nation of Islam working with Crips and Bloods and realizing we're all on the same team. We're all working together, and I think that unity is certainly a threat to national security, but it's something that has been happening nonetheless.

Zaza Ali:

We have an abundance of technology at our hands right now. I can go on my phone and pretty much find out anything about the history of the world. So, our conditions have improved greatly, and I think that we have to make sure that we honor that and are grateful for that. I'm not giving credit to white people, the system of racism white supremacy, or to the west. I give all credit and praises to The Creator.

Boyce Watkins:

What makes me optimistic is that you really see a black awakening. You see the convergence of critical thinking, proactive behavior, [and] self-determination laced with self-love. Everything has to start with love. If you love yourself, and you love people like yourself, then you're going to take care of the things you love. We all do. We love our car. We keep it shiny and clean. When we don't care about our car, it gets dirt and nasty. When you own a home, on average, you take good care of it. You make sure it's nice and neat. When you don't own the home, on average, people don't take care of things. They don't feel it belongs to them when they don't feel any sovereignty and ownership.

When we start to feel sovereignty and ownership over our destination, over who we are as a people and where we are as a people, then you'll start to see us taking better care of that. You'll see black people in droves making moves. In The Black Business School, I see thousands of parents that say, "I want my children to be in a better position than me. I want my children to know how this economic system works, how to position themselves to be empowered in America." I think that this is going to be part of what I see as the black economic revolution.

Zaza Ali:

I see in us endless potential. I see the impact that Hip-Hop has had around the world. I see the impact that our athletes have around the world. I see the impact that black actors and entertainers have around the world. Instead of necessarily exploiting the negatives in our community, we could take that energy and take the responsibility of civilizing the world. Being studious. Teaching about diet. Teaching about health in our lyrics and rap songs with our celebrities. Everybody has a platform now. Everybody has a *Twitter*. Everybody has an *Instagram*. Everybody has a *Facebook*. If you're not using those platforms to raise the conscious of the masses, then you're wasting your time.

We have all of these celebrities and entertainers. I'm only using them as a focal point because they have a collective attention on them, and you only want to post pictures of yourself. It's very selfish, and it's our duty to civilize the world, in my opinion. Because we are so beautiful. Because we have this very powerful experience in history. The greatness as well as all of the pain and suffering that we've been through. We can turn that into gold. You talk about alchemy and the idea of turning lead into gold. Well, that's a spiritual concept. So, if we understand that we've been through lead, you know. Slavery produced a mindset of death and despair, but we're still here. If we took the lead of that situation, and said, "Okay, look at where we are now. Look at what we've endured." Studied our history, studied nature, studied the planet, studied mathematics and science, all of the things that the universe are actually built on. If we took those things, we could cultivate the experience, as well as the wisdom of God, as well as the knowledge of our ancestors, as well as the knowledge of who we are right now. I think that we could create a culture in our people that could absolutely not only lead all of the indigenous people around the world and Africa but could lead the world back into the mind and into the nature of God, and rule this planet, as Dr. Frances Cress Welsing talked about, as an army of God with the justice and righteousness.

Boyce Watkins:

Anybody who says that you have to be poor, and there's no way to be anything other than poor probably needs to study economic systems a little more closely. I'll give an example. Over any 30-year period in American history, if you simply invested $100 a month in the stock market your children would have over $1 million in financial assets or close to $1 million. It wouldn't matter which stocks you bought so long as you bought a bunch of different stocks and spent $100 a month in the stock market in 30 to 40 years. At the very least, whether it's $800,000, $1 million, or $1.2 million you're not an economic victim. You're not in a situation where your whole life has changed, because you can't get an extra $2,000.

While America is the country that creates a lot of this oppression, it's also the country that does create some of this opportunity. There is no "whites only" sign on the stock market. There is no sign that says it's for rich people only. You can buy stocks for as little as $1. The same way anybody could buy a pair of shoes could buy a share of stock. The difference is that because we've been locked out of certain opportunities, we have fear of the unknown. That fear of the unknown can cause us to stay trapped and find a way to become comfortable in the middle of chaotic, unhealthy dysfunction as opposed to leaving that dysfunction and going to a place that's healthier and more productive for us.

One important thing for people to understand about America is that America is a rigged society. There is no question about it. It's rigged in favor of people who own businesses, who own property, and who invest in the stock market. If you look at the gaps between the richest Americans, the middle class and the poor, that gap between the wealthy and the middle class is almost completely defined by stock market participation.....At the end of the day, the pathways are very, very clear. I think the cloud was created by virtue of the fact that we just didn't understand where opportunities were. By teaching our kids where the money's at and where opportunities are, we can create a more prosperous community. I truly believe that.

I'm Dr. Boyce Watkins, co-founder of *Your Black World*. Also, the founder of:

- *TheBlackBusinessSchool.com*
- *TheBlackWealthBootcamp.com*
- *TheBlackHistorySchool.com*

I was a finance professor for over 20 years. I've taught at the University of Kentucky, Indiana University, Syracuse

University, the University of Rochester, and Ohio State University.

Zaza Ali:

My name is Zaza Ali. My website is *www.ZazaAli.com*. I am the author of *Black Matters, Volume One: The Scientific Intervention in our Affairs, Volume Two: Plagues of Dysfunction,* and *Volume Three: Lifting the Veil on Racism White Supremacy*. I am the founder of Cooperative Economics Support our Schools, as well as the Sister Cipher Support Group. You can reach me on *Facebook* @Zaza Ali. I'm on *Twitter* @Zaza_Ali7, and *Instagram*, @ZazaAli_78.

TRANSCRIPT

A NEW PARADIGM FOR BLACK AMERICA TOUR WASHINGTON, D.C.

Michael Tapscott:

On behalf of President Steven Knapp, Provost Steven Lerman, and Vice Provost for Diversity and Inclusion Dr. Terri Harris Reed, I'd like to welcome all of you to George Washington University...My name is Mike Tapscott. I'm a D.C. native for those of you who appreciate that. I wanted to share with you quickly that this program is sponsored by Black Student Union, our Black Women's Forum, our Black Men's Initiative, our Directors Program for Black Men's Initiative, [and] George Rice, my associate director behind me. Please give him a round of applause.

I'm also seeing our Vice President for Safety, Darrell. Please welcome him as well. We're glad to have him here on our panel. I'm currently the Director of Multicultural Student Services Center. We've had the honor of sponsoring this event here tonight....Now, we're going to get down to business of the program, and I'll get out of your way, and just welcome Dr. Boyce Watkins. Thank you.

Dr. Boyce Watkins:

What's happening? We are here the Sunday after Thanksgiving on the day of the big Redskins game. I am not the smartest Negro on the plane right now, but nobody's complaining. We are here, because there are quite a few of us in our community who still give a damn. I applaud you for that, and I appreciate you for that. I want to say, first of all, thank you so much to the university for hosting us and allowing us to hold this event here. This is the third New Paradigm Forum that we've held this year.

The goal of the New Paradigm Forum is to bring ideas from all perspectives in our community and lay them all out on the table. To decentralize black leadership, if you will. Black leadership is a lot deeper than Jesse and Al. It goes back to what we all do in our homes. In fact, Dr. Wilmer Leon always says, "Black leadership starts in your living room." How do you lead your family? How do you lead your children? How do you lead the community? In the space in which you live. So, all of us are black leaders if you ask me. That's what I think black leadership should be in the 21st century.

Now, if you think about where we are, when you think about the community in which we live, and the problems that we see, you also have to look at the hope that exists in our community. Janks just showed me literally an hour ago that the black male graduation rate is actually higher than it's been in a very long time. In fact, the dropout rate was, I think, 8.1% down from double digits 10 years ago. So, there are lots of rays of hope and potential and opportunity in our community that we can't overlook. We can't look at this as a doom-and-gloom scenario.

At the same time, we have to think about why all of us play a role in dealing with what we're experiencing right now. You look around, and you see that mass incarceration has absolutely obliterated the black family in America. If you look around, you see what's going on in the educational system. If you look around, you see what's going on with economic inequality and black unemployment. It is about as bad as it was during the March on Washington on 1963. We know that we have a lot of work to do.

I would also argue that in order to understand the purpose and reason we do the things we're doing right now, we have to look at the first runaway slave. The first runaway slave was not the most popular slave on the plantation. We like to glorify and glamorize what that must have been like, but it wasn't fun to be the first person on the plantation who wanted to be free. You probably didn't have any friends. Your best friends probably told on you. You had a lot of people there claiming they love you and giving you the "good" advice, "You better not try to do that. Just go get a good job in the house with the massa, and you'll be comfortable. You'll be safe." We also have to realize that first runaway slave probably didn't succeed. When that person was brought back to the plantation – bloody and beaten and burning, and whatever else they did to that person – there was always that Negro standing over the top of him saying, "I told you. I told you so. I told you not to do that."

We have to realize that while we might glamorize that experience and the decision to break through a system that's designed to oppress us, it doesn't always work out the first time you try. Also, it doesn't always work out in the generation in which you try it. We must also understand that even though that first runaway slave probably didn't succeed, that individual planted the seed of freedom that existed in his children and grandchildren. That's what led the other persons to say, "Well, maybe there is something wrong with this system. Maybe there is a way for me to get out of this system." If you really look at it closely, you realize that you can't have the first black president without the first runaway slave. We are really a pack of runaway slaves. We're looking at the plantations on which we live, the situations that we work in, the discrimination we face in the workplace, the things we see in our communities, and we want something better.

When you go out and talk about liberating a community, making your community better, people look at you like you're crazy. When we confronted the rapper Li'l Wayne and killed his endorsement deal with Mountain Dew six months ago, people called me a hater. "You hatin' on that dude trying to make his money. You hate rappers. You hate this. You hate that." I said, "No. It's not that I hate you, Li'l Wayne. It's that I love my children more than I like your lyrics. You agree with me that the messages you are spitting out into our community are not helpful to our kids. Nothing great has ever been accomplished by a group of people sitting around getting high and drunk every day."

This gathering is the third one. The first one we did was in Chicago. Minister Louis Farrakhan joined us. I love his ideas, because Minister Louis Farrakhan, like him or not, is one of the freest black men in America. He's done things for black men that nobody else can do. We went to New York City. Dr. Cornell West joined us. Again, if you ask my opinion, Dr. Cornell West is the closest thing we have right now to Martin Luther King, Jr., and they hate him just like they hated Dr. Martin Luther King, Jr. right before he died...Dr. Steve Perry's here. Dr. Wilmer Leon. Etan Thomas, who was formally with the Washington Wizards. Dr. Towanna Freeman. James Borden. Just people that I wanted to bring to you to have what I would call a politically incorrect conversation about what it's going to take to save our communities. I'm not here to fit this into a liberal box. This is not a conservative box. This is not Democrat or Republican. This is about us. For us, by us. And that's all that really matters to me.

That's all I'm going to say. Thank you so much from the bottom of my heart to those of you that did come out. Consider me a friend. We will remain connected forever, and understand this. There will probably not be a day in our lifetime that we look outside into the black community and see that everything we're working for is bearing fruit. We're not going to look outside and see the sun is shining. We're not going to look outside and see that another baby didn't get shot or that somebody else didn't go to prison. That's not going to happen in our lifetime. We have to accept that. We are fighting a battle that's going to look like a losing battle for a very long time, but just like that first runaway slave, we're not doing this for ourselves. We're doing this for our children's children. That's what I want you to hold onto today. Without further ado, I would like to bring up Dr. Wilmer Leon.

Dr. Wilmer Leon:

Good evening, everyone. Thank you, Boyce. As I was thinking about my comments, Etan. As I was thinking about my opening remarks in terms of saving our community and what I wanted you all to be able to take away from this conversation this evening, to me it really comes down to this. There's a very popular narrative out there that's been constructed primarily by the dominant culture. It perpetuates a very unfortunate stereotype, and unfortunately, there are some of us that do play into it. That narrative is, that stereotype is, that we just don't care. We don't care about education. We don't care about our families. We don't care about our communities. When I say that some of us play into this stereotype, some of us do. But unfortunately [and] in too many circumstances, the anecdotal and negative stereotypes are used to describe and caricature our people. We do care about our families. We are great fathers. We are great husbands, mothers, parents, [and] wives. We do care about educating our children. We do care about working every day to control our communities and to protect our communities. We have a very, very, very long documented history of such.

How many of you all have seen the film *12 Years a Slave*? For those of you that haven't, you really, really need to see that incredibly powerful film. How many of you all have read the book? Those of you who have seen the film and haven't read the book, you really need to read the book. Everybody needs to read that book. Particularly when...In the holiday season give it as a Kwanzaa gift. Give it as a stocking stuffer, because it is an incredibly powerful narrative.

There is one element in the book that I wish received more attention. That was Solomon Northup's focus on family. Now, he was born in 1808, 205 years ago [and] 189 years after those first 20 and some-odd so-called indentured servants disembarked from that Dutch Man-o-War in Jamestown, Virginia, in 1619. He writes in chapter one the following, "From the time of my marriage to this day, the love I have borne my wife has been sincere and unabated. And only those who have felt the glowing tenderness a father cherishes for his offspring, can appreciate my affection for my beloved children which have since been born to us. This much I deem appropriate and necessary to say. In order that those who read these pages may comprehend the poignancy of those sufferings I have been doomed to bear." What Solomon Northup was doing was placing his struggle to regain his freedom into a context: the family context. That's what kept him sane amidst those 12 years of insanity: his need to be a father to his children and his need to be a husband to his wife. That's what motivated him, kept him from accepting his plight, and struggling until he was eventually free.

Now, the dominant culture has attempted to destroy our nuclear family. The structure of our nuclear family through slavery. Through separation of parent and child, husband and wife. Made it illegal for us as people to marry. We adapt[ed]. We form[ed] the extended family. The surrogate and the communal structure. Grandparents took in grandchildren. Surrogate aunties and uncles look after other folks' kids. Communities place their collective arms around individuals and families to instill discipline, bestow love, and provide support. A huge problem facing us today is that now our communities are under siege. From mass incarceration, underemployment, unemployment, wealth disparities, disproportionate impacts of subprime lending, to all of the things that so many of us are feeling victimized by or at least very familiar with.

In our prisons in the late '70s and '80s, America shifted from a rehabilitative model to a strict incarceration model. The introduction of tons of crack cocaine and weapons into the black community and resulting drug wars was documented by Gary Webb of the San Jose *Mercury News* and articulated by Congresswoman Maxine Waters. The political response and solution to a rising crime rate in the mid-'80s was the mass incarceration model: no more than a war on the black male. Removing him from the community, the family, and branding him with the stigma of felon. Today, the fastest-growing demographic in prison is men: particularly black men.

So, here's the takeaway. Yes, our communities are under siege, and too many of our families are struggling. [However] Solomon Northup, Frederick Douglass, Harriet Tubman, Miss Fannie Lou Hamer, Ella Baker, the Deacons of Defense, [and] the members of the panel I'm about to introduce prove beyond a shadow of a doubt that we are a resourceful people. We are a resilient people, and – what the dominant culture fears most – we are a brilliant and a powerful people. Our beautiful history is evidence of that.

I mentioned the panel, so let's bring 'em out. Our first panelist is the principal consultant for Towanna Freeman and Associates, an active consultancy in the greater Washington D.C. Metro area, the creator of the Black Life Coaches Network, a successful life coach, management consultant, inspirational and motivational speaker, and advocate for young women. She is the co-author of the award-winning *Purposeful Action: Seven Steps to Fulfillment*, which reveals a seven-step method for identifying and effectively pursuing personal and professional goals. Please [give] a warm welcome to

Dr. Towanna Freeman.

Our next panelist is without question, the most prolific African-American filmmaker of his generation that 90% of African Americans have never heard of. He is a groundbreaking international award-winning documentarian and a founder of iYAGO Entertainment Group. He states, "The company came into existence to reflect both the conscious and unconscious soul of black America." He has been in the entertainment industry for more than 20 years, and he is a much sought-after teacher, lecturer, communicator, and motivational speaker. Please welcome Janks Morton.

Our next panelist is more than an athlete. He's been called a gentle giant, a rebounder with a cause, the poet. He defies the stereotype of the apolitical athlete and plants his roots in his budding literary career with the conviction of a Bill Russell and the poetic finesse of Muhammad Ali. He is a recipient of numerous awards. He has started a fatherhood movement in which he goes from city to city holding panels and town hall meetings to discuss fatherhood. In each city, he recruits different celebrities to join him in inspiring an entire generation. Please welcome Mr. Etan Thomas.

Our next panelist's heart pumps passion and produces positive change. He is the founder and principal of what *U.S. News and World Report* has cited as one of the top schools in the country, Capital Preparatory Magnet School in Hartford, Connecticut. Capital Prep has sent 100% of its predominantly low-income minority first-generation high school graduates to four-year colleges every year since its first class graduated in 2006. He's a strong advocate of personal and civic responsibility in all aspects of life. His secrets to success and calls to action are revealed in his new book, *Push Has Come to Shove: Getting Our Kids the Education They Deserve — Even If It Means Picking a Fight*. Dr. Steven Perry.

And, you all know our convener, Dr. Boyce Watkins. What we decided to do instead of having each of the panelists give an opening statement...[is start] with questions and let them go at it from there. The first question is for Dr. Towanna Freeman. And the question is...Yes, you're the first one...Ladies first. What can be done within families to help our children see that fighting or other negative physical behavior as a main coping skill is not the way to resolve conflict?

Dr. Towanna Freeman:

How many of you, by a show of hands, saw the video of Sharkeisha? Okay. I was born in 1970, and we fought, but we didn't have video cameras. So, we know we've had that...The way to help our young people resolve issues without it being physical is to first let them know the consequences of videotaping things. The consequences could serve you some time. That's the first thing you need to get real quick. This young lady will be [in] or potentially find herself in jail. With that being the case, that is a perfect model from this point further. Remind every single one of the youth you influence that unless you want a Sharkeisha charge, you may want to re-evaluate how you engage in negative confrontation. Point real issues out. Give real-life examples.

The other thing I would recommend...[is this]. Anytime and every time you see young people engaging in conversation that encourages or causes one to believe it is socially acceptable to fight or disrespect your brother or your sister, call them on it. You see everybody that's in this room. I don't think you're the ones that we're necessarily talking about...Here in this room are people who are about change. With that being the case, we're talking about youth identifying something and addressing it. See something and take action to do something about it. Point out the issue. Give them a real-life example. Then, turn around and encourage them to be more respectful to one another. Be accountable to one another as brothers and sisters in this community. Those are just two basics. I'll stop there.

Dr. Wilmer Leon:

Anybody want to –

Etan Thomas:

Yeah, I saw the Sharkeisha video.

Dr. Wilmer Leon:

Go ahead.

Etan Thomas:

It was...I don't know if anybody else felt as sick and disgusted by what you saw as I did. I mean, it was interesting, because it also made me think about what media's done to exacerbate the wrong value systems with kids. It's not going to go away. *WorldstarHipHop* makes probably $10 million to $20 million a year running these videos and making these kids into overnight celebrities. I went to Sharkeisha's *Twitter* account, and I actually tweeted at her. I saw that she had 25,000 *Twitter* followers and was really embracing the celebrity of what she did.

It's also interesting, because you see. In terms of media, you also have these basketball wife shows which teach young women how to interact in very unhealthy ways. I think that really, to some extent, we know our kids are already being educated by what they're hearing on the radio, seeing on TV, and seeing on the internet. That's an education. Anything that's entering into their brain and that they're absorbing is part of their education. So, I say that we have to offer a counter-education. We have to be just as diligent, just as angry, just as willing to pick fights, as Steve is. That's why I love Steve. Steve will pick a fight for his kids. We have to pick fights over this in terms of understanding that if we don't approach the education of our children with the same energy that the enemy is educating our children we're going to lose this battle. This isn't really a fight or a war built for kind, passive people. This is a war that's built for warriors.

Dr. Wilmer Leon:

Janks.

Janks Morton:

Yeah.

Dr. Wilmer Leon:

Oh, you were smiling and nodding. I just wanted to be sure I didn't move on before –

Janks Morton:

It's the hallelujah praise chorus. Of course, being on the filmmaker's side and in the media, we know the power of what these images have done to our perception of acceptable behavior. So, and this is where...whatever. Y'all are gonna get mad, but it is what it is. Sharkeisha's not my problem. Sharkeisha's mom and dad are my problem. I'm real guarded in what I do in working with young people and knowing that the outcomes we see with them...Yes, they have to own up at a certain age, but most of the time they're a direct reflection of a lack of socialization by a generation that let them down. I say this all the time, and it gets me in trouble. I really don't believe we have a black youth problem in our community. We have a black parent problem. Until our generation owns up to what we did not do for these kids, the Sharkeishas are going to keep coming. The Lil Waynes are going to keep coming. Lil Greezy, Lil Cheezy, and Lil Meezy are going to keep coming, and it's going to take a maturation of the baby boomers, first, before any significant impact can be made on these young people's lives. Thanks.

Dr. Steve Perry:

First, if I can...I wish you could see what I see: how amazing you look on a Sunday night that we have come together to have this conversation. Can you give yourselves a round of applause?...Really, you are what makes this whole thing matter.

We are at a point where we've lost two generations and counting. The report from the front lines is bad. We're getting beaten up really badly. By ourselves, really. It's our own inactivity: our comfort with the uncomfortable reality of children walking around dressed or undressed in the public sector. In ways in which just a generation ago, they wouldn't have allowed you to see them in their own home. We've lost a lot, and we don't know what we've lost.

You know. We can sit and have a polite conversation, but the blunt truth is that we've messed up. It doesn't have to stay this way, regardless of what your faith conviction is. It doesn't have to stay this way if we decide that it isn't going to be this way any longer...Each one of us could do something right if we reach inside ourselves. This young lady is the symptom. She's the blood on the dress. There's a cut somewhere, and it's deep.

We're here this evening to have a conversation about solutions, and in my sphere it's education. That's what I do. I believe that you can't get out of the situation, regardless of your socioeconomic status, until you have an education. Not just go to school but learn something. You can't learn something in places where learning isn't occurring. It's hard to learn the lessons that we need to learn in what are essentially baby prisons: places where the people who work in them would never send their own children...So from my sphere, this is a conversation about what we can do in the public sector where education is something that's supposed to be compulsory and a human right.

We know everything that is good in life gets better when you get more education. Dr. King said that in 1967...He said, "Everything that is good, we have half of, and everything that is bad, we have twice as much of." Can't keep telling this story. It just can't keep being. We have to get sick and tired of being sick and tired and start to make the changes tonight...There's too much power in this room for us to walk out of here the same...If we can make a commitment tonight to promise ourselves [that] we ain't leaving here how we came, it's going to be better tonight, because we're going to make it better...This won't be just conversations.

Etan Thomas:

There's a saying that it takes a village to raise a child, but what happens when the entire village is afraid of all the children? I think that's where we are today. My passion is working with young people. I want to go and speak with them, hear how they're feeling, and have them bounce ideas off of me. Not just talking at them but also listening to them. They get a lot of criticism all the time. They'll get that from everywhere. You know. Criticize how they talk, how they dress, how they act, how everything. You know what I mean? Sometimes they don't feel that they're being heard, and I think there's such a disconnect right now from two generations. When you ask them, you see how much of a disconnect it really is.

I want to say this real quick. I don't want to spend too much time on it, but young people respond to respect. There's a big thing with young people who feel disrespected. A lot of bad stuff happens from that point on. Once the disrespect happens, they don't feel that the older generation respects them at all. If you're coming into a situation where an older person is criticizing you and you don't feel that they are respecting you, then you can't hear anything that they say. At all. Now it's interesting, because when we're doing these panels in different places across the country and talking with young people, there's a lot that they have inside. You know what I mean? If you can get past their exterior.

See, sometimes as adults, when their package isn't the way that we want it to be presented, we want to just throw the whole thing away. Like, we can't even see them. We don't like the way they're dressing, their hair, their clothes, or anything like that, and they feel that rejection. They do. One of the issues that we have is that, as adults, we're not embracing our young people the way that we should. I think that's the honest truth. I can't blame them for everything, because you know what happens? They get embraced by the wrong people. [People who] don't care how they look, how they're talking, how they're dressed or anything like that, but we want to turn our noses up at them. You know what I mean? Act like we're afraid of them. Like, "How could she possibly wear that outfit?" You know what I mean? Most of our parents didn't like how we dressed when we were younger, either. That's the truth. The generation before you don't like how the generation after them dress, act, talk. That's what happens, but sometimes we have short-term memory.

They're going through so much right now, and I can't criticize them when they're acting out. When they feel nobody else is willing to take them on and help them out. That's one thing that we have to do 'cause we're losing them. We're losing our young people right now, and we're losing them by the truckloads. It's not gonna get better before it gets worse, so we definitely have to figure out something.

Dr. Wilmer Leon:

Dr. Freeman?

Dr. Towanna Freeman:

Yeah, I just wanna close it out with ... I will say this. In addition to what they all just said, an important word that I'd like to throw out here is patience. We've lost patience. It's one thing, yes, we have our fears. We are afraid of who they've become and do not understand them. Their language has changed. We don't relate to them well. We're critical. They don't understand. They don't respect us. They're not showing the old school respect [of] be seen and not heard – all those types of things that we were raised under. It's patience. You have to formulate a way to communicate that will allow them to open up...[and] feel comfortable enough to have a conversation with you without judgment. So, when I work with young people I have a strategy for when I approach them. The first thing I'm gonna talk about is not what they're not doing but what they are doing right, first. [I] allow the conversation to develop to the point where I am patient as I listen – actively listen – to everything that's coming out of their mouths. I can then interpret what to do next based on what they've said.

You see, all of us know how to address issues. We're problem solvers. Once you know what the issue is, you can work on a solution, right? You just tell me what the problem is, and let me help you. A lot of times we're trying to help without listening. I didn't ask you for all that. What I need you to do is hear what I'm saying and then offer a solution based on what I'm telling you. So, patience is important.

Dr. Boyce Watkins:

I have a quick word I want to add. She mentioned the word patience. I think it's a very important word. I think another really important word to add to that is love. I think love is the most powerful thing in the universe. I've found that kids respond very strongly to those they know love them. Raising one child taught me a lot about children, parenting, and all that, but I have some others that I kind of scooped up along the way. I remember one day, one of my daughters called me, and she was crying. She told me about this little boy she babysat who was about three years old, and the little boy had been shot in the head. I didn't understand how a three-year-old child could get shot in the head, so I asked her what happened. She told me the boy's mother had gotten into an argument with a neighbor. The mother was maybe about 20 years old. The neighbor was about 19. So, I guess he was a wannabe gangster. He went home, got a gun, came back and fired off unloading the clip into the house. He didn't care who he hit. He was just shooting at the house. He didn't know that there were 10 kids inside the house playing at the time. A little boy got shot in the head and died about three days later from swelling of the brain.

When I heard the story, I cried. I didn't cry just for the three-year-old who died. I cried for that little boy who killed him. I realized that...just a few years ago that 19-year-old gangster was also an innocent, loving, sweet, kind three or four-year-old child who could have been anything. He could have become the next black president. He could have become an attorney, doctor, lawyer, [or] whatever. He could have become anything we wanted him to become, but somehow, the world shaped him into the monster who could unload a clip of bullets into a house full of kids...When this child was growing up, there's a very good chance that when he reached out for us to love him all we fed him was hate. When he needed somebody to embrace him, we neglected him. When he looked to us to lift him up, we only crushed his soul. So, he went from being a sweet, loving, innocent child who could have become anything to a 19-year-old killer who unloads a clip into a house full of kids.

What I figured out right then is that when God puts a child in front of you who does not have a parent...We always say, "Well, look at the parents. Look at the parents." What if they don't have any parents? When that child is in front of you and that child has no parental guidance, it is your obligation to step in to provide the love that child needs. Whether you choose to act or not, there will be a ripple effect. What you put into that child, that child takes into the world.

You don't have to have a child in order to be a parent. I encourage you to remember that. I guarantee you that if somebody had stepped in and been a parent to that little boy, he never would have killed that three-year-old child. He would have protected him and loved him instead of killing him. Those are the ripple effects that we're seeing in our community.

Dr. Wilmer Leon:

In talking about the Shanquisha video...whatever her name is.

Dr. Boyce Watkins:

Sharkeisha.

Dr. Wilmer Leon:

Sharkeisha, my bad. Steve talked about [the fact that] he's not angry at her. It's her parents. That made me think about when my son was about four. I was down in my office working on an article. He came downstairs, and he said, "Daddy, I'm ready." I said, "Ready for what?" He said, "Ready to do my show." I'm typing. I said, "Oh, okay, okay," as we would tend to say. "Go talk to your mother. I'm working."

He comes downstairs about 30 minutes later. Got a sport coat on and a tie, and he says, "Daddy, I'm ready." I said, "Ready for what?" My son replies, "Ready to do my show just like you on CNN with Lou Dobbs." In that moment it hit me. Children are like sponges. I mean, we hear that all the time, but he, even at four years old, was paying attention to everything I did. So, if I'm sitting on the couch, drinking a 40, and smoking a blunt, he's gonna sit on the couch, drink a 40, and smoke a blunt. But, if he sees his father reading, writing, and loving his mother, he will most likely think that reading, writing, and loving his mother are the right things to do. So, I took him upstairs, and we set up a tripod and mic'ed him up. He interviewed our niece who was living with us at the time. He did his show. Now, if any of you all happen to hear my show from time to time, the little voice that closes the show every Saturday that he's with me in the studio is number four. He's just doing what I do. Our kids are doing what we do.

Dr. Steve Perry:

Let me, if I may. One of the things...We didn't all come up here for a love fest to agree on everything, so this is where I step in. I don't think it's ever a good idea to put a child in a situation where they have parents who are not necessarily as effective as we want them. How nice would it be if everyone could grow up in a community where everything was hunky-dory? But, that ain't what it really looks like. I submit to you that while it is important for us to have positive home role models, the fact is that much of what's happening to our community is happening within our schools. We're being crushed in our own schools by the weight of our own public education system.

There's an over feminization of primary education whereby black boys and Latino boys are made to stop raising their hands by the time they're in second and third grade. They think school ain't really for them. They don't really feel like they have a place in this system. And so, children who were fired up about going to school when they were three and four years old – practicing doing homework because their older brothers and sisters were doing homework, getting their new

Trapper Keeper together, and new sneakers to run faster – somewhere along the way stop liking school, because they believe school doesn't like them.

I believe it's so easy for us to demonize sisters who are raising kids by themselves. It's just so damn easy, but it's not the facts. The facts are that just because you grow up in a single parent household doesn't mean it has to go terribly wrong. I was born on my mother's 16th birthday. Just because your father goes to prison doesn't mean you have to follow behind him, as mine has. I recognize that we can create a more compelling experience through our...We use so many clichés about communities and villages. I'm telling you right now. Your local school can be that place when it's run right.

A job of an educator is really like a magician. They have this capacity to reach into the child's mind and convince him that he can be something that he never imagined before – even if that something is something bad. We have to own our messes as a community, no doubt. We could all be better parents. I'll grab a fistful of shirt in a minute, but that's not where it's falling down. We're sending our children to places [where] we trust they will be educated and prepared for the next part in life, and they're not.

There's no one who can tell me [that] because a child lives in a particular zip code they're less intelligent than another. You just can't convince me of that. Last time I checked, children are still manufactured the same way they've always been. Since that's the case, we keep allowing conversations around poverty and parenting to wash away the real issue. We send our children to places where they're not loved, respected, or treated like they're supposed to be. They come home not one day smarter. You ask them, "What'd you learn today in school?" What do they say?

Etan Thomas:

Nothing.

Dr. Towanna Freeman:

Nothing.

Dr. Steve Perry:

All over the country. And they're not lying. The data is too clear. Why is there an achievement gap between black children and white children? Because black children are less intelligent? Because black parents are worse parents? I mean, come on. We can't let that dog hunt forever. At some point we have to recognize that there's a hole in the system. It's called our schools.

It really is. The difference between many people's lives is where they went to school. It really boils down to that, and that cannot be determined by the ball in the lottery.

We have to begin to fight sometimes the very people we thought were always on our side. We're so quick to give every vote to a democrat. So quick to jump behind anybody who says that they're in a union. Do we ever decide to ask them, "Damn, man. When was the last time you did something for us? I sure would like to look at your record for real." We can focus on the outliers: the parents who are...Look, I'm a principal. Don't get it twisted. I've had the mothers [saying], "I'm gonna bring down my husband." Number one, he ain't your husband. Number two, leave that little man at home before he get sent out the way he came in...Yes, grown people, y'all can be aggravating, no doubt, but the real issue is we have a system that is fundamentally flawed. [It] constantly suspends, expels, and punishes black and Latino boys. [It] constantly and consistently undereducates people of color [and] has since its inception. If we don't do something about it, then we have nothing else to discuss. Game over. You could pump all the money into the community. You could talk about giving everybody free lunch. All the things you wanna do. But if they cannot read, write, and compute anywhere near grade level...There are schools here in

D.C. in which 5% to 10% of the kids are reading at grade level. That's a 90% fail rate. Enough has to be enough. Y'all gotta say, "I'm tired of this. I'm not giving you another one of my children." I believe every single parent sends us the very best child that they have in their house, and every single parent is doing the absolute best that they can. Doesn't mean that I think it's the best...I think everybody's doing the best they can. It's just [that] our schools have failed us miserably.

Dr. Wilmer Leon:

Janks Morton. You, sir. Janks Morton, what is the deficit model approach to black identity in activism, and what is its impact?

Janks Morton:

The deficit model approach to black identity is the thing that gets you on these kinds of panels all over the country. I can sit up here and give you negative statistics about black people until the sun comes up tomorrow morning, guaranteed. The deficit model is part of what I'm pushing against in what I call the not-for-profit industrial complex. What you know and what your formulation around what it means, from a statistical standpoint, to be black is probably very, very negative. So, if I were to ask anybody in this room to give me one positive statistic about black people, it would be a hard pressed conversation. But if I say give me something negative, we go all day. Everybody knows how bad everything is.

I wrote a piece for *Ebony* a couple years ago, and it got me in a lot of trouble. I stay in trouble. Terry Glover, a dear woman who passed away last year, said to me, "I get what you're trying to say now. You're not saying that we don't have problems. What you're trying to say is that we have to shine the light on our greatness along with those problems." That's a tough thing for us to do, because it's kind of a twisted reverse psychology that we have.

About six or seven years ago, I was the guy who proved there have never been more black men in jail than in college. Never. It's never happened. Never been true. But some special interest organization comes out with a flawed study, and we go to the barber shop, and the beauty salon, and to CNN, and everybody else, and say, "Oh, Lord Jesus. God help us. Save us. It's more black men in jail than it is in college." Right? Oh, I'm tripping?...Don't even try. Don't even try. I see the looks. Y'all know what I'm talking about. This is everywhere over the country. Our generation has done a disservice to the younger generation.

Etan talked about how we [need to] uplift, elevate, and encourage, not constantly berate and tell [youth], "You don't know your history. You don't know where you came from. Pull your damn pants up." They heard that. [How about], "Do you know that you and your generation, despite being given the greatest handicap in the history of blacks in this country, are enrolling in college at a higher rate than any time ever? You know that you're great. This is the bar of expectation that we want to drive you to. One out of three of you [age] 18 to 24 is not going to jail. You are going to college right now." That's where we are. What if we began to frame our conversation differently around this generation and tell them that they are phenomenal when they are?

And the statistics...Like right now, I cannot get this story out. It drives me freaking crazy. Right now as we sit here today, 50 blah years past Brown versus Board of Education. Black women enroll in college more than any other group in this country – including the Asians. More. Yeah, yeah. And it's not even close. A full percentage point: 9.6% are enrolled in college, of a group, and 8.6% are Asian men. A full point ahead. Where's the press release? Where's the pat on the back? Steve is complimenting single mothers. Well God bless America for the ones that are 30, 'cause that demographic is...What they're doing...They went to school, and they're going back. We have got to see ourselves through a different lens, because if we go through the lens of the deficit – of our inadequacies, of our shortcomings, of our less than – [we] can join the Klan. They got those all day all on the boards. [We] really can. They can tell you how bad black people are.

At this juncture in our history, I believe that there is some greatness that is emerging that we need to give to one another to begin to see ourselves with clarity in our entire mosaic. That will give a renewed message: a renewing of the heart, mind, and soul to a people that I think are desperate for over 400 years...Actually, take it back to Nimrod. That's how long black folks have been castigated in this world. That's what the deficit model...to see black people as inadequate, first, without their greatness.

Dr. Wilmer Leon:

And unfortunately, to that, it permeates our politics...There's a whole dynamic that is to a great degree pushed by conservatives, but unfortunately it does get supported by some of the democratic camp. Blaming the poor for their plight.

Janks Morton:

I would like to stay apolitical on this, because it's both. The republicans don't care, and what pisses me...can I say piss?

Dr. Wilmer Leon:

Yep.

Dr. Steve Perry:

Yeah, after you said it.

Janks Morton:

What pisses me off to know...is the low expectations based upon my skewed perception of who you are as a...The liberals see you as inadequate, so I gotta help you out. Get out of my way. I am not a black man that you...No one has ever in the history of the human condition...Black people, take this one home. Take it to the bank. In the human condition, no other group has ever elevated another group to equality. It just doesn't happen. If you think that the white man's ice is colder and that's where you need to go, look at the Asian data first. They will never bring you to equality. It just doesn't happen.

And us looking for, you know...this concept that God is coming. It's just not gon' happen. So it's back on us, and what are we gonna do? What I'm saying is, as Steve said it earlier, if you could see the beauty of what we see out here on a Sunday night when my Skins are playing...They're probably losing by now...That we have every single wedge of resource we need to begin to change this conversation, to begin to start, but we have to see the beauty as well as the shortcomings first. I'm gonna shut up. I'm sorry.

Dr. Boyce Watkins:

He had a good point about equality. I loved what he said about equality.

Dr. Wilmer Leon:

Go ahead. Go ahead.

Dr. Boyce Watkins:

The equality thing, I think, is an important conversation, because the last time I checked nobody ever gives you equality. Just the idea that you would look to the descendants of your historical oppressors to validate you and give you the things you need to feed and educate your children...is a mental illness. That's sick. And you know, when we started doing these panels, which honestly, it was just sort of a spark of God that made me just say, "Okay, let's try this. Let's see how it goes." I'm not an event planner. I didn't know if it was gonna work. People started comparing it to what Tavis used to do: Tavis Smiley with the State of the Black Union events. I thought [those] were very helpful to the community in their own context. People said, "Well, if you wanna pay for this, why don't you go get corporate sponsorship? Go get McDonald's. Go get Walmart. Go get these corporations to give you the money that you need to go around the country and do this, so you don't have to bother people like Steve Perry and Cornell West to do things for free." I said, "I don't want to bring black leadership brought to you by McDonald's." Okay? The revolution will not be televised, and it will not be in a damn Walmart commercial. The fact is that if we're not willing to pay the cost for our own freedom, then we do not deserve to be free. Period.

Dr. Wilmer Leon:

Etan, you've started your fatherhood movement traveling across the country. Your book. Your CD. You and Janks may want to get into a debate. The statistics can't be denied that kids from broken homes do worse in every category. Teenage pregnancy, dropout, in a gang. Just much more likely to fail. With this reality and so many young people growing up in broken homes, talk about the chances.

Etan Thomas:

Well, as Steve said earlier, it doesn't have to be that way. No matter what the statistics say, you don't have to fall into that category. I think that one thing we have to do is uplift our young people to know that they don't have to fall into that category. When you lower the expectations and they think that's all they're gonna become, that's what they become. You know what I mean? But if you speak life into them, show them positive examples...that's what I wanted to do in the book: get men from all walks of life that young people would recognize. Rappers, actors, athletes, or whoever. They tell them their stories. 'Cause you don't really know how somebody got to where they are. You know what I mean? You see the end mark. You see Kevin Durant on the court. You hear Talib Kweli and Styles P in the studio and their albums. You see Taye Diggs in the movies and things like that, but you don't know how they got there. You don't know. You know what I mean?

People have had to overcome a lot that we're not shown. The only things that you'll hear about athletes [are] all the negatives. All the bad people. All the people that did something terrible. All the eight baby mamas. The worst stories you could possibly hear. That'll be what they show you as the norm. They'll have you thinking that *Basketball Wives* is really how athletes' wives really act. My wife does not act like that. She does not, at all.

There's always an element that you see like that, but it's not everybody. You hear the stories, and they'll be on the top of *Sports Center* [and] the main outlets. If the athlete does something wrong, they're plastered right on the top. Right? So then you start thinking all these athletes are doing all this terrible stuff. They're all having babies out of wedlock. They all having eight or nine baby mamas. They all doing all...And same with the rappers. You know what I mean? That's what you would think, but that's not reality. You have to know that what you're given is not the [whole] truth. If we start thinking that everything that we're given is the truth, then we start getting all messed up.

It's funny, because I was talking to my son, and he was learning about Christopher Columbus Day. He was like, "Well, Dad, how can somebody discover something when some people [were] already [there]?" I was like, "You're right. So, what does that tell you?" He's like, "Well, they kinda invaded it, like Avatar...The fire nation invaded the water tribe." Anybody who has kids knows what I'm talking about....I told my son...You can't always just take in what you're given as being the truth. Then we started talking about Thanksgiving. He asked me if the Native Americans were really all cool sitting down all peaceful and loving like they tell us. I asked my son what he thought, and he said, "No. So what point did they start killing all of them?" He was asking all these questions, because I'm telling him, listen...It's like in the movie *Malcolm X* when Elijah Muhammed poured the water in the glass and then he put the iodine in there. Then he said, "If you give this to the people, they have no choice but to drink it." Then he poured the other glass, and he was like, "If you give them this option, they can make their choice." We're only given one option of ourselves in the media. You know what I mean? They're only giving us one option about who we are as a people, what we can do, and what our possibilities are. Our young people are feeling it.

[All our youth see is] negativity all the time thrown at them on the radio, in movies, and on the news. There's a reason why all of the negative Hip-Hop is what's played on the radio 24 hours a day. There's a reason for that. There are not just all negative rappers. There are a lot of positive rappers, but they'll play all the negative stuff nonstop. The worst possible images of our women. Telling them that this is who you are. So, they're going and thinking, "That's what I have to do to be successful. I have to be like that. I gotta show my body. I gotta get some fake everything, and I gotta...just keep doing all of this stuff to be able to get a man to pay any attention to me." It starts early.

The worst thing on earth is to see a young person emulate what they see on TV, and you know exactly where they got it from. That's the worst thing on earth, but we're not telling our young people how special they are. We did a panel at Rikers Island, and we told the young people how special they are...It was a group like this of all young people under 18 that all looked like me. It was terrible to see. I said, "Listen, y'all deserve better than this. This ain't living. Somebody telling you when to eat, when to sleep, when you can see your family, all this stuff. That's not living. Y'all deserve better than this." They looked at us like it was something that they had never heard before – that nobody ever told them. "Like what do you mean we deserve better than this? This is where we're kinda supposed to be." That's how they looked at us. That's awful. We gotta tell them how important they are, how special they are, [and] the rich heritage and history they come from. When you know your history and you know your heritage, you know you're part of something bigger. You know you have a tradition that you're carrying on....If we only allow our schools to educate our children, then they're not really educated. That's what it is, and that's the honest truth.

Good school or bad school. If that's the only education they receive...because they're not being told about themselves.

We gotta pump our young people. When they see and hear all these negative images telling them how if they come from a broken home they're probably gonna end up dead, in jail, dropout, get pregnant, or something terrible, they can know instantly, "No, that's not gonna be me. I'm gonna defy the odds." That's what they have to [be able to say to themselves]. They can't let [the negativity] soak in and say, "Oh, well I'm gonna go in this direction, so this is probably what's meant for me." [That] is what's happening now. We gotta pump our young people up. I can't say it enough. We can't just criticize them. We have to lift them up, as well. That's what we have to do if we want anything to get better. If we just criticize them, we're gonna just keep losing them.

Dr. Steve Perry:

So, we're losing, right? No matter what my partner says, we're losing by a lot. You can run around happy-go-lucky all you want, but I'm telling you we're getting our asses beat. We're down a lot, and this is a locker room speech. We can't come out the second half the way we went in the first one. Where we are right now, we have to decide...I don't know what you know how to do...I don't know, but you should do something. Tomorrow tonight, you've gotta do something. That's really what this has to be about. When brother Boyce and I spoke about this, I said, "I ain't going all the way down anywhere just to talk, 'cause that's not cool. We gotta come out with something." Right?...I'm not in charge of who gets called on, but I will call him, because I really like [his] outfit. Think of what you know how to do. Think of...the thing that keeps you up at night, the thing that makes you want to do something, that thing right there, and throw it in the pile, man. We need all hands on deck. We are losing.

Dr. Wilmer Leon:

You know, when we were in Brooklyn, somebody asked the question, what organizations should we support? What things should we do? Tell us as we leave this room where we should go. My answer was, I don't know, because I don't know your circumstance. So, I may tell you that the place for you to go is the PTA, but you may not have a child in school. I may tell you that the place for you to go is to your homeowner's association, but you may not have a home. You may live in an apartment, or you may live in a box. To your point, Steve...you can do something, get off of the bench, and get in the game. It's amazing how what you deem to be a little thing – an hour, two hours, or three hours in a week – can have a tremendous amount of impact. You wind up touching people you didn't even realize you were touching until one day you're walking down through a mall, and you see some little kid that comes up to you and says, "Hey, you were in our school. Thank you." You're like, "Who is this kid?" Never even saw them in the hallway, but it made an impact.

So, the solutions. What are the solutions? Well, the solutions are for some of y'all to figure out based upon your circumstance. Towanna?

Dr. Towanna Freeman:

It looks a little something like this. Everyone in this room, how many of you are small business owners? Alright. So every last one of you who are small business owners have a passion for delivering a service or a product to the community for goods and exchange, right? For dollars. You did that based on the fact that you saw a need, and you wanted to fulfill that need, right? You saw an issue. You wanted to address it. The same works in a community. If there is something that you see that resonates with you, a problem that absolutely drives you crazy every time you see it, something that pisses you off that you wish you could get in arm's reach to, those are the things you are called to address.

One of the things that I'm very good at doing as a life coach and as a business strategist is helping people understand how to fine tune those things. So in this room, if you're a small business owner you know how to apply that. If you are a productive citizen, and...you're an educator and you're always giving [but] so tired of giving, you need to take a break. Take a time out. [When] you're giving, giving, giving [and] you're not seeing results in that situation you need to separate yourself from the outcome. If you are not getting results in the thing that you are actively participating in and driving...you're in the wrong stream. You need to be getting results...If you have a child in a school, Dr. Perry, and your child is not producing...based on report cards, interims, all that kind of stuff, you see that something is wrong. It's broken. You actively go in, and you address it. Start at the top and work down. Start with the teachers and work up. Whatever, however it functions.

We're in the DMV: D.C., Maryland, Virginia. There are more non-profits in this area than I think there could be between here and the west coast. We have a ton of non-profits. We have lots of churches. We have tons of food banks. We can volunteer until we turn blue. It's not about volunteering anymore. It's about effective change by putting your hands into something that you know...For the people in this room, you know what it is that you can do. You know what it is that drives you crazy [and] that you want to address...Fine tune that, and get very specific. When I say specific I mean as simple as this: "I want to work with women ages 25 – 30 who are living in Hyattsville, Maryland, have kids, [and] whose parents are incarcerated." So specific. Identify your target. If you are a small business owner you know what that means. You identify the target market. The same thing with volunteering. You absolutely have to know the color of the hair of what it is that you're trying to do. If you can't tell me who you are trying to help, don't go out here making a mess, because you're going to make it hard for me.

Don't go out here and start stirring up stuff trying to do a little over here and a little over there. You're making a mess. It's like when you're in the kitchen cooking, "Honey, I did not ask you to boil the water, and go over here, and start this, and do all that. You done messed up the whole kitchen. The dinner's going to be off." I need you to stay in your lane. Basically, [if] you don't know how to cook, get out the kitchen. So, identify what it is that you're good at. That's what you have to do. That's real. Talk with yourself...even with the people that you care about [and] who know what your best skills are. Have that conversation, get very specific, and take action. Or call. Call me. Email me. I'll help you.

Dr. Wilmer Leon:

And, too, find a friend. Find someone that has a similar concern or a similar interest as you do.

Dr. Towanna Freeman:

Right.

Dr. Wilmer Leon:

And the two or three of you in your community, put your arms around. And how many of y'all have one of these? I think they're called smartphones, right? Well use your smartphone to make you smarter. Stop sending me all of this crap, emails, and all of this foolishness and silliness. Start sending some people some information that they can actually use to improve their circumstance. You know, prayers are great. Can't go nowhere without them. But, if that's all you're sending me on this so-called smartphone...You can communicate with China. You have the ability, with this thing in your hand, to impact the world through *Facebook* and other social medial. Too many of us are just using it for foolishness.

Dr. Boyce Watkins:

I want to add to that point. I think that what I [have] found through talking with a lot of my friends over time is it seems to me the plantation analogy is appropriate. I think a lot of us have a life that we are trying to escape from, right? If you think about the structure of a life, there are pretty much two decisions that you make that are the most important. One is what you do for a living. The other is who you spend your life with: relationships, marriage, all that stuff. Everything else is kind of a blur, right?

I remember when I was trying to escape my life, what I considered to be my plantation. I felt like I was in a situation where I wasn't fulfilling my purpose, and I wanted to do other things. I saw great people doing amazing stuff, like the Steve Perrys of the world. I always looked up to Cornel West, Michael Eric Dyson, and Julianne Malveaux. Those are three of my greatest heroes of all time. I love them to death. I didn't know how to get there. There's a simple idea that basically says no matter how far the distance is, if you take baby steps every single day and consistently move there's no distance you can't travel. If you took three steps every day and went west, you'd eventually hit the west coast. Now, walking to California doesn't seem possible. It seems so far away. There are so many things that might distract you along the way, but the truth is, fundamentally, if you take those three steps every day [and] move forward, you'll get there.

The way I started off, nobody believed in anything I was doing. Nobody listened to me. Nobody let me do any of the stuff I get to do now. I kept a little spreadsheet, and I literally would give myself a point every time I did any little thing that moved me toward my goal. My promise to myself was not that I was going to succeed, because I knew I was going to fail. I didn't know what was going to happen. My promise was [that] I was just going to be consistent. I was going to do five things every day that was going to get me a little closer to my goal. And so, I did that every single day, week after week, month after month, year after year. Then one day I woke up and looked back six months earlier and said, "Wow, look at how far I've come just by being consistent." When you talk about finding your purpose in life and taking action to get to that life, that's what this is about. This is not just talk. This is about action. This is de-centralized black leadership.

Everybody in here is a leader of something, someone, or some space. When you talk about taking that action to move to the life you want to move to, to get off your plantation, just be consistent. Take those baby steps and go back to what we know as black folks which is, faith. Faith says that if you believe, continue to move forward, and don't stop you will eventually get somewhere that you're meant to be. That's my two cents. Whatever you do, don't sit still.

Dr. Wilmer Leon:

I have a two-part question here. Dr. Freeman, I'm going to start with you. I know, Boyce, this is an issue for you, as well. A growing number of girls suffer from low self-esteem. How can parents help establish a sense of self-worth within our girls? The second part is what advice can you offer a single mother raising black children in 2013? Go ahead.

Etan Thomas:

Well I think...You wanna start?

Dr. Wilmer Leon:

No, you go ahead.

Etan Thomas:

Okay, okay. Well number one for our black girls, we have to tell them how special they are from a young age. They are going to hear all the negativity, as with our young men, as they grow older. We have to be real with our young people. Let them know that they are in a system that is set up for them to fail, and that's the honest truth. I go, and I speak at schools. I've loved to do that since I was in college. The schools look like baby prisons, like you said. I be honest with them. "Listen, you are not getting the same education as the kids in the suburbs. I don't want you to think that you are, so you have to work twice as hard. You have to [work] twice as hard to get half of what they're getting. You don't have any time for any foolishness. Know that you deserve this even though that's not what you're getting. You have to expect more. You have to go the extra mile."

We've got to be real with them. We have to tell them how special they are and how much they deserve more than what they're getting...It's great to talk about fatherhood from the impact of what should happen, but we have to deal with what is happening at the same time. The fact is, there are a lot of young people, myself included when I was growing up, who were raised by a single mother. My single mother is right over there. She's down here for Thanksgiving. Put your hand up, mama. Alright, she's down here for Thanksgiving. That's my single mama.

We have to tell them that it's going to be alright. That you can do it. It's not going to be easy. We don't have to discourage them. It's interesting, because you're dealing with a battle. There are some women who say, "I don't need a man for anything." Then, there are some women who will admit they do need a man for some things, so they can't do anything. It's like two extremes. When I was growing [up], there were so many guys I [knew] that should have been in the NBA before me. I can say that very easily. You know what I mean? They made bad choices and bad decisions. Any professional athlete can tell you that. They go back to their home. They can name 10 to 15 guys, spin them off the top of their head, that should have been there before them, right? Somewhere along the line they made one bad decision, and it changed their entire life.

We have to tell young people that one bad decision can really change your entire life. Everybody in prison is not just a horrible person. That's not what it is. I work with the young guys. A lot of times they're scared little kids who didn't get enough attention from their fathers. They didn't get enough love at home, and you know what? We have to tell them, "Listen, when you get in front of the judge, the judge don't care if you didn't get enough hugs from your daddy. They don't care at all." They're trying to send our kids to jail at a faster rate. This is a game that you can't play, because you're not going to win. You're not. There are sets of rules for this group. There are sets of rules for you. You do this crime?

This is what's going to happen to you. We have to be completely honest with them, and let them know that they deserve better than that. It hurts me when I talk to young people, deal with them, and they don't know that. Nobody has told them that they are special.

That's one thing that we have to do, because everything that they're being told [says] they're terrible – that they're negative. The women ain't nothing but sexual objects. The young girls get over-sexualized. It's so interesting. I love Hip-Hop. I always loved Hip-Hop. You know what I mean? When you get a little older you start looking at it a little differently. You know what I mean? When you got little daughters you're like, "What the hell is this they playing on BET?" You know what I mean? You just look at it differently. You look at the videos and what's being shown is nothing but poison in every aspect. Then you gotta look at who is at the top of those record companies. Who are the people putting that on the station day after day, record after record? Who is the one doing it? And, why are they doing it? You know what I mean?

They ain't putting images of themselves out there like that. They wouldn't do that, but they're going to put images of us out there like that. We have to ask them why. Why do they want our young people to look at themselves so negatively? You know what I mean? Why are they trying to promote nothing but a negative culture to them? We have to tell them that this is happening, because if they don't know, they're going along singing lyrics to terrible songs and letting it influence their lives. They're going down a certain path that's going to take them on a pathway right to prison. That's what they want.

I tell them, "This is where they want you to end up, so they can put you on their walls saying, 'Look, we're going to keep your streets safe by putting all these people,' that look like us, 'in prison.'" That's what's going to happen. You have to be real with them, and let them know you can't sugar coat anything. It's not about blaming the victim. You can fall into the holes that have been dug for you. These holes have been dug for a long time. Many people have paid the price for you to get around these holes, but you have to know the holes are there, or you're going to fall right into them. So that's what we have to do with our young people. We gotta let them know that they deserve more than what they're getting. Then they'll expect more out of life.

Dr. Wilmer Leon:

You know, one thing about establishing a sense of self-worth within our girls...As the father of a son, I have to be sure that my son understands the self-worth of women and the self-worth of the girls in his class. Because we can't just look at it...Whatever you do on the left side of the equation, you have to do on the right side of the equation, or the equation isn't balanced. As we focus on self-esteem issues with young girls, we also have to be sure, as men, that we are instilling in our sons how they are supposed to treat the women in their lives.

Real quick story. My son's class had a PE test where they had to run around the track in a certain amount of time. He came home, and he said, "Daddy, there was this one girl in the class, she was kind of big and slow. She didn't make it and pass the test." I asked him if he passed the test, and he said yes. I said, "Well then, the next time you have PE why don't you run with her? Why don't you do whatever you can do to see to it that she at least makes the minimum standard." So, he came home the next week, and he said, "Daddy, I did it, and she got through"...I said, "Well, see to it that you stick with her, and when you see her falling short you do whatever you can do to move her forward." Those are the kinds of little things, as fathers, we have to instill in our sons. James.

Janks Morton:

I think I'm in agreement with both sides of this. The acknowledgement, affirmation, uplifting, and elevation of our sisters. I get that. About three years ago I went on this beautiful journey with black women. I was like Teddy Pendergrass. It would be me and 500 women in a room. It was the craziest thing I ever did. I did a movie. I'm sorry. I did a movie. It was called *Dear Daddy*. I wouldn't let men come in, because, ladies, y'all know how we can mess stuff up sometimes, right? Because we do. I think the most important thing that I learned...What we need to do for our sisters right now is, give them a safe space to decompress first. The average young lady, woman, mother, or grandmother who has grown up with father absence...Your daddy was not there the right way. Y'all ladies know what I'm talking about. He could have died, been a deadbeat, or been with the lady down the street. It doesn't matter. You were the little girl whose daddy did not validate you in the right way.

The thing that broke my heart...It took me a long time to get this. Women have not been given a safe space to talk about what that means to them. Have you ever told someone, "My father was not in my life, and this is how I think it affected me. This is how I think my feelings...This is how I navigate and negotiate relationships. This is how I don't even get along with my co-worker because of my father not being there"? Then we can go into the validation, acknowledgement, affirmation, all of that. I think women truly, truly need to begin to...When I say de-compartmentalize, it's almost a mal-adaptive coping mechanism. You have the ability to take that trauma and put it in a little gift box. Then, you put it in the closet of your mind somewhere. What you don't realize is at the most inopportune time it comes out and tears your life apart.

So, for our sisters, to answer the question, the first step in this healing ... This is how I learned that...I talk to young boys about how you're supposed to treat girls. I'm not even worried about that anymore. If I have a woman who is actualized, validated, knows herself, and has healed, that little boy has no room to navigate at all. He can be the biggest fool you ever want to be. If a girl and a woman knows who she is, I'm not worried about him. I think that conversation that we used to have about young boys and respect your women, and all that. It's kind of okay, but if you heal a woman she has no desire to watch *Scandal*.

Dr. Towanna Freeman:

What's that got to do with it? What?

Janks Morton:

Her soul and her mind-

Etan Thomas:

You had them with you. They was with you.

Janks Morton:

I was checking to see if y'all were awake. No, but I really, really will say this though. There are things that you will not allow into your soul, because you know that it is no good for you. So yeah-

Dr. Wilmer Leon:

This is where you stop.

Janks Morton:

Okay, I'm gonna leave it alone. Let's back up. I'll give you [an] example. She'll have no desire to pursue *Real Housewives*. That's easy. No, I mean *Scandal*. I'm gonna leave it there.

Dr. Wilmer Leon:

Yes, go ahead.

Dr. Steve Perry:

Alright. First, I want to point out that I am a normal sized human being. It's just that I'm next to...I felt compelled to point that out. So when you say, "I saw you on TV. You look bigger." I am. Thanks.

Etan Thomas:

Ain't nobody think of that, though.

Dr. Steve Perry:

I was. All night.

Etan Thomas:

Okay.

Dr. Steve Perry:

That's number one. Number two, I think it's important to understand that up to about 10 years old, both boys and girls have pretty high self-esteem. If you see a little girl, she just thinks she's the finest thing she ever met. Somewhere around 10 or 11, things start to fall apart. This is where we, again...actionable steps. This is where we have to step in as the adults. We have to rally around these young ladies that think they're "too." They're too light. They're too dark. They're too fat. They're too thin. This is too big. This is too small. All the "toos." I wish I'd known that y'all have so many insecurities. I wouldn't have worked so hard.

Janks Morton:

He's talking about his single days, ladies.

Dr. Steve Perry:

That's exactly what I'm talking about. The point is this is where we, the adults, can step in and create these support networks for these children as they go through this space. A lot of y'all are still dealing with some seventh grade stuff. Somebody said something about you, and you're still thinking about it. It done burned you up. Well, somewhere in there...This is where we as adults, not just the parents...can create meaningful structures whether it be sororities or some other groups. Go into the schools and work with young ladies around this area. Or, it [can] be you going in and working with some young ladies and helping them go through that. Or later on in life. Going with the women who are still dealing with the seventh grade stuff.

We can create structures that build up people in such a way that they can feel good when they don't really feel good. We all go through that same thing. Similarly with young men. Ours is a different time. It doesn't happen with us the same way. It happens a little later when we start to doubt certain things about ourselves and wonder if all the things that the guy is saying he did with the girl, he really did. You're like, "Wow, an hour?" So, our insecurities are in a different space, but they're there nonetheless. This is where men can jump up and say, "Hey, he's lying." For real, I hope. We can create a space where this level of communication can occur. Believe it or not, sometimes this communication is easiest when it's not with your parent. This is actually where you get to be the auntie or the uncle or the cousin. This is where you get to play a meaningful role in children's lives, the most meaningful.

Sometimes the daughter or the son is more willing to tell somebody other than their mother about what they're going through. So if you're looking for something to do, help bolster young people's self-esteem and – at the backend –the adult self-esteem. There are so many women and men making decisions, because they're trying to get rid of this low self-esteem. They're with somebody, because he or she just said that they were pretty. That's pretty much the whole story. [If you ask], "What do you like about him?" [You may very well hear], "He likes me." End of story.

When we can be there in a more meaningful way...This is the last part about this. As a black community, one of the things that we do really poorly is emote. Really. We have a tough time communicating our emotions. It's always over the top. Right? Your grandfather doesn't speak at all. The brother just doesn't speak at all, and your grandmother will not shut up. We don't have a middle. We haven't found the ways to function within our emotional sweet spot. These are the things that we can help one another through and help people understand. Yeah, sometimes you feel some kind of way, and you can work through that. Whether it's young or old. Each one of us still has this need to feel like we belong to somebody. That's where the whole abandonment thing starts and ends. We can make our community feel like they belong to somebody.

The last thing is, so many of us walk past each other like we weren't taught. You know when you see a black person you're supposed to say something. You know damn well you supposed to say something. If you don't know he's black. He looks kind of fair, and he's got glasses on. You could give him something. This all, believe it or not, adds to our overall self-esteem. You feel some kind of way. Somebody hits you. Nothing expensive about a compliment. We can do better. Large and small, we can do better. We can do better than this. If nothing else, we can do better.

Dr. Towanna Freeman:

I'm going to...may I?

Dr. Wilmer Leon:

I've been waiting for you.

Dr. Towanna Freeman:

Boy, I tell ya, I wanna get some...the two young people that came with you? Where are they? Okay, I need you two to stand up for me. Okay, I want the audience to turn around and look at these two back here. Okay. There's my daughter against the wall behind that camera. Any more teens, teenagers, high school age? Stand up, please. Teen, stand up. Oh, there you go. Where you at? Okay. Alright, this is how we step outside of our comfort zones. This is how we...Thank you, young lady back there, for standing up. I appreciate you for that. This is how we do it. Every adult in the room, please clap your hands for these young people. Let them know that coming out here tonight means something. Now did that cost y'all any money? Did it hurt at all? Young people, I want to thank you for taking time out of your evening for coming out here and being a part of this forum. Because of what you've done tonight, you don't know it now, but you will not forget this night in years to come. Why? Because we took the time to single you out in this crowd to let you know that we appreciate you for taking the time to be here tonight. Now y'all can have your seats.

When we talk about actionable steps and what we walk away with, that is how we do it. That's how you step out of yourself and say, "You know what? I see someone that looks like me, and they matter." It doesn't hurt. We've given to them something that they could not pay for. And so, we look at validating each other. When Obama was elected, we were some happy black folk. Truth be told, when we walked down the street we were speaking to each other, because we were so happy about being black...Come on now! Weren't y'all happy about being black after Obama-

Dr. Steve Perry:

They even said hi to me.

Dr. Towanna Freeman:

At the end of the day we were, "Hey, how you doing? How you doing? How you doing?" Smiling. Then Obama gets in trouble, and we be like, "I don't want to be black no more." Y'all start hiding again. But the deal is, look. There has to be a sense of pride. The days of being proud about being black, today. Today. I am so proud of the people that are in this room that look like me. I am so proud to see you all here. I have a teenage daughter and a three-year-old son. I know. But at the end of the day, she's about to graduate high school, and I'm starting all over again. Y'all pray for me. I know.

But at the end of the day, my investment of my time, everything I gave to her, I have to recycle and now frame it for a young man that I'm raising in this world. Every day I show up for him. Every day. As a strong, black woman. Loving. Caring. I can't teach him how to be a man, but I'm going to love him and give him everything a mama needs to give a son. Let him know what it means to love and to show love and respect.

But let's say I did not have a husband around to be a part of his life. Then I would be knocking on doors of these gentlemen and letting them know that they have a responsibility to see into the life of my son. To ensure that he is a productive citizen in the United States. To ensure that he takes pride in being a man in this world. I will hold them accountable to make sure that they do something. Whether it's five minutes or three minutes. When they stood up and we applauded, give them an applause. It didn't take much, but I will hold them accountable just like I will hold you all accountable. If you see him cutting up, say something. I didn't say get in his face. I said say something to me. Let me know. Let me know what I can do differently. If I'm not doing something right, tell me.

We have to be open to doing something different, changing patterns, changing our parenting styles, [or] getting some help. Why is it that we have insurance before...obviously with the state of Obamacare and everything else. Why is it that before we all had options we would not exercise the option of getting counseling and therapy? Why are we so afraid to let other people see us in lack or in loss? Why do we care so much about what other people think or perceive about us? So much so that you will walk around with some type of mental health issue or hurting pain and will not seek help for it. You don't love yourself enough to go get help? You love somebody else's opinion of you so much so that you want to suffer? Those days have to go. We see every day on the news people who are committing suicide or taking other people's lives because of mental health issues. Doing things that just...Literally, there is a prescription for that. I'll get my soapbox.

Janks Morton:

Can I give a quick-

Dr. Wilmer Leon:

Let me say this before you do. First of all, thank you all. We're at the point now where we've got to wrap this up. And so what I want is just to let y'all know, I saw hands. We were taking questions from your RSVPs, so we could maintain some flow and control. With that, I'm going to ask each of you...We'll start with James since you wanted to weigh in. We're going to ask each of you, about three minutes, to wrap up.

Janks Morton:

So, the thing that kind of got me. My background is from healthcare. I hate crutches, but we talk about mal-adaptive social coping mechanisms. Basically, they have their lineage in slavery. I'm listening to you talk about mental health issues. Well, you know, we could never get the perception of...It was a weakness to ask for help anywhere. You're absolutely right. We are so past that right now, but we may have to reframe what that is. We are a hurt, broken, and shorted people throughout our experience in this country, and we are carrying some baggage.

I just had this conversation with my wife. I want to be the first in the history of my family to be able to say [that] when my son walks across the stage to graduate high school, I never laid a hand on him. Never. Now I'll talk them to death. My goddaughter's right back there – the one in them stripes. She know I run my mouth, but I will talk to you, credited. But if you don't understand our...and I'm a Kappa, too. If you do not understand the lineage of slavery, corporal punishment, and hazing. And I got scars...My father played pro football. I got the scars to prove it...The burden that we have carried as a people since our experience and how it affects us today. These scars that we are carrying. The first step I believe we need to take is taking the life away from the thing that has hurt us by giving a voice to it.

We don't talk about nothing. We don't say nothing. It is a crazy statistic that, I mean...I'm doing a movie on it right now. Like one out of four women in this room right now have been molested...The scarier part is that you've never told anybody. You never sat down and talked even with your own mother, sister, best friend, preacher, pastor, or therapist. No one. So, you take in that lineage of that trauma, because the slave master molested. You don't see it. I'm talking crazy. I got a bunch of lost hives. Do you understand where this stuff comes from?

Then as we begin to construct...what it means to be black, that this lineage has its negative connotations that are not authentically black. They're more Scott Irish, cracker white, the things of alcoholism, poverty, molestation, incest, abuse. That's not us. It's them. And I refuse to...I will continue to be the crazy one. I refuse to put that tag. We ain't losing. We might be having some challenges. We're not a group of losers. We are not a group of inadequates. We are not a group of less-ness. We are the greatest creation God has ever been put on this entire planet. Period.

I'll leave you with this. This is what I tell my kids. I teach at a charter school. Think of it in these confines. I started with the lineage of slavery. What if we as a people begin to embrace what we were sent here to do as opposed to what we have been brought here to do? When you understand that. That it was slaves all over the place. It was native American here. Why did they cross back over the water and go get us? Why? Then you'll understand that this position through stereotypes, through poor systems, through whatever it is, has been put in place to keep people permanently subjugated in this artificial construct of a larger white supremacy IDIA law. When you begin to fight it with everything that you have, you will never call black people losers again. Ever.

Dr. Wilmer Leon:

Steve.

Dr. Steve Perry:

One of the most important things we can do is give our children a great education. It is the most important thing, because so much comes from it, and we as a community, need to become more sophisticated in our understanding of the conversation around school choice. Very often you hear people fighting for schools to remain open not realizing that you can't call a school that doesn't educate, a school. Simply because people work there and it's got "school" in its name doesn't mean that it's a school. The data says otherwise. Too many of our children are going to buildings that are good places for bomb shelter or [being] a voting booth, but not [good] for your children. How do you know that? The people working in those (buildings) don't send their kids there. If it's not good enough for your kids it's not good enough for mine. We need to become more sophisticated in our understanding of what school choice is and isn't. We also need to become more sophisticated in our understanding of who is and is not working for our children.

Teacher unions are not working for your children. Period. The more they fight to maintain the status quo – i.e. failure, the achievement gap, high expulsion, suspension, and punishment rates for African-American boys – the more they're fighting against our community.

The same is true of people who were heading up once proud organizations like the NAACP who support many of those same zip code discrimination policies. They suggest very strongly that you should go to school where you live. When that was suggested back in 1954 it was found to be unconstitutional, because it was inherently racist and therefore unequal.

So when I say we need to become more sophisticated in our understanding, what I mean is that all children deserve access to a quality education no matter where they live. If the school at the bottom of their street does not produce a quality education that the people who work in it will use...your child should not have to go to it. You cannot be bamboozled by terms such as privatization and incorporation, because the United Way is a private corporation. Boys and Girls Club is a private corporation. This college is a private corporation. Just because it says private doesn't mean it's bad. Just because it says public doesn't mean it's good. Good is good, and bad is bad. The conversation that we as a people have to start being more astute on is...school choice. School choice simply means this. You will get to decide where your child goes to school. Period. That you shouldn't have to win a lottery in the United States of America to get access to a quality education. You shouldn't have to have money when the money was set aside for you. You believe in vouchers. Let me tell you how I know. Because you believe in financial aid, live on Medicaid, Medicare, believe in Section 8, food stamps, all the things that are vouchers. Private money, I mean public money, used for, in some cases, private goods and services.

When you're for school choice what you're for, ultimately, is the opportunity for a child to go to a quality school. Just because it's a charter doesn't mean it's quality. Just because it's a local neighborhood school doesn't mean it's failed, but failed is failed. Every single time we fight to keep a failed school open we hurt hundreds if not thousands of children. We can do all that we wish to do to build our kids' self-esteem, but they get to a fine institution like this and have to take a bunch of remedial courses, because the diploma they have doesn't mean a damn thing. Then, they drop out, and they stop out, and they never come back.

I'm telling you that in all that we do, if we do not ensure and fight – and I mean fight. Get out there and be part of the political process. Be on a board of education. Support candidates who are going to push forward a progressive agenda. If you don't do that, every other thing that you do will fall apart. Nothing. No community, not even post slavery black America, is going to move forward without education. Some of the first institutions that we opened were colleges. That's in our history. That's in our present.

You have to fight for school choice. You have to fight to have a better understanding of it. You have to stop looking at who used to be on our side. Who's on our side? Look at the purpose. If a school is not educating to grade level the majority of its children, it's not a school. It's not because the kids are poor. Every black kid ain't poor. Every Latino kid is not poor. We keep hearing that. We keep buying. So as I close as your educator here, specifically I'm asking you – begging you – please educate yourselves on this conversation around school choice. Our children need a choice right now in the same way people with means have choices. You shouldn't have to win a lottery or be wealthy to have a good school in the United States of America. You don't.

Etan Thomas:

I think that is great, what he said, and he's the educator. What I try to do is attack the problem and the issue from a standpoint of motivating young kids' minds, spirits, and hearts. You know, I was that young kid that didn't talk about anything. You know what I mean? I kept everything inside. So when I work with young kids who also keep everything inside and don't talk about anything, I know where they're coming from. You know what I mean? The therapist's way didn't work for me. I wouldn't have done that. That wouldn't have been my method of doing things. What I did was write, so I wrote. I wrote poetry. Wrote spoken word. Got my frustrations out that way. So, I have young people start writing what they feel. When you see some of the things that come out of them, it's amazing that they're walking around with all of this anger inside of them and no way to release it until one day it just explodes.

I want to show [youth] different people who were dealing with situations that might have been worse than [what] they're dealing with. [It's important for our youth to see that those people] were still able to be successful in life and didn't let those situations ruin them. So, I'll show them people like Kevin Durant. Everybody here, you know, they know Kevin Durant. Young people know him, because he grew up here...Young people can identify with people they recognize. The issue is that they're always being shown the negative aspects of the people they recognize. We have to start showing them positive, and that's where we need like what Dr. Watkins is doing with his public spaces.

We need other people to recreate the story and reshape us in the eyes of our young people. It's so important, because then you see them going through a situation where they don't know how special they are.

They're not getting the love they need from home. They start turning towards things as gangs. Now when I grew up. I told you I had so many young people that I grew up with that went in that direction. Not because they were evil little kids. The gangs became their family. You know what I mean? The OGs were like their father figures. The guys were like their brothers. That's why they were willing to die for each other, because it was like dying for family – not just dying for a color. It's something that they really took to heart.

When you talked about how you would be knocking on our doors and holding us accountable, that's what my mother did. My mother saw a connection that I had with an AU coach who's also a pastor. She drove clear across town to make sure that I had a connection with him. His name was Reverend Potter. My mom wasn't even Baptist. She was never Baptist, you know what I mean? But she saw the connection. She saw the importance of what I needed. I needed that. If it hadn't been for Reverend Potter, there were so many different directions I could have gone in just because I was a young person who was angry at not having his father there as much as I wanted him to be. If you don't know what that feels like, you can't even understand how some of these young people feel. You know what I mean? If you have a big event, say a basketball game or graduation, and other people have their fathers there, but your father's not there? You have no idea what that feels like.

A young person told me I could tell his story. It was so amazing to me that he was right here in PG correctional facilities. I work a lot in prisons. He said that he, you know, was in school and the teacher walked by [wearing] the same cologne that his father used to wear. He snapped. He was like, "Etan, the next thing I knew I was on top of him beating his face in. That's why I'm here." But there's so many. There's case after case, situation after situation, and I can tell you stories like that of our young people dealing with anger inside of them. We got to give them different ways to deal with it. You know what I mean? Different ways that are positive. They cannot let it ruin their lives, because it's there. We can't act like it's not there.

Some young people are going to need some counseling. Some people are going to need some writing. Some people are going to need to have a mentor reach out to them to let them know that they understand how they're feeling. That's why I kept going back to the point of we can't be afraid of our own young people, because they need us. That's the honest truth. They need us, and we're afraid of them. They're going to go to all the wrong people and then we're going to really lose them. There's nothing worse than seeing a group of scared young babies 14, 15, 16 years old in orange suits. You know what I mean? Locked up with their wrists bound together, so they can't move while they're sitting there listening to you. That's a terrible sight to see. When they're talking they start crying, because all the tough ones, you know. They can be as tough as they want to be. The tears come real quick, real quick once they start talking about their real issues. You see that they're not tough guys. They're little kids that needed guidance. All they needed was somebody to talk to.

As everybody is fighting in different ways...we could all just kind of work together. We need to be able to encourage them from the beginning, or they're going off the wrong path, because everything is set up for them to fail. Some of the schools that I've spoken at...it hurts my heart. I'm like, ain't nobody learning in here. This is terrible. Forty kids in the class. It's hot. The air conditioner don't work. The heat don't work. The teachers are all frustrated and then you're going to get them the same standardized tests that you give the kids in the suburbs? With 13 kids in the class, the teacher's aide, and they all got iPads? It's not fair. It's not a fair setup, and then they're going to say, "Well see this test. Their test scores aren't the same. That's why we don't need a private ration in colleges, and that's why we don't need to lower our standards" and all that stuff. That's the setup. You know what I mean? Then they're on a path right to the prison pipeline. That's where I come in. The reason I'm so passionate about it is because I'm tired of seeing it. I'm seeing it way too much.

I've seen it all my life. I've seen it growing up. Talking about different guys that I grew up with, they're all terrible stories. They're dead or in jail or something terrible, and it doesn't have to be that way. No matter what negative statistic they say like, "You come from a single parent household," you don't have to go in that route. As a single mother, you can raise successful children. You can do it, because there are too many examples of people who have done it and are successful. President Obama was raised by a single parent. You know what I mean? I could go down the list of people who were able to do it. It doesn't mean it's going to be easy. Nobody said anything about being easy. There are gonna be a lot of challenges. There are gonna be a lot of things that are going to be tough, because sometimes mama got to be mama and daddy. Sometimes she got to be the disciplinarian and the one that gives you the extra hugs. It's hard when 60% or whatever of households in our community are growing up by a single parent household. It's hard. I'm not going to say it's not hard, but it can be done. We have to just keep encouraging.

Dr. Wilmer Leon:

Towanna.

Dr. Towanna Freeman:

So, I was thinking about what I had not said that could kind of add two more actionable steps, and you know, kind of dovetail some things that these gentlemen have articulated before Boyce speaks. One of the things that I would encourage each and every one of you to do is take full advantage of the follow-ups that these forums present to you. So if you see in your email or see any announcements that say, "Hey, in the local area, this event is coming up to discuss how to do something," take full advantage of that. I would put it in your mind right now before you walk out of this room that you will invest in yourself, so you can now develop the story you want to tell in the community where you can make and affect change. Alight? That's the first thing.

The second thing I would like you all to do is go and research some of the best books that you can possibly find that speak to the heart of our children. Books that are authored by men like the individuals on this panel. Books that are written by women. Hill Harper has books: *Letters to a Young Sister* and *Letters to a Young Brother*. There are plenty of people in our community who have well written books that you can purchase. What do you do with the book? You write a note in the book, [and] address it to an unknown youth. Tell a quick little note, "This is a gift to you, because I believe in you." Something simple. Have some of those handy.

The reason why I say that is because every now and then you're going to run into somebody that's going to need something. They may take the book, [and] look [at you] like you're crazy. They may just put it somewhere in their room underneath a pile of clothes that they never bring out until it's time to pack up and or when they're in trouble. You never know where that seed is going to show up. So, I would encourage you all to do some research. Find some books. Get some books together. Write a little note, and be prepared to pass out those books, and plant those messages into them. You can't say everything that's in those pages within five minutes of meeting them. You can't articulate what you really want to seed into them in those few seconds, so let someone else who has taken the time to do that work do it for you. So, you purchase the book, make a note, and give it to them. Those are two actionable steps. Thank you.

Dr. Wilmer Leon:

Before we go to Boyce to close, I will say as I started, *12 years a Slave*. Hell of a movie. All of us need to see that and read the book. Solomon Northrup was born 205 years ago. After you see that movie, after you read that book, when you're in the car going back home, think about the fact you're in a car going back home. When you look at what that brother went through, what our ancestors went through, when you get to your home, sit back for a moment and think about yourself and where you are today. With that, you will truly start to appreciate that we are a strong, resourceful, powerful people.

The other point is our politics have to mature. We struggled to get the vote and now we have that ability, but our politics now have to mature. We have to move away from the politics of pigment and the politics of personality and start focusing on the politics of policy. It's all about outcome. It's all about educational policy. It's all about healthcare policy. It's all about social services policy. It's all about small business access to capital and seed money policy. If we stay stuck on the pigment and if we stay stuck on the personality, we're going to stay stuck.

Dr. Boyce Watkins:

Well first, I want to say thank you once again for coming out here. I really mean that from the bottom of my heart. What I think we might want to do...I'm not in the business to tell anybody what to do, but this is my two cents. Understand that this, number one, is not a one-time event. This is not just a powwow, just a conversation. This is something that is permanent. We're in the trenches together. This is going to be a marathon, not a sprint. We know that. When I think about my life and I'm thinking about what I'm trying to do with this little time I have on this planet, I try not to think about the year 2013. I try to think about the year 2053, 40 years down the road.

What are we doing today that is building the world that our children will grow up in? Now we know, for example, if you are a single parent, you can do it. We know if your schools are broken, you can do it. We know that if there are no job opportunities, you can do it, but are we laying the same landscape for our children when they're reaching adulthood and trying to overcome their struggles in life? Do we just expect the next generation of mothers to be single mothers, or do we raise better boys to learn how to be better fathers and women that know how to keep a family together with a good man? Are we going to move forward in such a way that we understand this is not about us? This is about people down the line who are not yet born. If it were not for people in the past doing things that they did, we would not be who we are where we are right now.

So, [there are] a couple of very tangible things I want you to carry away. Number one, when you talk about freedom in America and you talk about equality, you cannot talk about equality without talking about overcoming the oppression the capitalist system has put upon us. Every year Black Friday comes. We get all our money, [and] we give all our money right back to the companies that don't want to give us any jobs. Again, mental illness.

When I talk about economic empowerment, I can lay something out for you very simple. It's four letters: C-O-S-T. I talked about paying the cost for your freedom. Look at the word cost. "C" should stand for contribute. Again, I would hope that everybody in this room commits right now to giving a percentage of their income every month to some black organization other than their church. If we do not support our organizations nobody else will. Howard University, one of the best institutions in the country, is struggling financially, because we don't want to give them any money, but we will run right down to Walmart and give them $300 on stuff that we don't even need.

What does the "O" stand for? The "O" stands for ownership. You must own something. You must understand the difference between having money, having a good job, being rich, and being wealthy. We must build wealth. The act and the art of black institution building has been lost. Integration screwed us. I'm sorry, but it did...Black Wall Street and all these great black businesses and everything were prospering. They kept the money in the community. They owned the land on which they stood. It all got burned down. Now, we still have not yet recovered. So, teach the value and the importance of ownership. It doesn't matter if you're not working for the biggest, brightest, shiniest cooperation with the highest salary. There is pride in owning something that's yours that you can give to your children.

The "S" stands for saving and investing. We must build a culture that rotates around saving and investing – not borrowing and consuming. America as a country has an addiction to consumption. That's why Black Friday is so exciting. They've expanded it out to Cyber Monday. Then, they stretched it out to Cyber Week. They said, "These people are so stupid. We can just create spending holidays where they'll come and beg us to take their money." Don't buy into that. I'm a finance professor. That's what I do. I looked at the data. We're stupid when it comes to money. There's a reason why they don't teach financial literacy in school. They don't want you to understand how to keep your money.

"T" stands for target. Understand that your money is your power. Do not just give your power away. Target where you spend your money. Target black owned businesses. Target it with everything you've got. That is so important to the future of our community.

Next couple of quick points. Number one, I believe that every black child in America should be homeschooled even if you go to school somewhere else every day. When the child comes home during the weekends [and] the summer, that's when the real education begins. That's when that child should learn how to buy a home. That's when they should learn the fundamentals of black history. That's when that boy learns how to be a good husband and a good father. Those are the lessons that are taught by the primary teachers, which tend to be the mother and, I hope, the father. Call me old fashioned and stupid, but I do believe we should at least try to give our kids a daddy. At least try. If you can't do it, then that's fine. You work with what you got, but at least try. Even Etan's mother went to find role models for her son, so he could be the great man that he is right now, and I don't say that lightly. I consider Etan to be one of the greatest black men in

America. I'm not kidding when I say that. He's harnessing the power of the black athlete – many of whom have been puppetized, corporatetized, and emasculated – and he's taken that and taken us back to a time when athletes did things that actually mattered for the community.

Now, I'm going to finish on this quick point. When I was in Kentucky, somebody told me a great story about Simmons College. They said that the way Simmons College was founded was a group of ex-slaves got together. Now, this is right after slavery. You think we're broke now. They really didn't have no money. They pulled their money together, and they said, "We want to give something to our children, our grandchildren, [and] our great-grandchildren." So, they pulled their money together, and they created this campus. They didn't have any equipment, books, anything, any buildings, nothing, but they created this place of learning. They built this institution 150 years ago. Since that time they have educated thousands and thousands of black children.

Imagine what the world would have been like if those slaves had not understood their power. If they did not have the ability to see a vision greater than themselves. The ability to invest in something that wouldn't benefit them directly in their generation. Those kids wouldn't have been educated. So what I'm asking you today is this. I'm asking you to really harness the spirit of those individuals. Harness the spirit of the runaway slave and understand that we are in a scenario right now in our community where we have been obliterated. I agree with Steve that when you look at the data there's a lot of evidence to say that we're not winning the game right now. A lot of it goes back to mass incarceration, drugs, and all these other things that have happened which we can go into later, but we know that it has hurt our community. It's destroyed the integrity of our family, so we are in a rebuilding phase. We have to tap into the spirit of those slaves who built their raggedy institution 150 years ago and realize that we're here to build something that is going to benefit people who are not yet born. Hold onto that when you look around and everybody thinks you're crazy, because you believe in a better future for black America. It is possible. Let's go make it happen. Thank you very much.

Dr. Wilmer Leon:

Class is dismissed.

TRANSCRIPT

A NEW PARADIGM FOR BLACK AMERICA TOUR BROOKLYN, NEW YORK

Dr. Watkins:

First of all, I wanna say thank you so much for coming out. By the way, my name is Dr. Boyce Watkins. I am part of the Your Black World Coalition. We reached out to put together this event as kind of a clarion call to everybody in our community who still gives a damn. Basically, we reached out to Medgar Evers, such an amazing institution, and they were gracious enough to allow us to gather to talk about us. I'd be remiss not to give a sincere thanks to Dr. Byron Price who opened that door and made those connections. Without Dr. Price, this would not be happening. Also, thank you to the president, other individuals with the university who allowed us to come into this place, and the students who helped us as well.

Now, why are we here? I can't tell you exactly why each of you decided to come out. We all came for our own reasons, but I can give you an idea of the nature of the thinking that led to the creation of the event. This event was really created in the spirit of the runaway slave. Most of us, when we think about slavery, like to glamorize. We like to believe that if we were slaves 300 years ago, we'd be that runaway slave. We wouldn't tolerate that kind of abuse, right? We like to glamorize and believe that would be the case. However, most of us are probably lying. Most of us would have gone right along with the program. If you think about it, nobody really wanted to be the runaway slave.

The runaway slave didn't have any friends on the plantation. The runaway slave was the crazy one. That was the unrealistic one. That was the one that was gonna get everybody else in trouble. Also, we can't glamorize what happened when most slaves tried to run away. A lot of 'em got caught. That first runaway slave, when he ran off the plantation, got caught, and was brought back to the plantation all bloody – because they'd beat him to an inch of his life – had haters standing there saying, "I told you so. I told that Negro if he kept on talking crazy about trying to be free, this was gonna happen."

But, we also understand that the runaway slave was the greatest visionary on the plantation. They had this seemingly unrealistic idea that, somehow, all men and women are created equal and that all of us deserve to be free. The runaway slave had the ability to give to something greater than himself. The first runaway slave that got caught and was punished planted a seed of inspiration. It was that seed, that inspiration, that gave others the courage they needed when trying to find their way to freedom.

So, if you really think about it, you can't have the first black president without the first runaway slave. We have to understand that, to some extent, the task that lies in front of us is a depressing one. We're not here to do things for ourselves. We're here for our children, our grandchildren, and our grandchildren's grandchildren. We're here to fight for things that we cannot yet see. I hate to break it to you, but there's never gonna be a day in your lifetime or mine when we wake up and the sun is shining in the black community, and everything's just wonderful. We will not open the newspaper and not hear about a baby being shot. Somebody getting a 150-year prison sentence or something terrible happening in our community. We know that is gonna always be the case for many of us for a very long time.

But, just like that runaway slave, I encourage you to rely on your faith. To understand that sometimes you plant seeds. Sometimes you make investments in things that you won't see in your lifetime. Nonetheless, you have to be committed to that, because look at where we are as a community. Right now, we incarcerate more black men in America than South Africa did during the height of apartheid. If apartheid's considered to be the most racist regime in the history of the world, and we incarcerate more black men than they did during apartheid, then what does that say about America?

Today, in the newspaper, I read that there was a study that says that African Americans are worse off economically than any other ethnic group in America. There are communities where a black man has an easier time getting a gun than he has of getting an education. Black unemployment right now is 30% higher than it was during the March on Washington in 1963, so the goal of this gathering is really to realize that if we approach old problems with the same old solutions, we're going to get the same old results. Therefore, the idea of a new paradigm is to say that we need a new paradigm of thought. We need 21st century solutions to solve 21st century problems.

If we do not adjust our thinking, adjust our actions, and make that spiritual journey to dig deeper into finding out who we are, then we're gonna end up in a perpetual purgatory. We're gonna be like rats in a cage who are running on a wheel. Although the wheel's spinning and spinning and spinning we're not going anywhere. Now, my background, I'm a finance professor. I don't know why I chose to study money and finance. I guess I studied money, because I didn't have any money growing up. Perhaps I figured that if I studied and learned about money, somebody would pay me money to talk about money.

And so, I know capitalism pretty well. We live in a capitalist society. I know capitalism better than a man knows his ex-wife. One thing I know, also, about this country, is that when you run away from educational empowerment and when you run away from financial responsibility, you are running right towards slavery. That is just a fundamental fact. When you are living deep in debt, paycheck-to-paycheck, without your own business, without multiple streams of income, without your money right, then to some extent, you end up feeling like a slave every day. There's no group angrier in America right now than the black middle class: the people who have all the PhDs, JDs, MDs, and all these other degrees that make you feel like you're better than somebody else. Yet, they go to work and wonder, "Why do I hate my life?" Well, for many of us, we are enslaved by capitalism. Every time a situation calls for us to stand up, there's somebody right over top of us telling us, "Sit your black butt right down." That's exactly what you do. There's no greater amount of control that I can have over another man than for that man to know that I'm the reason his kids get to eat every day. Think about the sheer hilarity of relying on the descendants of your historical oppressors to get the things that you need. That does not make any sense. When you are addicted to a commodity that you do not control, you are giving away all of your power. In a relationship between a pusher and an addict, the addict never has any power. We have to think about that.

There are three quick concepts I'm going share with you. It is my hope that these concepts will help in your thinking as it pertains to achieving your individual empowerment as well as our collective empowerment. The first thing is that we have to pay the COST for our freedom. That is COST as in C-O-S-T. The acronym means something. "C" stands for contribute. Everyone should make it a point to contribute to some black institution outside of your church. If we do not build our institutions, nobody else will. Number two is own. Own something. You have to own something. You do not wanna be like Jay-Z and the Barclays Center where you own 1/15th of 1%. I am talking about really owning something. Own the land on which you stand. That is how you have power in America. Number three is save. Save and invest. We must embrace the idea of saving and investing. Unfortunately, too many of our kids get their brains poisoned by what they hear from their favorite rapper. They tell you that when you get money you are supposed to go to the club and "Make it rain, shorty." Throw your money in the air and go buy a pair of Air Yeezys and all this other stupid stuff. No, that's not going to empower you. You know that. Saving and investing our money must become a fundamental part of who we are. Number four is "T" which stands for target. That means your money is your power. When you spend your money, you must target your money. Target your money to black-owned institutions. Target your money to institutions that have value for the people that you care about.

The second concept I wanna leave you with is the idea that every black child in America should be homeschooled. Even if they go to school somewhere else there are valuable lessons they can learn at home, so that doesn't mean you yank 'em out of school and keep 'em home all day. It simply means that even if your children go to the public school down the street, you've got time for what we call extracurricular activities or extrication. Look at the word extra. Extra means in addition to. It means to extricate yourself from something. We must understand that the only thing worse than being uneducated is to be severely miseducated. So, when children have that extra time after school, weekends, and summertime, that is when they should be learning the basics of black history. That is when you have a list of all the things that every African

American should know, so they can have a sense of pride and dignity about their history. They can take pride in knowing where they come from. Their knowledge can go beyond believing that everything great done in the world was done by a white man. That's also the time when you might teach them the things they need to know in order to be a successful person in this world. Maybe that's also a great time for you to teach them how to buy a home. Teach them how to be a good spouse and parent. It's a good time to teach them all the things that they are not going to learn in school.

The third thing I wanna leave you with is that every black child in America should be taught the basics of entrepreneurship. That is learning how to cultivate his or her own business. Even if you work for somebody else, everybody should learn how to grow their own money the same way you learn how to grow your own food. Even if you have a job working for someone else, you should never get all of your money from one source. Then, you are pretty much vulnerable to that one source. Furthermore, we cannot depend on corporate America to give us the things we need. Considering the aforementioned, you should find a way to have a business on the side. Find ways to have multiple streams of income.

Entrepreneurship must be a part of who we are, because that is the root of black unemployment. If companies are looking to hire new employees, who are they gonna hire first? People they know or us? So, understand that when you talk about how we can succeed and thrive in this society, we have to remember this fundamental principle. It's a simple principle that comes from physics: force = mass x acceleration. That means that if I wanna have a lot of force, then I need two things: a lot of mass and I need that mass to accelerate. If I wanna move this podium I must use my force. I must accelerate. I must push. I must do all those things in order to make the podium move. Well, what is mass? Mass is all the stuff that we have that makes us feel like we are powerful. It might be your education. It might be your status. It might be your money. It might be all these things that you have that make you feel validated. They might be the things that make you feel successful. That's great. Congratulations. I'm glad you got it. However, understand that mass means nothing if you are afraid to accelerate. If you are a powerful, educated person and you have the ability to do all these things and you're doing nothing with that, then guess what? You will live, and you will die. The world will not care that you were ever here, because you will have left no impact on the world. So, again mass means nothing if you are afraid to accelerate. I have heard Dr. Wilmer

Leon say that when you talk about black leadership, black leadership does not start with Jesse and Al. Nor does black leadership start with the people you see on TV. Even as I am before you today I declare that black leadership does not start with the people you see on this panel. Be it known that black leadership starts in your living room. All of us are black leaders.

Now without further ado, I'm going to introduce somebody that I consider to be the most talented and most brilliant political scientist in the country. When Dr. Ron Walters died, he was the person that I started turning to for political advice and information on issues of importance in our community. Dr. Wilmer Leon.

Dr. Wilmer Leon:

Good afternoon, everyone. Thank you all for coming. As I thought about how I would kick this off, I decided to open this discussion the same way that I open my classes each semester at Howard. Each semester I open with a story. It is a story about a guy. Well, let me ask this. Any history majors out here? Any historians? Anybody ever heard of a guy named Dr. Ephraim Thaddeus Millage Devore? You have? Okay. Well, I'm glad one person has. He was born in 1880 on the Devore Plantation in Greenwood County, South Carolina. That's 15 years after the 13th amendment was ratified. When he was 18 years old, a riot broke out in a small town called Phoenix, South Carolina. Phoenix is in Greenwood County. The riot is what has now become historically known as the Phoenix Riots. Some of the African-American residents were trying to vote in a local election. A lot of the white residents didn't really take too kindly, at that time, to black people trying to exercise a franchise. Even though voting for them was legal. So, what happened was a fight broke out at the polling place. A big fight broke out. We now know that to be what today we call voter suppression. During this fight a shot rang out and this white guy named "Bose" Ethridge fell to the ground with a bullet in his head. And when the shot rang out, everybody scattered. White folks scattered. Black folks scattered. Nobody really knows who fired the shot.

Now, according to the New York Times on November 10, 1898 and over the next few days, whites from across Greenwood and surrounding counties converged on Phoenix to avenge Ethridge's death. Bands of armed whites scoured the countryside looking for the "usual suspects," and we know who those suspects tended to be. So when the mobs were done with their handiwork about 12 people had been lynched. One of whom was a guy name Wade Hampton McKinney. Wade Hampton McKinney was Ephraim's older brother. So after wade got lynched Ephraim's family decided that they had to get him out of Greenwood for his own safety. What they did over a period of a year or two is begged. They borrowed and they probably even stole a little bit to get everything that they could to get Ephraim out of the county.

Ephraim's family decided to send him north on September 25th, 1901. Actually, this Wednesday will be the 112th year. At the age of 21 and never having gone to high school or even finishing elementary school, Ephraim Devore enrolled at Howard University. He attended what, at the time, was known as the Normal School. He went to undergrad. He went to grad. Then, Ephraim left in 1911 with his doctorate in dental surgery. He was a dentist of the highest order. Then Ephraim moved to New Orleans where he practiced dentistry for about 65 years. He led an amazing life. Ephraim and his wife Mabel raised five daughters. All of whom were college educated and all of whom received advanced degrees.

Ephraim would go into the fields of Mississippi with his oldest daughter in tow, under the guise of providing free dental care to the sharecroppers there in Mississippi. However, while he was in Mississippi Ephraim would convince the sharecroppers to come to New Orleans in order to get them off of the farms and out of sharecropping into the city. When the sharecroppers got to New Orleans Ephraim would find them employment. Also during the civil rights movement and the struggle for civil rights in the South when protestors and those involved in the sit-in movements were arrested, Ephraim would be one of the blacks in the professional class who would write bonds to help bail the protestors out of jail. Most folks in New Orleans called him Doc. I was blessed to be able to call him Granddaddy. Dr. Ephraim Thaddeus Millage Devore was my maternal grandfather, and that little girl, that daughter of his that he would have in tow, I called Mom. Now, I tell you this story not because it is unique and not because I think it makes me special. It is not unique, and it does not make me special. Rather, I tell you this story, because as we convene here today to engage in a nation building discussion it is important to remember that we are a strong people. We are a resourceful people. We are a resilient people. We are a powerful people with an incredibly powerful and compelling history.

Now, at this point of the story, if we were in class, I would be saying to you all as my students that this tells us that failure is not an option. I would tell my students, "I don't care where you're from. I don't care how dire you think your straits may be. That if my grandfather could walk across the yard of Howard University coming off of a plantation, never even having finished high school, then you all as my students have to find a way or make one. Failure is not an option."

Now for this discussion, I believe the story is relevant because, as a community, we are facing some horrific realities. As Dr. Watkins talked about employment rates and using government numbers such as 17% which is twice that of the national average. Wealth disparity. White wealth accumulation is on the average about $123,000 per household. Average wealth accumulation in a black community is about $5,300. Mass incarceration is a subject that Dr. Byron Price can speak to much better than I. Then we talk about the home foreclosure rate due to the financial products that were targeted at our community. These communal statistics represent the realities of individuals. Many of whom are sitting in this auditorium today. Therefore, I hope my grandfather's story can provide just a little bit of motivation for you. Combine that motivation with the practical knowledge and information that is going to be departed or come from our panelists today. Then we all will be able to move just a little bit forward. We'll all move a little bit further forward. So, I stand here today with this suit on and with these letters behind my name at 54 years old. I am just three generations removed from the plantation. In 2013 at 54 years old — I know I only look 53 — three generations removed from the plantation. We are a powerful people. We have a powerful and compelling history. So, the question is if each of you leave here today saying, "Enough. Not on my watch, not on my block, not in front of my home, no longer in my living room am I gonna tolerate the circumstances as they exist today." That is what I hope we leave here today moving just a little bit closer to.

Our first panelist has spent more than a decade following her passion, which is journalism. As an editor, writer, and TV correspondent, you may recognize her face from CNN, E!, or MSNBC. She worked at an array of pop culture magazines including *Entertainment Weekly*, *Teen People* and *In Touch Weekly*. In addition, this panelist is a trained life coach and licensed therapist who authors "Do Better, Be Better," an advice column where she tackles issues with her signature candor and practical tips. She's a native New Yorker. She attended Brooklyn Technical High School and graduated magna cum laude from Howard University with a BA in legal studies. She has a master's degree from Columbia University, as well as a master's degree from New York University. Let us bring with applause to the stage Ms. S. Tia Brown.

Our next panelist is an associate professor in the Department of Mathematics, Science, and Technology at

Teacher's College, Columbia University. There he also serves as Director of Science Education at the Center for Health Equity and Urban Science Education. He is also a Caperton Fellow and Hip-Hop Archive Fellow at the W.E.B Dubois Institute at Harvard University. He is the co-editor of #HipHopEd social media movement. In addition, he is a public speaker on a number of topics that include Hip-Hop education, STEM education, politics, race, class diversity, and youth empowerment. He holds a PhD in Urban Education with a concentration in Mathematics, Science, and Technology. He also holds a Master's Degree in Natural Sciences as well as Educational Administration. Let us welcome with applause Dr. Christopher Emdin.

Our next panelist is a professor in the Center of African American Studies at Princeton University. She is the author of two books: *More Beautiful and More Terrible: The Embrace and Transcendence of Racial Inequality in the United States*, and *Prophets of the Hood: Politics and Poetics in Hip-Hop*. She is also the author of numerous scholarly articles in the fields of law, cultural studies and African American studies. She edited the Barnes and Noble Classics edition of *Narrative of Sojourner Truth*. She writes book reviews for *The New York Times*, *San Francisco Chronicle*, and the *London School of Economics Book Review* blog. She provides occasional commentary on radio, television, and web-based broadcast media. Let us bring to the stage Dr. Imani Perry.

The next panelist is an associate professor of education at Teacher's College at Columbia University. He also holds an affiliated faculty appointment in African American studies at the institute for research in African American studies at Columbia. He is the host of the nationally syndicated television show, *Our World With Black Enterprise*, which airs Sunday mornings on TV1 and broadcasts in markets all around the country. He also provides regular commentary for CNN, MSNBC, and Fox News Channel where he was a political contributor and regular guest on *The O'Reilly Factor*. He is also a columnist and editor at large at the *Philadelphia Daily News*. He holds a PhD from the University of Pennsylvania. Dr. Marc Lamont Hill.

Our next panelist is an actress, producer, and owner of Reel Righteous Entertainment, and that's R-E-E-L, Reel Righteous Entertainment. After several years of working on and off screen, she was unhappy with the lack of diversity-

Dr. Hill:

She was mad.

Dr. Wilmer Leon:

To create balance, she launched the Reel Network. It's an online television network that strives to create riveting, thought provoking, and hilarious content for African Americans. Currently, she is producing projects intended for film, television, and the internet. She has a graduate degree from Xavier University in Louisiana. She got her undergrad in public relations, creative writing, and speech pathology. Ms. Tiara Williams.

For our last panelist, all I need to do is tell you who he is: Dr. Cornel West. In lieu of each of panelist giving prepared opening remarks, I will ask each of them an opening question then allow them to go with that. We will start with Dr. West. As we look at the current condition of the black community, what would you say are the top three issues that, from a community perspective, we have to focus on and attack?

Dr. Cornel West:

First, let me just say I am blessed to be here. I salute brother Boyce Watkins and Maria for bringing us here. I also salute Medgar Evers – special place. Brenda Green. And others. I salute each and every one of you for being here. But, for me it is a spiritual crisis. It has to do with how do we preserve integrity, honesty, and decency in an age of such pervasive lies and cowardice? It has to do with...How do we deal with folk who are willing to sell their souls for a mess of pottage? Those are fundamental questions.

When we talk about economics, can we generate trust with each other in the name of integrity, honesty, and decency. We are talking about politics. Can we be accountable and render our politicians accountable in the name of — not your skin color — integrity, decency, and honesty? When it comes to our culture, the quality of our music, the quality of our mosques, and synagogues, and churches are they led by persons who are fundamentally committed to integrity, decency and honesty? Brother Kevin knows what I'm talking about. Good to see you. That for me is a starting point. Because if we don't have those, we can have all the high black faces in high places, but it will be like sounding brass and tinkling cymbals, because they're too dishonest. They're too indecent. They're too willing to sell their souls.

Dr. Wilmer Leon:

Dr. Perry, following on that theme of honesty, integrity, and decency one of the primary issues that I think we see in our communities has to do with our children. What would you say are some of the things that we can do as parents to promote these ideals and support our children in the midst of the incredible issues that we find facing our community?

Dr. Imani Perry:

Thank you. That is a great question. I think the first thing – probably an obvious thing to say – is to turn off the television set. That's for multiple reasons. One, because of the kind of messages that are being communicated to our children. But also, research shows that the longer black children watch television the worse they feel about themselves. The only kids who feel better about themselves from watching television are white boys. That is for obvious reasons. So when I think about what do you do with the time that's left when you turn off the television, I think it should be devoted to reading and literacy. I also think about that becoming a life practice. A practice that is both about developing the kind of deep thought, developing skills, and developing the kind of personal reflection that is necessary in order to address these kinds of issues. I think that doing that in the context of community is really important, right? Also, the kind of literature that we expose them to must have values that potentially are incorporated with the material.

We do a lot of talking about the failures of the educational system, and that is appropriate where it's applicable. However, there's also a lot we can do in the context of our communities. I actually like to give practical solutions, so for example, most cities, public school systems, or public libraries have public passes to go to museums. That means you can have a kind of quality time that is connected to children learning by simple acts like that in addition to literacy. There is a lot of that kind of educational support that is free. There are websites like *Kahn Academy* and *Starfall.com* that actually provide the kind of academic support that sometimes is not available in the classroom. So actually, I'm a mother. Thus I lean towards very practical things. I think praxis in life that puts children's development at the center is what's essential for us to pursue.

Dr. Wilmer Leon:

Dr. Hill, following on the idea of our children and the problems with our children and our community...That has become a funnel, unfortunately, for too many of our children as it relates to incarceration. Mass incarceration is a very serious problem that is harming the stability of families and communities all over this country. What are some of the effects of the prison problem as well as some things that we can do within our communities to combat this issue?

It is having such a devastating...I mean just strictly the numbers...We've got almost 2.5 million people that are incarcerated or that are in the system. We make up about, last time I looked at the numbers, 52% of those people.

Dr. Hill:

Yeah, yeah, thank you all for being here. I want to extend my gratitude once again to Boyce Watkins for organizing this event and for making sure that the panel is strong and that you all came out. He didn't have to do this. You notice he is not sitting here although he is brilliant and perfectly capable of being up here on the panel. He made a commitment to organizing something for the benefit of this community and not for self-aggrandizement. I think we should give Boyce Watkins another round of applause.

It's funny that I was visiting Mumia Abu-Jamal last Sunday and Dr. West was there the week before. On my way back home I called Dr. West, and I was talking about how heartwarming it is to stand in that visiting room. You watch prisoners stand there as their babies come in, as their sons and daughters come in, as their wives come in, as their partners come in, and you see these prisoners' faces light up. They are so excited. They are so happy to see them. Then I thought about how sad it is as you are leaving when they have to walk out and give that final goodbye hug. You see the prisoners. Their whole appearance change and those babies cry, you know? They break down.

When you think about Mumia's book *Live from Death Row* he talks about one of the saddest moments being when his grandbabies couldn't touch him through the glass. When you read Assata Shakur's memoir she talks about the moment she knew she had to leave prison was when Kakuya was pushing up against the bars. She was trying to bend the bars and finally felt defeated realizing that she could not. For me, a big part of why prison is so troublesome and so dangerous is because it dismantles families. It breaks spirits, and it has broken so many spirits in our community. We are disproportionately, as you pointed out, represented in those spaces. So for me, prison becomes one of the key areas that we need to deal with in our community largely because it is connected to everything else. Crack has disproportionately impacted our community over the '80s, '90s, and 2000s. Other drug addictions have impacted us. Mental illness has affected us. Homelessness has affected us. All these things have an impact on our community. The problem is we live in a country that criminalizes everything. So a medical problem or a drug addiction is criminalized. You are on crack, and you get locked up. You have mental illness. They close the facility then you end up on the street. In places like New York, for so-called social decency, we criminalize homelessness. We criminalize loitering. Therefore people who are homeless, often mentally ill, and self-medicating on drugs are now triply affected, because now they are incarcerated. We have essentially criminalized mental illness. We have criminalized poverty. We have criminalized homelessness. Then because we are disproportionately affected by all of that, our community becomes disproportionately criminalized.

However, the deeper problem is that it has become normal to us. It has actually become normal that we are criminalized folk. We have created this sort of moral narrative around it that we think people who smoke crack are actually bad people. Now, it might be a bad decision. I do not advise anybody here to smoke crack, but seriously. We have decided that people who smoke crack are actually bad people. Subsequently, when we find out that people are in jail for smoking crack it kind of makes sense to us. Nevertheless, it does not make sense that white boys in corporate boardrooms snorting coke should be incarcerated, because that is just what they do. Still yet, when people smoke crack they should be in jail. We have decided to criminalize so many things that when prison gets overstocked it's just normal to us.

So anyway, I don't want to take up too much time. So for me, the problem is that we have normalized criminalization. We have normalized mass incarceration. We have allowed ourselves to become the problem. School is just another space for that. When you walk into school...Go to Westinghouse. Go to any school. Go to school in East New York. Go to school in Harlem. Go to school in Philly. You see the very infrastructure of prison: dogs sniffing, cameras, more surveillance equipment in schools than in prisons over the last five years. There are parole officers, probation officers, police officers, and all this stuff. It takes you literally 20 minutes to get into school from all of the searching. Then when you finally get in ain't nobody stopping you from leaving, right? So it's a kind of public pedagogy that says all of our investment is on containment, blame, and criminalization – not on the other. We can talk about it more, but for me, that's the problem. The solution for me is I'm on the far left. I am not an Obama democrat. So then my argument would be...Yeah, clap for that. But for me, the answer is prison abolition. In a very practical way though since prison abolition is sort of a long-term goal we can talk about. First of all, we should be voting against these laws. We should be voting against these so-called get tough laws. Stuff like stop & frisk we need to be voting against. Zero-tolerance policies in schools we need to be voting against. It's us we're locking up.

Dr. Wilmer Leon:

Tia, Marc in that incredibly concise and to-the-point response mentioned broken spirits. One of the things that does not get, I believe, nearly enough discussion and admission within our community is the idea of depression. From a depressed person, thank you. How do we address the unspoken state of depression? Not only does depression compliment poverty, it is in many instances a result of oppression within our community.

S. Tia Brown:

I will say the answer starts with removing the stigma from being depressed. I think that in our community there is always an emphasis put on being strong, on persevering, on not being weak, and just dealing with whatever we are given. We are expected to accept the status quo. As a community we have to start talking about depression. We must grow to understand that being depressed does not necessarily mean that you are weak. It does not mean that you need to take medication. What it does mean is that you need therapy. Know that all of that therapy will not come from the church. So, when we talk about tools for addressing depression, we have to look beyond just going to church and praying. We need to look at getting help from licensed professional therapists. Let's be really honest. We might need more than Mommy and kitchen talk. We also need to talk about creating ways of changing things that are making us sad. A lot of times we talk about helping the kids. You just can't send a kid to a charter school and then send him home thinking that his life is going to be different. You can't do that when his parents are depressed. His family is depressed. When we talk about how crack and crime affect homes we're not just talking about people who are addicts. We are talking about the other people that have to deal with them. We are talking about the other people who also live in that environment.

I grew up in East New York. One of the hardest things with growing up in the crack epidemic was the constant state of fear we lived in. We always feared that people would break into our homes. We always feared that we would be robbed. We always feared that we would be hurt. That kind of fear creates an anxiety that you begin to live with. Fear then manifests itself in a very unhealthy way. It also robs us of hope. When we want to talk about depression the first step is saying,

"Yes, there are multiple things. There's nothing wrong with being depressed, and it is okay to get help." There are lots of resources that do not cost money. I've worked at free clinics. I've worked at different hospitals. Also, there are ways to have licensed therapists work with you in individual sessions and group settings, as well, that will not cost. However, on the other hand I have to say people buy sneakers. People buy Gucci bags. You need to invest in your own mental health. Sometimes you need to make a short-term sacrifice for a long-term gain.

Dr. Wilmer Leon:

You said something I'd like to see if I could get you to follow-up on. Let's see if you could quickly talk about self-medicating. Since there are other things that people use to self-medicate, it may not be crack. It may be the seventh beer that you've had today. It could be the fifth vodka and tonic that you've had, or it could be the two beers. Then the two...you know. Or, it could be the Gucci bag that you just went out and bought knowing good and well that you cannot afford to buy Gucci. For many people, buying things is the only sense of control that they seem to have over their lives. So then I would just like to get you to quickly talk about self-medicating.

S. Tia Brown:

We have to work on developing natural coping skills to trauma. Since when you talk about self-medication, we're talking about alcohol, wine, shopping, all of the things that we do on the surface level to make us feel better. Looking at the big picture, we know that by doing these things we definitely haven't solved the issue. We have to look at solutions that we can do to really deal with the problems that are plaguing us. Being honest with ourselves about the issues is also a must.

There are so many different topics that we need to discuss in our community. My girlfriends and I frequently talk about sexual abuse in the community. These are things that are not often addressed. In the black community we talk a lot about things that happen to men, but we do not talk about things that happen to women. Now then, when you see women acting over-sexualized. Women who think it is okay to act like a hoochie. Women who think it is okay to be a baby momma. All of these things they are coping with in a negative way. We tend to want something on the surface level that makes us feel better. We tend to need that immediate sense of love, that immediate sense of appreciation, and that immediate sense of gratitude. On the other hand, we're not dealing with the underlying issue.

So, we self-medicate in a lot of ways, but the biggest step is to be honest with ourselves about the issues. We need to remove shame from so many things. We need to remove shame from dealing with people who have had drug addiction in their family. Remove shame from being abused. Remove shame from being abandoned. Once we start looking at the heart of those issues we can say, "It's okay to be hurt. It's okay to be embarrassed. It's okay that I wasn't chosen. It's okay that I did something bad, and now, how am I gonna be resilient to move forward in my life and not stay in that place?" So, I would say resiliency is the biggest thing. Resiliency doesn't always mean, "I'm getting up and going to work." Resiliency means, "I'm not continuing that cycle. I'm not going to pick someone who was like my dad or pick someone who was like my mom. I'm not going to drink just a little bit less and say I'm not an alcoholic. I'm not going to do an illegal substance and say I'm not an abuser." That's what resiliency really is, and we all have to push ourselves to do it.

Dr. Wilmer Leon:

One of my real issues, particularly now being a parent, is school and the impact that schools are having on our children. In many instances it is impact that we are not having on our schools. You talk about a concept called Occupy Your School. Talk about that concept and why you think it is so important for us to occupy our schools?

Dr. Emdin:

The notion behind occupying your school is actually not novel. It's actually a norm in communities that are not ours. If you went to an upper-middle-class community that's overpopulated with white folks, in those schools, the parents or the community members are a fixture in the school. They walk into the principal office and make demands at the drop of a hat. If a grade is not the way they want it they go and have a conversation with the teacher. They make sure that the students are prepared for SATs. They make sure that the students are prepared for ACTs.

So, the notion of occupying your schools, in essence, is saying that if other people who are as American as you and I are feel like they have the passport to be able to enter into the school and ensure that their children are getting the kind of education that they want, why is that only a norm for them? Why not for us? And so, the notion of occupying schools in our community is understanding that in a public school or a charter school, or oftentimes public schools, that, as a taxpaying citizen of the United States, not only do you have a responsibility to ensure that you focus on your child's education, but you have a right to do so. You have the right to do so on your own terms.

So, if you're working and you can't be there on open school night, then you have the right to be able to have a conversation with the principal or assistant principal and say, "This is when I can come into the school. I would like to have a meeting with you to discuss my child's progress." So, what I mean, occupying your schools, essentially, is saying that the barriers that we feel like we have between an institution and ourselves are oftentimes barriers that people create for us. However oftentimes, they are barriers that we have created for ourselves.

You may have gone to the school once, and you didn't like it. Consider that you send your child back to the same school. You're scared to go to the school to talk to the teacher, because you feel like you don't have the degrees or you don't have the diction? It doesn't matter what you bring to that space. Each and every one of us is intelligent and brilliant in our own right. Each and every one of us has a responsibility to our children. Each one of us has the ability to go into the schools and demand the best education for our children. So when I say occupy schools, I speak to just that.

Dr. Wilmer Leon:

And, let me real quick. My son is 11. When he was nine, he was being bullied. I went up to the school. I'm walking Wilmer to his class, and I say, "Hey, Boo. Where's that kid who was bullying you?" He said, "Oh, Daddy, he's standing right next to you." That boy didn't bully my son anymore.

Dr. Hill:

You leaving some details out, bruh. Go ahead.

Dr. Emdin:

"After I yolked him up."

Dr. Wilmer Leon:

You really wanna know?

Dr. Hill:

Wait, they videotaping this. Tell me afterward. I don't want you to get in no trouble.

Dr. Wilmer Leon:

As the president said last week, sometimes it doesn't matter the path you take so long as you get there. That's what matters. That boy isn't bullying my son anymore. Dr. West, we've been talking. We've been hearing about depression. We heard about baby mamas and this whole idea that now it's almost acceptable to have children out of wedlock. Is there a value crisis or does there just need to be a refocus on value? Talk about...Where we are now in terms of a value system and a value structure?

Dr. Cornel West:

Well, one is that we live in a capitalist society that is obsessed with moneymaking and profit taking by any means necessary. And so, you end up with a culture of superficial spectacle, obsessed with visibility and profitability. It produced spiritual blackouts. That's what we're dealing with. And so what is a spiritual blackout? A spiritual blackout is somebody who has given up on integrity, decency, and said, "I'm gonna get over by any means, and it's just gonna be for me, me, me, and maybe a little of mine."

Well, you see, the thing is, historically, black people...'Cause we gotta be very honest about this. We got 400 years of being terrorized, traumatized and stigmatized. The only thing that kept us going in our song and in our religion and in our politics was some spiritual commitment to something bigger than us. That had to do with integrity, decency, and honesty. That's not to say all of us did the right thing. We're all gonna fall on our faces. We're all human beings. At least we know the difference between being dishonest and trying to be an honest person before you meet your maker. Once you lose that, then we've lost what our foremothers and forefathers sacrificed for. I don't care what color your mayor, your governor, your president, or your pastor is.

Dr. Wilmer Leon:

One of the big influences that we see on our culture, particularly on our children, is media. Can you talk to — whether it's the music, whether it's the visuals that we are seeing on television — the power of the messages, the power of the images? Can you even talk to your own personal experience as an actress and the conscious decisions that you've made not to buckeye, buckdance, and shuffle along? Talk about that.

Tiara Williams:

Working in Hollywood has been an experience for me. Most of you probably don't know who I am because of a decision that I made a few years ago. I noticed that when I was going to auditions they would have us ... you would go in and be a regular person, you know? "Hi. My name is Tiara Williams. I'm here to audition for whatever – Jiffy." You would find yourself directed by some point in the audition to be like, "My name is Tiara, and I love me some Jiffy, girl." You know somehow I realized I became a reflection of you all. Me working in the business, I wanted to represent you instead of just thinking, "Me, me, me, me, me." So it's across the board.

What's most interesting to me is when you go to middle America and all these different places there's people, whether you believe it or not, that have never seen black people before. Their first images of black people and how they get their dose is through television. Guess what they see? They see over-sexualized women. They see hos and bitches. They see black men as gangstas. What happens is if there's a black man walking down the street in a white neighborhood, they feel comfortable enough to shoot them because they already feel like they are dangerous. Not that that's happened anytime recently. I'm just sayin.' So for me, we started The Reel Network. Right now we're a small network, but the idea is to be dedicated to providing positive content for you all. We are just going in a different direction trying to be the balance to *Love and Hip-Hop*. Seeing us in a dysfunctional way on television, whether you know it or not, rubs off on you. You can't wait to see Stevie J. womanize women. Most of us think it's funny, but it's only — like you were saying — normalizing things. We think it's okay, because it comes on, and it's down your timeline, and you wanna see it on your *Facebook*. You wanna see what's happening, but then you just kind of learn to behave in that same way, and you don't even notice it.

The things we listen to in music. I find myself listening to a song, and I'll be like, "I hate this song. It's just so bad." Then after a while I find myself like, "That bitch, that ho, whatever." Whatever it is, and you can't help it, because it's all around us. I guess my point to you would be if...We could collectively be a little bit more conscious of the things that we digest into our spirits and the things that we watch. Dr. Perry said that turning the TV off would be the first step. I couldn't agree with her more although I work in the film industry. Turn it off, because unless we start to protest against the things that are on television and the way that we're seen they're going to keep giving it to us.

Dr. Wilmer Leon:

We have a question from Gavin. Gavin, are you here? Nope, okay, came through electronically. "What are viable solutions to the current subculture of ignorance and irresponsibility that inhibits our progression as a people?" Now, implicit in that question isn't irresponsibility and ignorance, which we may want to argue against, but, I'll just throw that open. Who wants to take that question?

Dr. Hill:

Let me...I'll just say one thing real quick. I worry that the language of indecency, irresponsibility, and shame gets imagined in a very particular way that often reflects bourgeois middle-class values. Often it is deemed a kind of shame that we have of the black poor. So we have to be careful even when we talk about...I don't want to take for granted that baby-mamahood, as it's been described today, is a signpost of some kind of moral decay or moral decline as such, right? What we don't wanna do is demonize and stigmatize single-motherhood, nor do we wanna create the kind of sexist patriarchal notion that we should be marrying our way out of poverty. 'Cause if women had access to jobs...I mean, there's a whole lot of layers to that. Again, I said I'd be fast.

But, I just think as a black middle-class people or a black working-class people that aspire to black middle-class values and/or sort of social standing, we need to be careful about how we talk about the black poor. We don't want to end up as a collective group of Bill Cosbys embarrassed by those people over there and seeing ourselves as socially disconnected from people over there. Boyce when you made the flyer it said "A New Paradigm." Part of what we might need to do is imagine a new paradigm of family, right? Because we don't wanna become romantic for the '50s and '60s for patriarchy, like, "This man is gonna come and save the day and rescue the family." 'Cause sometimes that man who came home every day to you also beat you. Sometimes he may have also been emotionally unavailable.

I mean, there are all these other things that came with daddy being at home sometimes. If we're gonna have a new paradigm for family ... I'm not saying fathers shouldn't be there, but there's other ways for fathers to be there. Black non-custodial fathers are as involved as any other racial group, so we also don't wanna overly pathologize black fatherhood. What we need to do is think about, how we can be more emotionally available and how we can construct models of family that involve the entire community. It's better for a child to have healthy parents than it is to have parents in the house always mad and fighting, right?

I mean, it's all this stuff that we could talk about, and that's just one thing. So when we look at 2 Chainz and you are embarrassed. We look at what's on the TV and we're embarrassed by that. I understand there are certain things that are embarrassing. However, we need to not become so reductive in this that everything that's seen as working-class or poor black culture becomes something that we need to run from and be ashamed of. That's us, too.

Dr. Emdin:

Speaking about education I think part of what we have to be able to do is push the education agenda to the point where we also bend the rules of what normalcy is in those spaces, as well. We need to force the schools to incorporate aspects of our culture into the instruction in schools. When we're talking about a new paradigm and we're talking about doing things differently, it also requires recreating and reestablishing norms within institutions. What we have to do first of all is watch the institution. You infiltrate said institution. You carve out a space within it. Then you repurpose and refashion that institution to meet your own specific needs. And so that process requires us, first and foremost, to understand the nuances of our culture, the multiplicities of our culture, and what is viewed as negative aspects of our culture. Then incorporate that into the school system. Allowing and forcing them to utilize and see the benefit of those things.

When I go into a school and they ask me to do a professional development or to work with teachers I say I wanna incorporate Hip-Hop into what's going on in the classroom. The first thing I get is, "Well, we don't wanna do that. It's negative. It's misogynistic. It is violent." My response is always, "That's what you have made it to be or that's what you see it as." I can utilize that same tool to push forth ideas in science, technology, engineering, mathematics, wordplay, creativity, writing, and history. So, I'm not gonna allow you to demonize aspects of our culture. What I want you to do is be able to take a step back and learn about the nuances of the culture and understanding the brilliance of that culture. It's the institution's responsibility to bend their structure to meet your specific needs.

Dr. Hill:

That's the point, right there.

Dr. Emdin:

And you know, there are various ways to do that. In every New York City public school, there's a position for a parent coordinator. Does everybody know that? There are schools in New York City that cannot find a parent in their school to apply for that job. What we need to do is make it visible that you could be a parent coordinator. Did you know that schools in New York City, despite the things we hear about the tests, the tests, the tests, a parent has the right to go into the school and opt out of the city-wide test? And, if you opt out of that exam, it is the school's responsibility to ensure that your child is still getting a top-tier education.

So, when we understand the power that we have, the beauty that we hold, and the complexity of our culture then we can go into those schools with that information. We can force them to do not what we want them to do but what's their responsibility to do.

Dr. Wilmer Leon:

This next question, I think, is very enlightening, and I think the answer to this will be very enlightening. This is from Percy. "How do we as a people begin to reclaim the unity we once demonstrated during the mid and late '60s?" I'm turning to Dr. West for that answer. However, I will say I believe that there is a lot of revisionist history in that question. I don't believe we were as unified as we now want to look back, reflect upon and romanticize about. Dr. King was pillory in the community, so anyway with that, Dr. West-

Dr. Cornel West:

I mean, you're right, though. When Martin died 72% of Americans said they disapproved of him. Also, 55% of black people said they disapproved of Bro. Martin. How come? Because they felt he was talking about poor people. He was talking about critics of capitalism. He was talking about Vietnam and killing innocent precious Vietnamese babies. He understood that those babies had the same status as babies in vanilla suburbs or chocolate cities. Now, when you have that kind of moral and spiritual witness, you're gonna scare some folk. Now that Martin is dead we love him in the grave, because he's no longer able to respond in the way that...Same is true of Malcolm X. What is the percentage of black people who approved of Malcolm X when he was shot down February 1965? We love Malcolm. Same is true with Nina Simone. How many folk really bought the albums of Nina Simone with her telling the truth in the way she did? How many made Curtis Mayfield the hero that he should have been? He never won a Grammy. How come? He was telling the truth.

So, the question is not the unity. The question is the love, the care, the concern. How do we express it? How you gonna have stop & frisk policies going on for almost 15 years, five million precious black and brown mothers and no moral outrage? That is not loving the

413

young brother at all. That's not showing love. They're uncared for. We can talk all we want. If we don't zero in on the policy or be willing to hit the street and go to jail, or die, then they look at us and say, "Oh, sounding brass and tinkling cymbals." You don't really love us. Forty percent of our babies live in poverty. Where is the love Donny Hathaway and Roberta Flack raised? That's the fundamental question.

The '60s was one of those historic moments when – after all of that terror, trauma, stigma, and loss of unity – we had an emergence of self-respect, protecting our weak, and willingness to live and die. What we don't have today are people who are willing to go that far. We want folk to be highly successful and end up being well-adjusted to injustice with their material toys, trophy wives, and husbands. That's a very different tradition. Martin Luther King, Jr. was maladjusted. Bob Marley was maladjusted to injustice. Where is that tradition today? Lupe Fiasco, Jill Scott, okay, it's there, but it's not strong as it was in the '60s, and the course is, "Can we come back?"

Marcus Garvey said...And I take Garvey very seriously. He said, "As long as black people live in America, the masses of them will live lives of ruin, disaster, and destruction." He's yet to be proven wrong. What does that mean? It means that even if the masses of black people are never treated with respect, we've got to proceed as if they are worthy of that respect. We've got to try to create all possibilities for them to be treated with dignity. Most importantly, we must create all possibilities for them to treat themselves with respect, dignity, and protection of one another. This is why the international dimension is so important.

I'm gonna end on this 'cause you all know that Martin and Malcolm were coming together in June of 1964. What was Malcolm doing? He said, "I can't conceive of how black people can overcome this system." He said, "We need revolution, but we don't have enough revolutionaries. The people gonna kill us — FBI, CIA, national surveillance, incarceration — so we're going to the international court of appeal. We're going to the United Nations and say, 'America, you have violated the human rights of precious black people in prisons, ghettos, and schools. We want the world to see your hypocrisy.'" 'Cause once you start tarnishing the image — even of the most powerful at the moment — you're in a different situation. You're in a very different situation. Now, Martin Luther King, Jr. put in a phone call and said, "Malcolm, I'm with you. Let's go together." When they did that they both signed their death warrants. Malcolm was poisoned the next month in Cairo. Martin Luther King Jr.'s FBI surveillance was doubled. He already had enough. So then the question becomes, "What do we do in this situation?" Do we smile, tell the truth, or bear witness? I'm a Christian, so I call on Jesus for empowerment. That's the only way you gonna keep loving folk who oftentimes have difficulty loving themselves then still bear witness and tell the truth and be willing to pay the cost.

Dr. Wilmer Leon:

This question, I think, is strong. It's simple but strong and comes from Patricia. "What can I do to save my sons from white supremacy and racism?"

Dr. Emdin:

Wow.

Dr. Cornel West:

Oh, no, no, no, no, no, no. No, no, no.

Dr. Wilmer Leon:

Imani?

Dr. Imani Perry:

It's a strong question. It's a heartbreaking question right? To be a mother of sons is to be fearful every time your child is not in your site. There's a deep sense of powerlessness attached to that question. I do think that there are some things that we have to do for ourselves in the midst of the struggle against white supremacy. One thing is we have to stop believing the mythologies about who we are. We have to stop saying that our kids want to fail. That they believe being successful, particularly our boys, is acting white. Stop saying that they all want to be thugs, that they don't have any aspirations, and that they don't wanna work. These things are simply not true. Part of the way that you know they're not true [is that] everybody points to somebody else who thinks that way.

We were devoted to demonstrating to ourselves and the world that the lies about what black people were, in fact, were lies. Right? [We were trying] to speak truth in the face of lies, [but] we've begun to allow the dominant narrative about who we are to seep into our consciousness and our thoughts. I think that does a significant amount of damage – particularly to the ability of our sons to soar. But also, all the questions that we talked about before about depression, sense of possibility, sense of hope, and so on. I would say, for me, one of the first steps is to begin the story as a story of triumph against the odds. Get rid of the deficit narratives, and develop a deep sense of confidence in our children in addition to all of the practical things you have to do. Have the talks about racism. Have the talks about how to navigate the world. My position with my children is not to tell them the story of oppression first. The story I tell is the story of resilience. Right? It's all about the extraordinary story of resilience.

Dr. Wilmer Leon:

I wanna say about your answer to that question that three books come to my mind: one, *The Mis-Education of the Negro* by Carter G. Woodson. That's a book that I think at just about any age, particularly once you get into middle school, is a good place to start. I would then go to *Where Do We Go From Here: Chaos or Community?*. That's the last book Dr. King wrote before he was assassinated. If you really want to understand Dr. Martin Luther King, Jr. forget the misrepresentation of the "I Have a Dream" speech. Go to *Where Do We Go From Here: Chaos or Community?* and get a real understanding of the man. I would also suggest the late Dr. Ronald W. Walters book, *White Nationalism, Black Interests*, which is an incredibly powerful analysis. He called out the Tea Party before the Tea Party was even called out. With that I'll go back to you all.

Dr. Emdin:

It's such a gut-wrenching question that when you first hear it you're almost speechless. Just echoing on Dr. Perry's sentiments, I also believe that the chief counter to white supremacy is black empowerment. If you get to a point where you are so put down by a structure that's in front of you, then a construction of self and understanding of your worth and value becomes a chief counter. Any person who has an understanding of self-worth and value when confronted with white supremacy cannot even use the term white supremacy. The term in itself is problematic. If you believe in the value of self you wouldn't even associate those two words together. I feel like the first step is always a value of self, what it is that you offer, and what you bring to the table. With that being said, it's like the path towards that is also in showcasing our history, resilience, and all the hidden stories about blackness. Not necessarily historically, but in the contemporary sense.

The reason why I say that is because whenever I go into a school I ask folks, "Alright, you have X amount of black boys in the school. You want us to work on getting them to be better?" That's always challenging, so I say, "What are you guys doing?" And they say, "Well, we have this Black History Month celebration and you should come in February." I'm like, "Alright." I go back in

February to check out what's going on. When I get there, they have an ode to powerful historic figures. I'm not at all making the statement that we should forget our history or where we come from. However, youth today want to see that there's somebody like them who listens to the kind of music they do and has the same bop in their step like they do. They want somebody who has been able to accomplish a multiplicity of things. Since they exist, you sometimes have to create an immediate history. You know what I mean? Like Dr. West is here. Imani's [here]. These folks are folks that I've engaged with before meeting them. The reason is because they are my heroes. They are contemporary black heroes that exist. Kids don't know that, but if they have that knowledge when they're confronted with issues that challenge their black supremacy, they will shrug that off. They will know the notion of white supremacy doesn't truly exist.

Dr. Wilmer Leon:

Anybody else wanna...Tiara?

Tiara Williams:

Yes?

Dr. Wilmer Leon:

From a visual and Hollywood perspective, white supremacy has an impact on what we see and what we hear. The decision-makers, the people who are deciding which artists get promoted, what's good, what's gonna sell on this album, what is not gonna...the whole conflict between what we would call positive Hip-Hop and rap music. Some of the stuff that is not so positive is impacted by white supremacy.

Tiara Williams:

You know, it's crazy to me, because a lot of times, people don't want to admit that white supremacy exists in that realm even though it's so, so visual.

Dr. Wilmer Leon:

Well, because Hollywood is so liberal.

Tiara Williams:

Right. Anything goes. Anything can happen. I'll just say that what I would like everybody to know is that it does exist. I think that the counteraction to that is we have to create our own media. We have to patronize and really listen to the stories of people who are like you that are writing stories and making films just so you can get a grasp of who you are. So you can celebrate who you are. Nine times out of ten the people that don't look like you, won't celebrate you. They don't even know you.

I guess my biggest issue with Hollywood is that there's not a lot of access for African Americans to write the main films that you go see. Even on the shows on television, you look at yourself in a way that white people see. They have black characters, but their roles are written by a white person who does not know your experience and lives in a suburban area of Hollywood. They just are out of touch. I think it does exist. The only way that you can counteract that is to really, really learn and patronize the people that look like you and support them.

S. Tia Brown:

I would like to add that I have worked in the entertainment industry for a long time. We see a lot of kids who aspire to be Jay-Z, Lil Wayne, and Dwayne Wade. We don't have people who are aspiring to be the person who manages Dwayne Wade or who is producing in the boardroom. In terms of being gatekeepers for the media a big issue is that our image is based on what Jewish people think about black people. That is also because we are not pushing to get into those positions enough. It is important for us to have our own mediums, but it is also important for us to talk to our kids about what opportunities are in the spectrum of careers.

I started out my career as a journalist. For a long time, I knew what journalism was, but I didn't understand all of the opportunities that were within the field. We need to make sure that we are educating our kids and looking at all of their talents. "You're a great writer. These are some options for you. You like making music. These are some options for you. You like sports, but you can't shoot a hoop. These are some options for you." Since these careers are not the only way kids can become well-to-do or happy, we also want to encourage them to pursue careers that are in line with their passion. We often say, "You do this or you become blue collar." There is such a huge spectrum of things that people can do, so really push to identify their talents and passions.

Tiara Williams:

You're right, Tia.

Dr. Wilmer Leon:

You know, you mentioned the various different jobs within journalism and you mentioned producers. A lot of people who watch MSNBC, CNN, or Fox don't realize that in many instances, the power behind what you see is rarely the host. It is the producers of those programs who decide the issues that are going to be discussed. They decide the individuals that they want to bring on the program. Producers go to their rolodexes and say, "Well, who's a good democratic Negro that we can go to who gets this particular perspective." Am I wrong?

Tiara Williams:

That's so true.

S. Tia Brown:

Definitely.

Tiara Williams:

And there are different types of producers, too. That is something that people need to be aware of.

Dr. Cornel West:

I think that relates to this question about white supremacy and our precious young people because-

Dr. Wilmer Leon:

Wait, say again.

Dr. Cornel West:

I mean white supremacy is the biggest lie of the modern world.

Dr. Emdin:

Yes, yes, yes.

Dr. Cornel West:

It is, but the problem is if you've been lying and your life was a lie then your kid is liable to believe in lies, including white supremacy. It's not the only lie. It's no accident CNN and MSNBC don't talk about the new Jim Crow. They don't talk about Wall Street domination of the government. They do not talk about the wages being flattened. They do not talk about minimum wage being locked into 1968. Every once in a while they touch on it, but why? Because both of these stations, just like both of the political parties, are dominated by Wall Street. They can't help but tell certain kinds of lies in order to perpetrate these stories. The aim of the stories is always to do what? To keep their advertising flowing. The money flowing. It's a capitalist society.

So, then, the question says, "Are we really prepared to face the truth?" White supremacy is inside of black people. You don't have to have white brothers and sisters around for white supremacy to operate. Just look inside the black people's souls. Look inside your own soul. You don't grow up in America and you're not somehow sedimented with white supremacist sensibility. That's what it is to grow up in this decadent empire. That's what it means, but you have to have resiliency. We teach the young folk, "Now, that white supremacy is going to be creeping in you must have the strength and fortitude not to believe the lies. Stand for the truth." The truth is black folks' humanity is real.

Dr. Wilmer Leon:

What type of programs can the community enhance, implement, or develop that will create healthy leadership for black American girls and boys?

Dr. Emdin:

The theme here is a new paradigm. A lot of the issues that we are discussing are issues that have been pervasive over a long span of time. We have offered some thoughts about ways to move forward. I think a way to address the kind of question that you posed is also, "What kind of new spaces are there for us to coalesce that are outside of the traditional norms? Spaces that will allow us to have the kind of conversations we need to have happen?" I think that is why when we talk about a new paradigm, we also have to find new spaces to inhabit. Find new spaces to infiltrate like social media, for example.

I think back on the Trayvon Martin case. I think that with any major issue within our communities we oftentimes will grumble about them in isolation or at the kitchen table. Then the issue dies, because it's usually just between two or three of us having these conversations in these small places. We have a platform now where we can coalesce under a hashtag. Coalesce under a shared ideal and meet every Tuesday night at 9:00PM. Then we can talk about the intersections of Hip-Hop and education on *Twitter*, #HipHopEd. I'm just saying. Whereas, we have spaces where we can create connections with people in multiple spaces, we're having these conversations in isolation where they will die. We need to create a block of folks that can make things happen.

You know, the Dream Defenders are right now on *Twitter* gathering votes and attention through constantly sharing information about what's going on post Trayvon Martin. You don't hear anything about the Dream Defenders on any major network. Anybody who is on that social media space understands that this is happening. It is growing and moving. Therefore, being part of a new paradigm is understanding, knowing what new tools we are afforded and how we can utilize them to push the agenda forward as a unit rather than in isolation.

Dr. Imani Perry:

I would also like to add that there are parts of old paradigms that ought to be made anew. For example, when I was a kid, I belonged to an organization called African American History and Culture Club. It was an organization that was started by a group of parents and children. We met every Saturday for most of the day. They provided us access to lots of history. We wrote a newsletter. We had elders come in and speak. So there are lots of old fashioned forms of civic organizations that can be revitalized. It is very important for this kind of work and familial structure to once again be a part of our tradition. Also, we need to have extended family networks. This idea of a nuclear family as the only legitimate model is something that was imposed by a white middle-class ideal. It is a social policy which they tried to enforce upon us. One reality is that when you are in conditions of economic hardship, you need as many adults as possible operating together to pool resources. So, I think part of the new paradigm is to actually embrace the older paradigms that worked for us. We need to restore the paradigms that allowed us to make it over instead of always trying to emulate those who are in positions of power and how they do things.

Dr. Hill:

Can I just say one thing real quick? I agree with everything that has been said. The other part of the question that I think is important is, "What kind of organizations? What should they look like?" There are so many issues in our community that I think we should be thinking about. Some in the new media model, the new models, and as Imani said, also holding onto some of the traditional models that have worked for us.

One issue in our communities that I think we should be talking about is food insecurity. Food deserts in particular right here in Brooklyn. You go up to Harlem, not the Columbia Harlem but the real Harlem, and you still have to go three, four, five miles for fresh fruits and vegetables. You know, it's not that people always do not want to eat healthy. It is that they do not have access to eating healthy. If you work 10 to 12 hours a day it is tough to then get on a bus and ride three or four miles just to get a banana or an apple when the store next door has pig's feet, Snapple, and a blunt. I'm not necessarily mad at the latter point. I am just saying that shouldn't be your only choice. My point is part of what we can do in terms of making these words action and actionable is having organizations that do things at community gardens. We need subsidies, but we also could use community gardens. We can build stands for fresh fruit and vegetables right here, you know? There are things we can do right now. We can demand fresh fruits and vegetables in stores just by not going to them. So, let's think about food insecurity.

Another thing that's an issue is...and it strikes me. My daughter is here. I was just thinking about how black girls are vulnerable at a very young age to issues like street harassment. If you are talking about organizing in the new paradigm, let's organize on some new stuff like food insecurity, street harassment, and sexual violence. These are things that we should be doing to protect young girls and also to educate young boys. Having different kinds of conversations. When you're in the Boy's Club, the Police Athletic League, when we're mentoring, or we're doing one-on-ones, we need to also educate. In fact, we need to primarily educate boys about what sexual assault looks like and what date rape looks like. Those are the kinds of conversations we have to be having in a new paradigm with our black boys. Sometimes it's very simple like, "No means no." Other times it's more complicated like language usage and the way we frame physicality. For example, if you're with your homies and you're 16 or you're 17 or even if you're 35 or 45, and you talk about sex, you might be like, "Yeah, I hit that. I tapped that. I pounded that. I beat that up." Y'all laughin', but that's how lots of men talk. So every image and every metaphor we have of sex is one of violence, right?

Dr. Wilmer Leon:

Hence, Lil' Wayne had a song where he equated a sexual act with the brutalization of Emmett Till.

Dr. Hill:

Right, when Lil Wayne says, "I beat that up like I was Emmett Till," it wasn't just the troublesome part where he was desecrating Emmett Till, but it's also the fact that we're normalizing sexual violence. You know that can't be the only way we imagine sex. We frame this. You know what I mean? So, sexual violence, food insecurity, and LGBT need to be a part of the new paradigm conversations. We have been here for an hour and haven't talked about gay people yet. That's exactly a metaphor for how we think about black culture, black life, and even new paradigms for black America. Everything is included but gay people. We know there are gay people in the room. We know there are gay people in our families. Sometimes, there are gay people in our relationship, and we don't deal with it. We don't talk about it. You know what I mean? We have to talk about this.

Finally, I swear this is the last thing I'm gonna say for the whole night. We have to come to terms with this Obama thing. I mean, we really got to. Maybe we can't do that today. Maybe, Boyce, you can organize something later, but we have to come to terms with this Obama thing. Right now, we are downright crazy. We have literally lost our damn minds. We got black people who are voting for war. Never in the history of America have black people voted for war. We are voting to drone people in Yemen and Afghanistan. We are talking about strikes against innocent people in Syria. When have we ever been warmongers? When have we ever been advocates of war and not peace? Black people have always been...No, listen. Don't clap. Listen. Black people have always been the moral conscience of this country. We have always been the signpost of morale.

Dr. Wilmer Leon:

Marc, Marc-

Dr. Hill:

Now, hold on. Excuse me, Brother.

Dr. Wilmer Leon:

In the world? We are the moral conscience of the world?

Dr. Hill:

We are losing our damn minds. We are voting for war more than anybody else. What is wrong with us? I don't even want y'all to...I am literally pissed off at this shit, man. We are literally voting for war.

Dr. Wilmer Leon:

My only point being-

Dr. Hill:

And it's strictly Obama. The same people that were marching with me, Cornel, Imani, and everybody else in DC in 2003 and 2004, "We're against war. We're against Iraq." We are now voting for bombs in Afghanistan. We are voting for strikes in Libya. We are voting for chemical strikes in Syria. We're doing it, because we have somehow become intoxicated by this Obama thing. It is causing us nothing but suffering and misery. I love Obama. This isn't anti-Obama. However, what are we doing, man? This is...You know what? Go ahead. I'm sorry. I'm sorry. I'm sorry, I'm sorry, I'm sorry, I'm sorry, I'm sorry.

Dr. Wilmer Leon:

No, no, no, no, no, no, no, no. No, no, no.

Dr. Hill:

This shit is crazy, man.

Dr. Wilmer Leon:

My only point to you is that we're not the moral conscience of the country. We're the moral conscience of the world. The world has looked to us for that direction. We have now, in many regards, put an African face on American imperialism.

Dr. Hill:

That's it. You're right.

Dr. Wilmer Leon:

One quick thing, as we look at the issues in our communities. We hear now they want to cut food stamps. Why? "Because we don't have enough money."

They wanna cut back on education. Why? "Because we don't have enough money." But, they are more than happy to rain Tomahawk cruise missiles onto Syria at $1.4M per missile. Now, I don't know what you could do with $1.4M, but because my main man is Boyce Watkins, I know what I could do with $1.4M.

Dr. Cornel West:

Don't forget about the $85 billion every month that the Federal Reserve is giving to Wall Street. Detroit only needs $17 billion to stay in place. They're gonna pay the banks before they're gonna pay the working people's pension. They're gonna take away their pension, but the banks get priority. That is spiritually obscene and morally sick. Where are the voices and the bodies? That's the question. It has a lot to do with the fact that we have become sleepwalkers. Oh yes, but we can wake up. We can wake up.

Dr. Wilmer Leon:

What are the programs in your community that are having the greatest impact on you? You have to figure that out. You've gotta go home today and look around your kitchen table. Look at your children. Ask yourselves, "Well, what's going on in my living room that I need to adjust?" Then, find some like-minded people in your apartment building. Find some like-minded people on your block. Then figure out how a group of you can figure out how to solve problems in your community.

As Chris talked about the technology, folks, how many of y'all got iPhones or the Samsung 4G? What we have to figure out is how to have our smartphones actually make us smarter. They talk about the digital divide, because not everybody can walk around with a smartphone. But, y'all got these darn phones which are powerful. But, you wanna spend too much time sending me silly prayers and jokes. I don't need that. Send me some information that I can use. I think, too many times, we get consumed by the national aspects of these things. We wanna try and solve either the national problem or the world problem. Just solve the problem in your living room.

Dr. Cornel West:

That's right. That's right. That's right.

Dr. Wilmer Leon:

Just solve the problem in your living room. When you do that, maybe then you can move out into the yard and solve the problem in the street. Then you can move into your child's school. You'll be amazed, because that's how these movements actually develop. The March on Washington was really motivated by the Montgomery, Alabama movement. They brought Dr. King into Montgomery, Alabama and said, "Hey, man, we got butt kickin' going on down here at a level that isn't taking place anywhere else in the country. Dr. King, you gotta come down here to Montgomery, down to Bombingham in Birmingham and help us solve that." When they got down there and dealt with that local problem then they said, "You know what, we can take this thing all the way to Washington." That's where the March on Washington came from. It came from the response to a local problem.

Dr. Cornel West:

I just wanna add something on. This is my brother from Sacramento. Give him a hand. Give him a hand. Professor Wilmer Leon. And then, I know Brother Anthony Daniels is somewhere here from Sacramento. But, I think that the history of black people is not really a history of being obsessed with being smart, but being wise. This is very important, because a smartphone has no soul, no compassion, and no courage. A lot of smart people were Nazis. A lot of smart people are white supremacists. A lot of smart people are homophobes, xenophobes, thugs and gangsters. Smartness to me has never been highly impressive. I learned that in Vacation

Bible School.

Dr. Wilmer Leon:

In Oak Park in Sacramento, California.

Dr. Cornel West:

The Devil can use smartness. When you're wise, you're courageous and full of compassion, but the Devil is a liar. You're fighting against evil. You're fighting against unjustified suffering. You're fighting against folk trying to put other folk down. We got a whole lot of smart Negroes out here come out of Harvard, Yale, and Princeton. I'm not impressed. How wise, how courageous, how sacrificial? What are they willing to pay? What cost are they willing to pay? That's the history of black people.

Now, I'm not saying stupidity is a good thing. I'm saying don't get tripped with the discourse about smartness after phones, but rather, the wisdom. See Curtis Mayfield was wise. That's what made him the genius. He was also smart, but that wasn't important. It was the wisdom. He dropped out of school in ninth grade: wisdom, courage. That's what we need to teach our young folk. In some ways, I'm agreeing with you. I'm just trying to give us some spiritual undergirding.

Dr. Wilmer Leon:

With all of the issues facing black America, how do you recommend we tackle these issues without becoming burned out?

S. Tia Brown:

I would say the first step is definitely self-care. We often talk about community issues. Some of the panelists [are] talking about taking care of the living room and your family, but you have to take care of yourself. If you are not in a place where you're happy, nurturing yourself, taking time to make sure you're physically and mentally healthy then you can't be of service to anyone.

Dr. Emdin:

You gotta make sure that what you do every day is what you wanna do. I think that's a really, really important thing that is definitely understated. Sometimes it takes a little bit of sacrifice to move out of a realm of the security of a job. Especially, if the job is probably paying you what you shouldn't be getting paid anyway. Yet, you're struggling to go through it. I just had this same conversation with my wife. She's working at a job that she hates. She's like, "But, you gotta have a job.

We just had a baby." I said, "Well, let's think about this. They're paying you this amount of money. It is about the same amount of money as the cost for childcare. How about you just don't work there? Try to find something that you really love that will allow you to work while you're doing what you have to do for the family?"

Thus, I think part of sustaining self is ensuring that you're doing something that motivates you, that you love, and that you're passionate about. Having a job that wakes you up at night thinking, "Man, I can't wait to get back to do what I gotta do tomorrow to impact the world in some way or another." When you do that your whole life is dedicated to something where the more work you do the more you reinforce your spirit. You're more productive as a worker, but your soul is fulfilled. If you're doing something every single day, because somebody says this is what you gotta do to get a dollar, where somebody is oppressing you, or somebody is hating you every single day then, you're spending most of your time damaging your soul and spirit. You gotta find something that you love to do.

Dr. Wilmer Leon:

Focus on what you love, and then figure out how to get paid doing that. You'll never work a day in your life.

Dr. Imani Perry:

Can I add a tiny bit of a damper on that? I think that's beautiful. Nevertheless, sometimes you just have to go to work, and you don't have options. A lot of folks don't love their job but have to hold onto them. Hence, I don't wanna contradict what has been said. I would add to it that you can follow passions in addition to sometimes having to work a thankless job.

Dr. Wilmer Leon:

Absolutely.

Dr. Imani Perry:

And so, I don't wanna suggest that...It is meaningful to put food on the table period, even if you do something you hate. I think there's a way to have that same kind of passion about something in your life outside of work and also acknowledge the limitations of the job market.

Dr. Wilmer Leon:

How can we build and sustain economic wealth in the black community and gain more resource?

Dr. Watkins:

You know, it's funny. I was riding over with Dr. West, and I was telling him, "You know I studied finance. I learned the reason I was so obsessed with money was because I didn't have any." Once I had a chance to make a little bit of money, I started to understand the power of money. I figured out that money can either liberate you, or it can enslave you. A drug can either make you well and healthy, or it can turn you into an addict. Fire can either cook your food, keep you warm, or it can burn you and your family alive. Obsession with money is one of the problems that we have right now. You see it mass promoted particularly if you look into Hip-Hop, and you see this sort of worship of money. "Imma call myself Yeezus and Yehova" and all this other crap. Then whenever you tell me that I'm doing something that is spiritually degrading myself and my people, the first thing I'm gonna do is say, 'Well, homie, look at my watch. Look at my car. Look at my private jet.'" Somehow that is supposed to make that all go away.

When we had our little issue with BET...I referred to them — I think quite accurately — as the new KKK. As you can imagine, that hurt my relationship with the network. When I said that, I remember hearing from one of the executives who basically said, "Yeah, I know you have your objections to the BET Awards. I know you have a problem with the promotion of artists like Lil Wayne." I said, "Yeah, absolutely. Lil Wayne is probably the most powerful mega-pastor in America, except instead of teaching the gospel of Christ, he's teaching the gospel of ignorance and self-destruction." He's a brilliant man, but he reminds me of Malcolm Little. He never met the honorable Elijah Muhammad. Can you imagine what kind of man Malcolm X would have been if he'd never met the honorable Elijah Muhammad? Can you imagine the kind of destruction he would have used his genius to cause throughout the world? That's what I'm seeing in Hip-Hop with these brilliant men who somehow have never been taught to think better of themselves and of their people. I remember when we had that conversation. The only thing that the executive could say to justify what we were seeing on television and teaching young boys and girls about themselves at early ages was, "But, do you know how much money we made from the award show? We made more money than we've ever made before." I said, "If that's all you got then I really feel sorry for you."

So, I give this financial advice with extreme caution. I'm here to tell you that, yes, you want to be economically empowered. Part of the reason that black people are enslaved to this day is because we have no economic power. We achieved a few gains in terms of political power in the '60s and '70s, etc., but those things can be taken right back. You know that.

In fact, political power without economic power is like having a driver's license when you can't even afford to buy a car. In that situation you only get a ride if somebody gives you one. You go in the direction they want you to go. When they take your car away you don't have a ride anymore. So, economic empowerment is critically important to how we solve our problems in the 21st century. What I will say to you is this. When you talk about developing economic power, I think that it's very important that we rethink how we talk about money. Even rethink how we teach our children about money. The black unemployment problem. Malcolm X talked about this a long time ago. A lot of other people said it before me, so I can't take credit for this idea. Malcolm made it very clear that as long as you never own your own businesses, you will always be out in front of somebody else's business with a picket sign hoping that they're gonna give you a job.

Dr. Claude Anderson said this in a speech...I don't wanna get his quote wrong, but I'm gonna tell you what I remember from it. He said that right after slavery, 99% of all black people worked for a white person. He said today, 97% of all black people work for a white person. This is not about hating white people. This is about loving yourself. Unfortunately, we somehow think that if you love black people you must hate somebody else. I am not talking about nobody else outside of this room. So, if you want to understand economic empowerment it's not a complex idea. I study finance at the highest levels, but it all goes back to simple ideas that I learned from my first finance professor. She was my late grandmother. My late grandmother never went to college. She never made more than $25,000 a year. She was married from the age of 15 to age 18. Then she got a divorce. She kicked him out and never got married again, but she never had to borrow money from anybody. She always had perfect credit. I cannot remember a single time that my grandmother had a financial problem. In fact, people would come to her to borrow money. So ultimately, how you think about money – thinking like a saver and an investor – is far better than thinking like a consumer and a borrower. Keep that in mind.

When I think about my own experience — and that's the best way to communicate this — I remember how painful it was to go to work every day. I remember dealing with all the racism that I dealt with and still do all the time. It doesn't matter who you are. Everybody goes through it. Even Barack goes through it in the White House. I remember that my life became so much better when I sat down and learned how to have my own business. I learned how to bring in extra money from different sources. Then, when pressure was put on me, and I was threatened with losing a little raise for the year, it didn't bother me as much. When I did eventually lose my job I didn't care. I had money coming from other sources.

When I spoke up about racial injustice Bill O'Reilly literally went on a strategic campaign for an entire week to get me fired from my job. The first thing I did was turn to my brother who is my business partner and say, "Alright, dawg. How much money we got? Where we got our money coming from? Are we gonna be alright?" He said, "Yeah, you good." I said, "Man, F Bill O'Reilly, then." So, the bottom line is very clear. We must educate ourselves and our children like our lives depend on it. We must build our wealth individually and collectively like our lives depend on it. This is not a matter of blingin' and ballin'. This is a matter of maintaining our pride and self-respect as a people.

So, I want to say thank you so much to these people who I admire so much for coming out here. Please give them a round of applause. Thank you. Yeah, if you wanna stand up please do. Just so you know, nobody got paid to come up here. They gave their time. God bless you for that.

Dr. Cornel West:

Wonderful panel. Wonderful panel.

Dr. Watkins:

Thank you all for coming out. God bless you.

ABOUT THE AUTHOR

Dr. Boyce D. Watkins is one of the leading financial scholars and social commentators in America. With a 23-year background in teaching finance, he advocates for education, economic empowerment, and social justice. He has changed the definition of what it means to be a black scholar and leader in America. He is one of the founding fathers of the field of Financial Activism – creating social change through use of conscientious capitalism – as well as a Blue Ribbon Speaker with Great Black Speakers and one of the most highly sought after public figures in the country.

In addition to publishing a multitude of scholarly articles on finance, education, and black social commentary, Dr. Watkins has presented his message to millions. He has made regular appearances on various national media outlets including: CNN, Good Morning America, MSNBC, FOX News, BET, NPR, Essence Magazine, USA Today, The Today Show, ESPN, The Tom Joyner Morning Show, and CBS Sports.

Educationally, Dr. Watkins earned BA and BS degrees with a triple major in Finance, Economics, and Business Management. In college, he was selected by *The Wall Street Journal* as the Outstanding Graduating Senior in Finance. He then earned a Master of Science in Mathematical Statistics from University of Kentucky. This was followed by a PhD in Finance from Ohio State University where he did his dissertation on the stock market and was the only African-American in the world to earn a PhD in Finance during the year 2002. He is the founder of The Black Business School which has 67,000 students and The Your Black World coalition. Together, these organizations have over 300,000 subscribers and 4.2 million social media followers world-wide.

Among recent honors was Simmons College's 2017 announcement of the creation of The Dr. Boyce Watkins Economic Empowerment Institute where the goal is to develop black economic leaders for the 21st century and beyond. Simmons College is an HBCU in Kentucky.